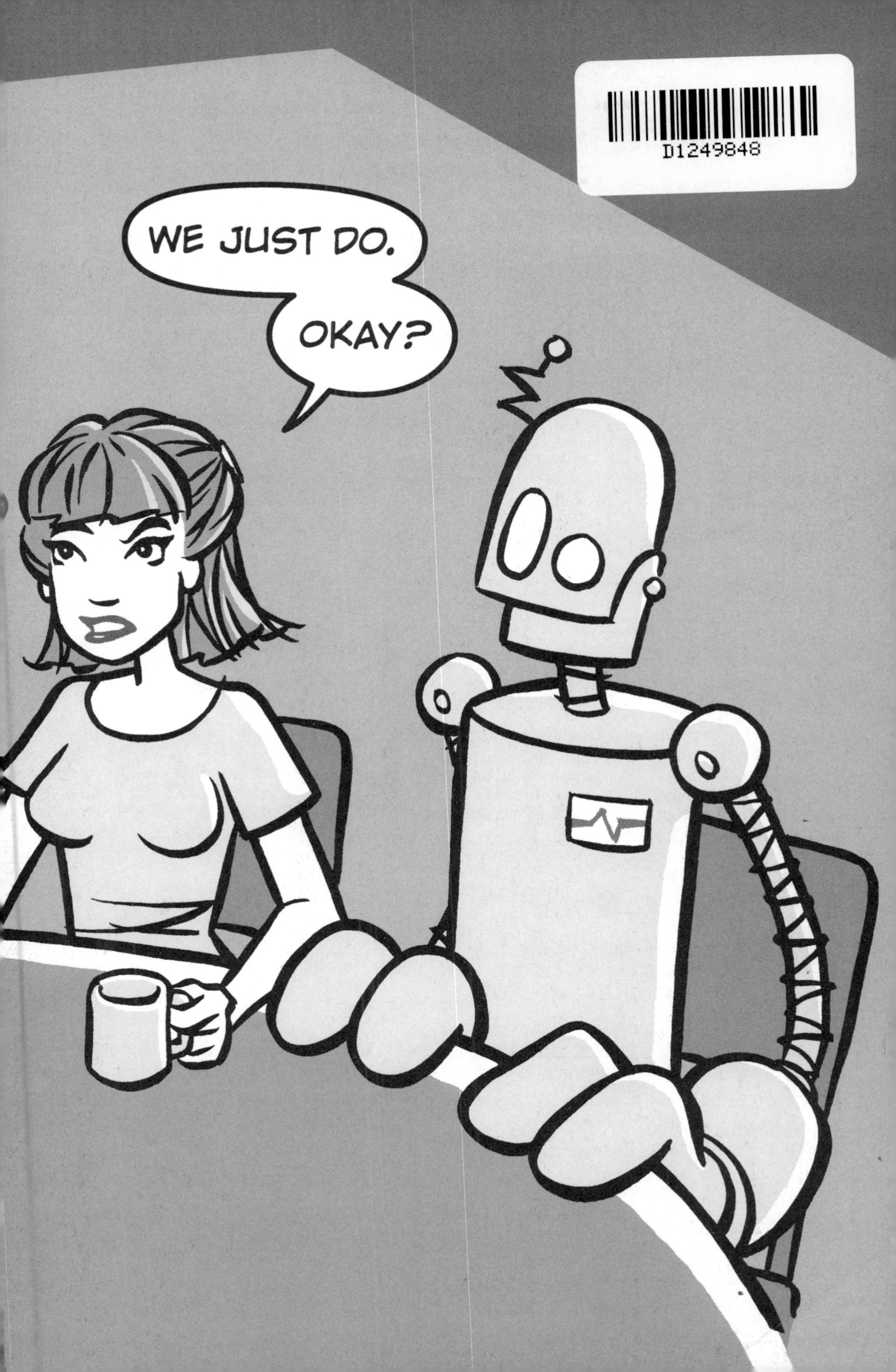
WE JUST DO.
OKAY?

A series by Kerry Callen   angelrobot@hotmail.com

For
Ellen,
Anna,
Chris &
Martin

Halo and Sprocket Volume 1: Welcome to Humanity

This volume collects Halo and Sprocket issues #1 through #4, published 2002, 2003. "Aw Heck" originally appeared in Slave Labor Stories, 2003. "Spontaneous Human Combustion Explained" originally appeared in Show and Tell #1, published by Void Pulp Press, 2003. All other material previously unpublished.

Published by Amaze Ink, a division of SLG Publishing, P.O. Box 26427, San Jose, CA 95159-6427.

Dan Vado – President & Publisher
Jennifer de Guzman – Editor-in-Chief
Deb Moskyok – Director of Sales

www.slavelabor.com.
Call 1- 877-754-7877 for a free catalog

Second Printing: June 2008

PRINTED IN CANADA

ISBN: 0-943151-81-3

HALO AND SPROCKET

Volume 1

WELCOME TO HUMANITY

by Kerry Callen

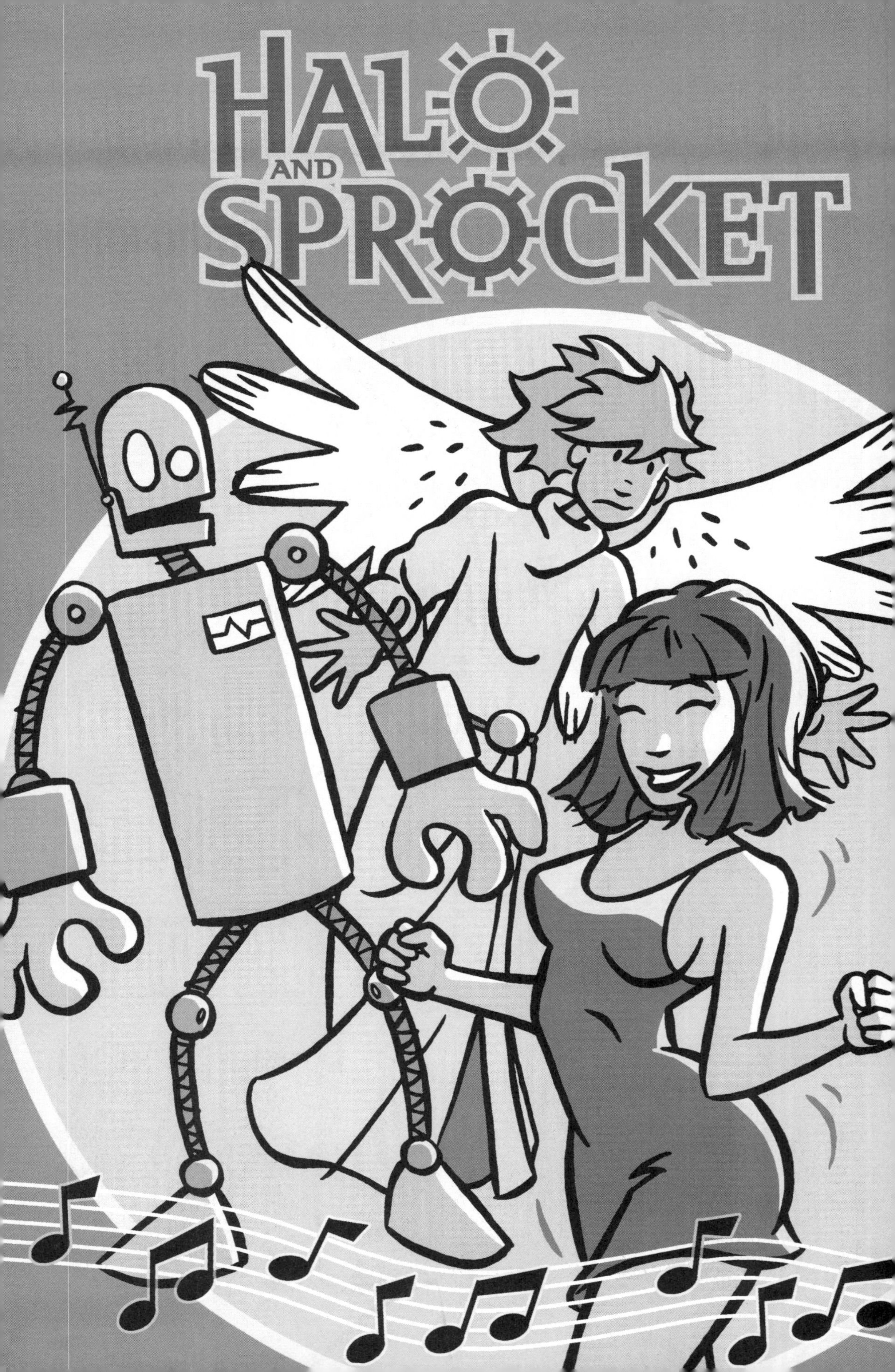
HALO AND SPROCKET

HALO AND SPROCKET™

"HALF WITS"

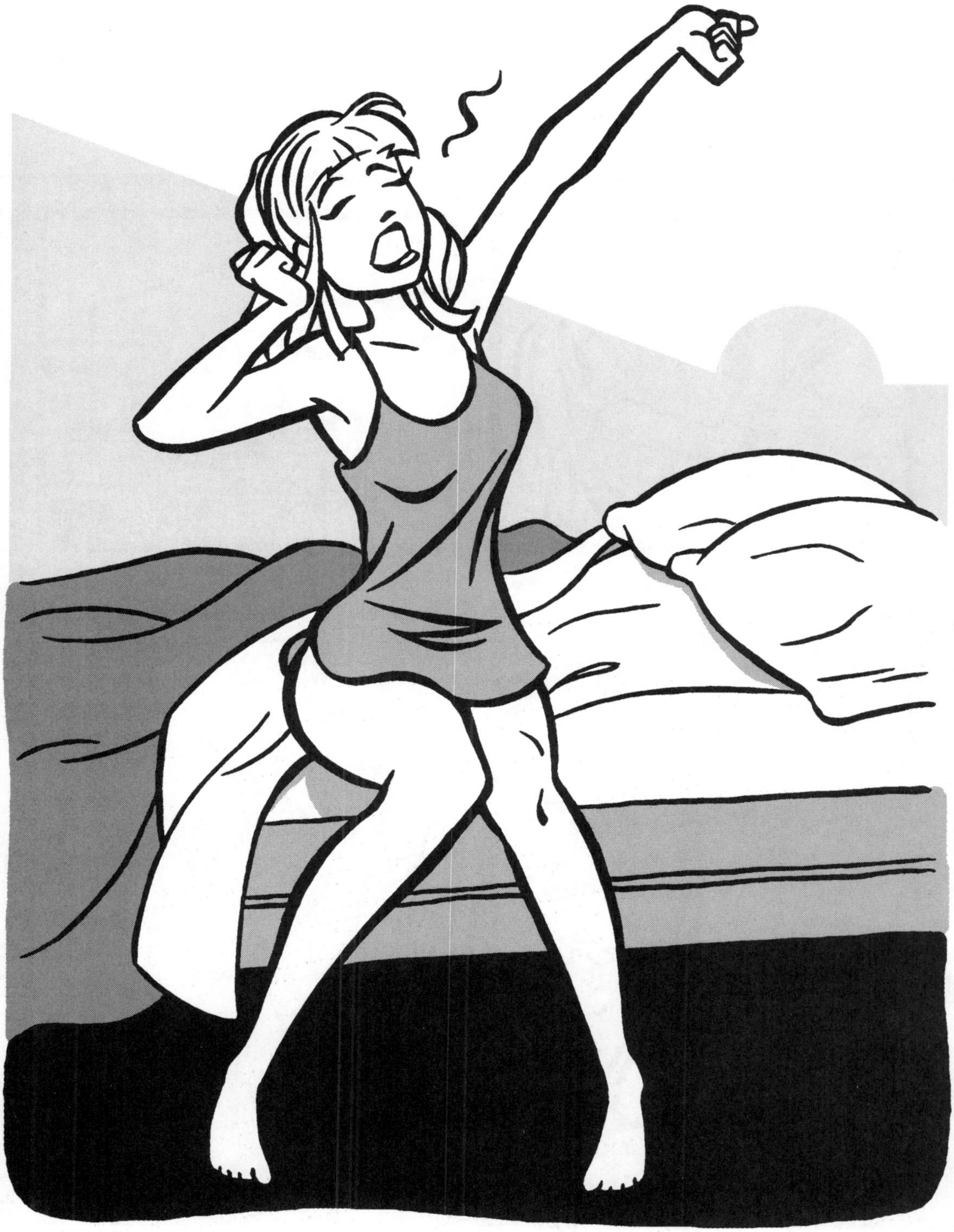

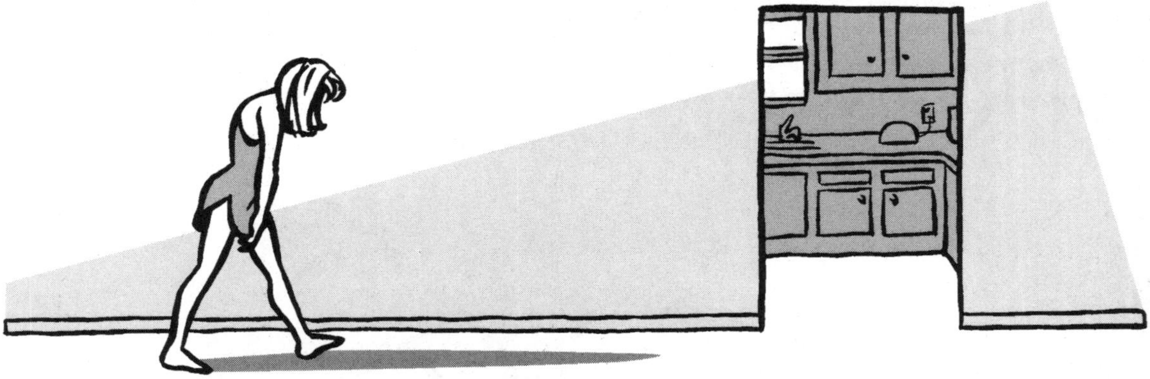

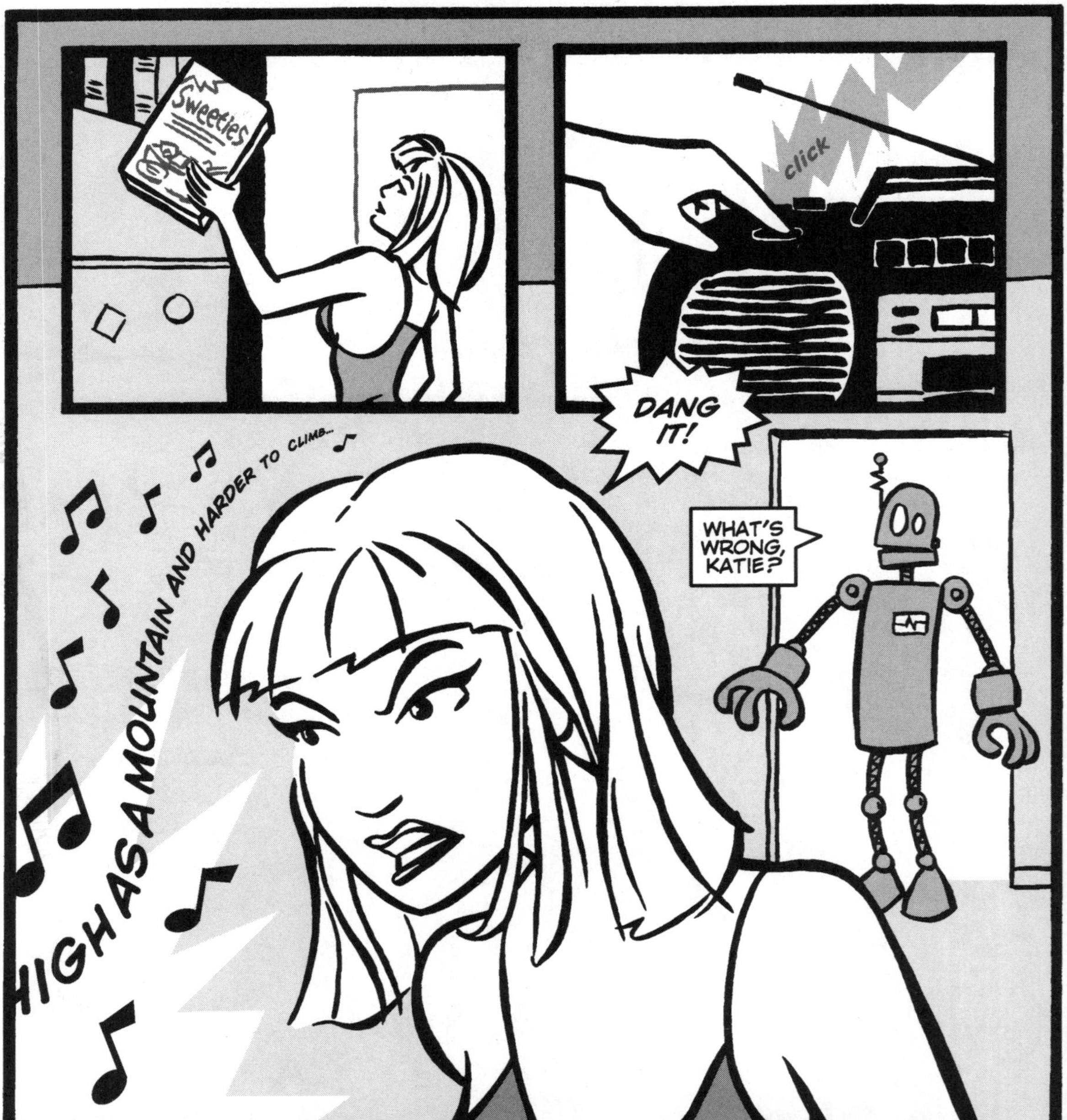
Sweeties
click
DANG IT!
HIGH AS A MOUNTAIN AND HARDER TO CLIMB...
WHAT'S WRONG, KATIE?

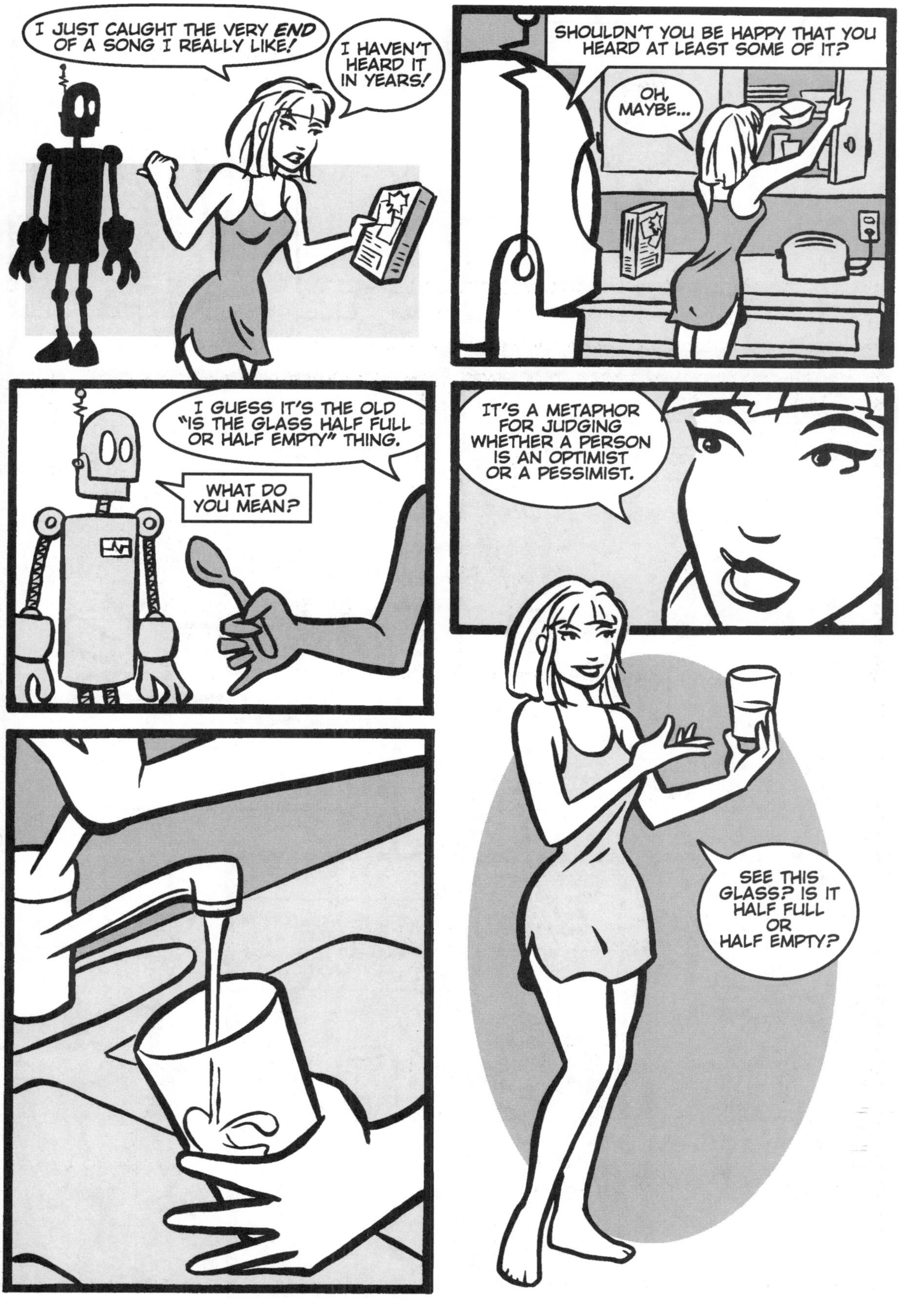
I JUST CAUGHT THE VERY *END* OF A SONG I REALLY LIKE!
I HAVEN'T HEARD IT IN YEARS!
SHOULDN'T YOU BE HAPPY THAT YOU HEARD AT LEAST SOME OF IT?
OH, MAYBE...
I GUESS IT'S THE OLD "IS THE GLASS HALF FULL OR HALF EMPTY" THING.
WHAT DO YOU MEAN?
IT'S A METAPHOR FOR JUDGING WHETHER A PERSON IS AN OPTIMIST OR A PESSIMIST.
SEE THIS GLASS? IS IT HALF FULL OR HALF EMPTY?

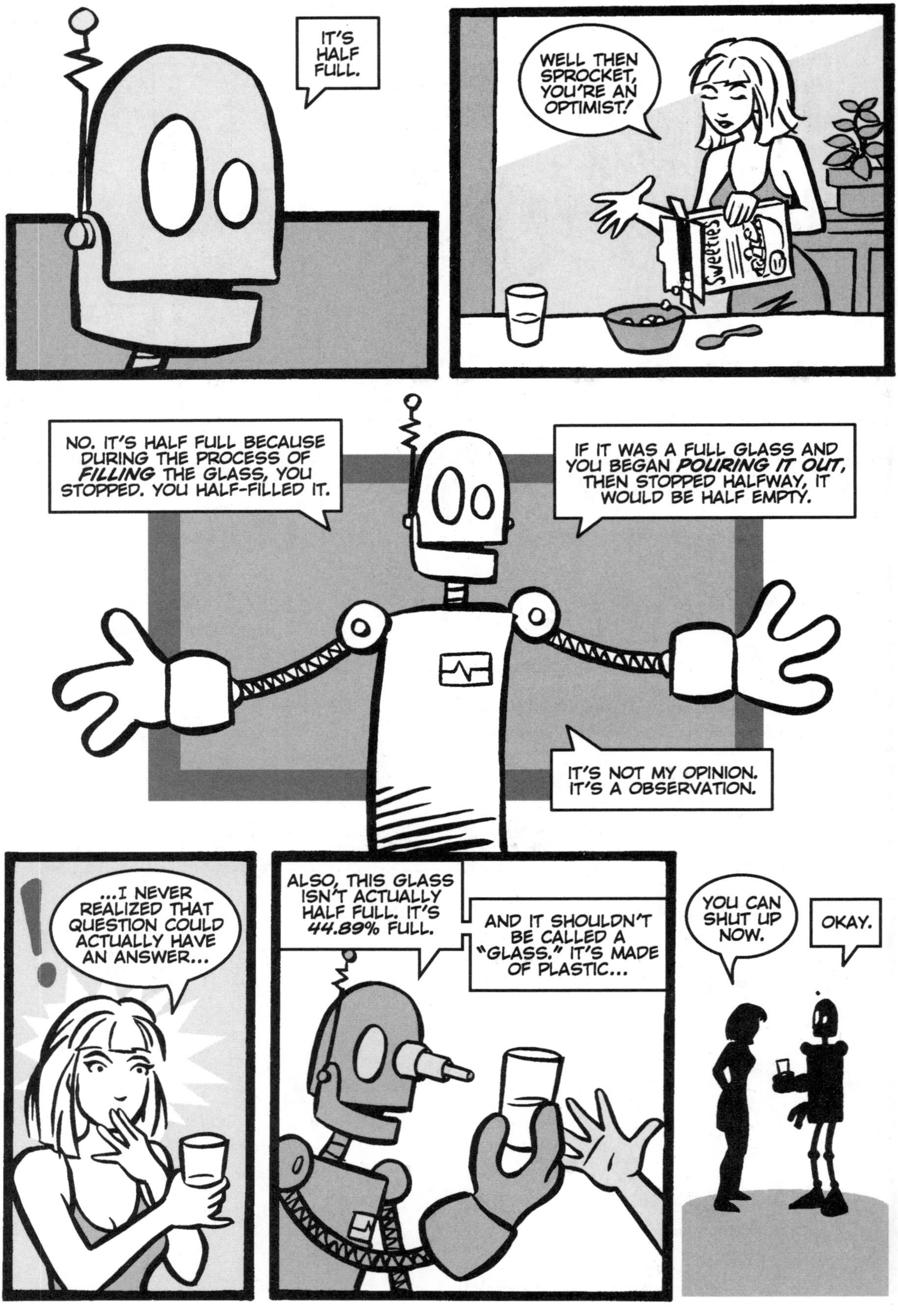
IT'S HALF FULL.
WELL THEN SPROCKET, YOU'RE AN OPTIMIST!
SWEETIES
NO. IT'S HALF FULL BECAUSE DURING THE PROCESS OF *FILLING* THE GLASS, YOU STOPPED. YOU HALF-FILLED IT.
IF IT WAS A FULL GLASS AND YOU BEGAN *POURING IT OUT*, THEN STOPPED HALFWAY, IT WOULD BE HALF EMPTY.
IT'S NOT MY OPINION. IT'S A OBSERVATION.
...I NEVER REALIZED THAT QUESTION COULD ACTUALLY HAVE AN ANSWER...
ALSO, THIS GLASS ISN'T ACTUALLY HALF FULL. IT'S *44.89%* FULL.
AND IT SHOULDN'T BE CALLED A "GLASS." IT'S MADE OF PLASTIC...
YOU CAN SHUT UP NOW.
OKAY.

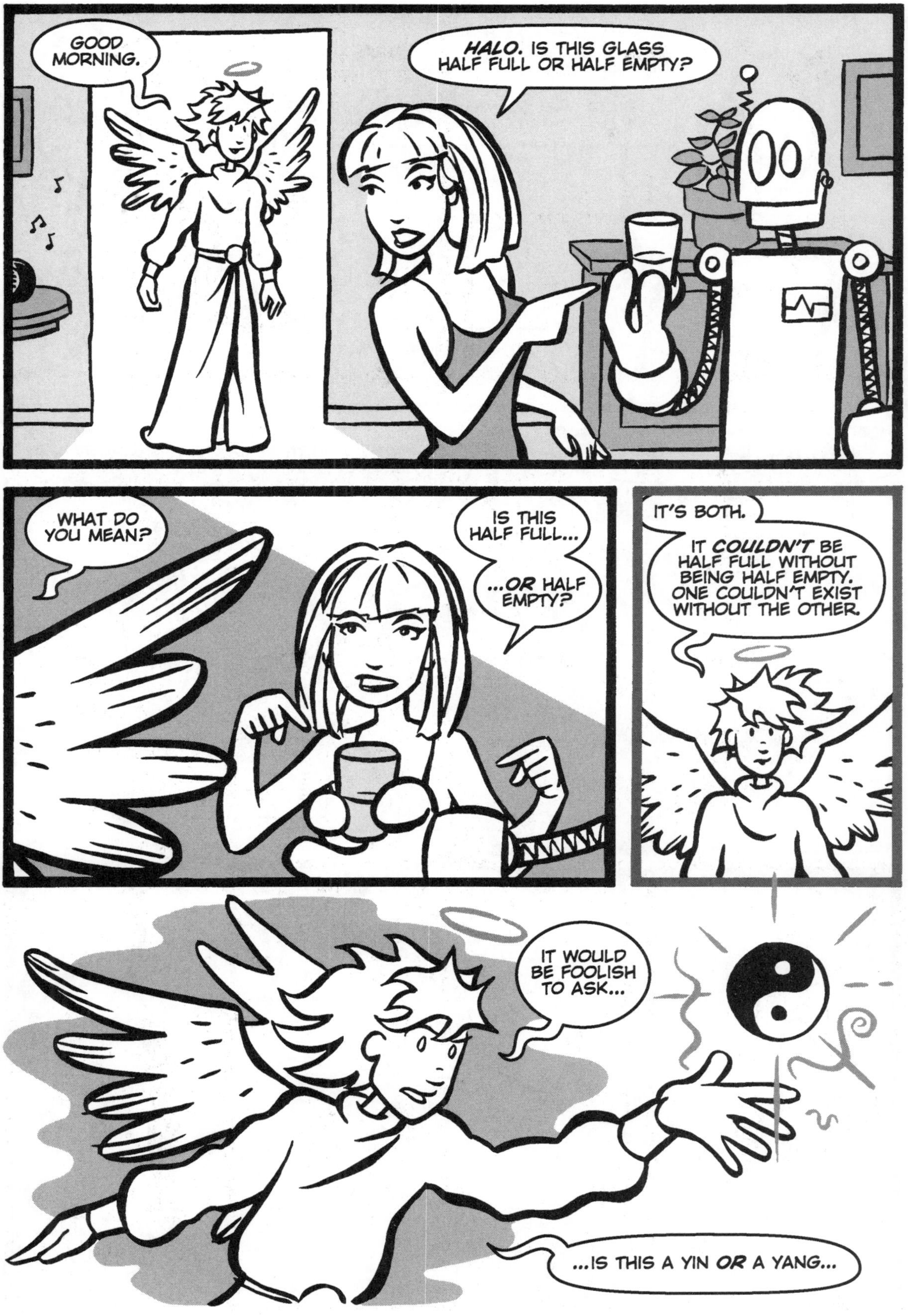
GOOD MORNING.
HALO. IS THIS GLASS HALF FULL OR HALF EMPTY?
WHAT DO YOU MEAN?
IS THIS HALF FULL...
...OR HALF EMPTY?
IT'S BOTH.
IT COULDN'T BE HALF FULL WITHOUT BEING HALF EMPTY. ONE COULDN'T EXIST WITHOUT THE OTHER.
IT WOULD BE FOOLISH TO ASK...
...IS THIS A YIN OR A YANG...

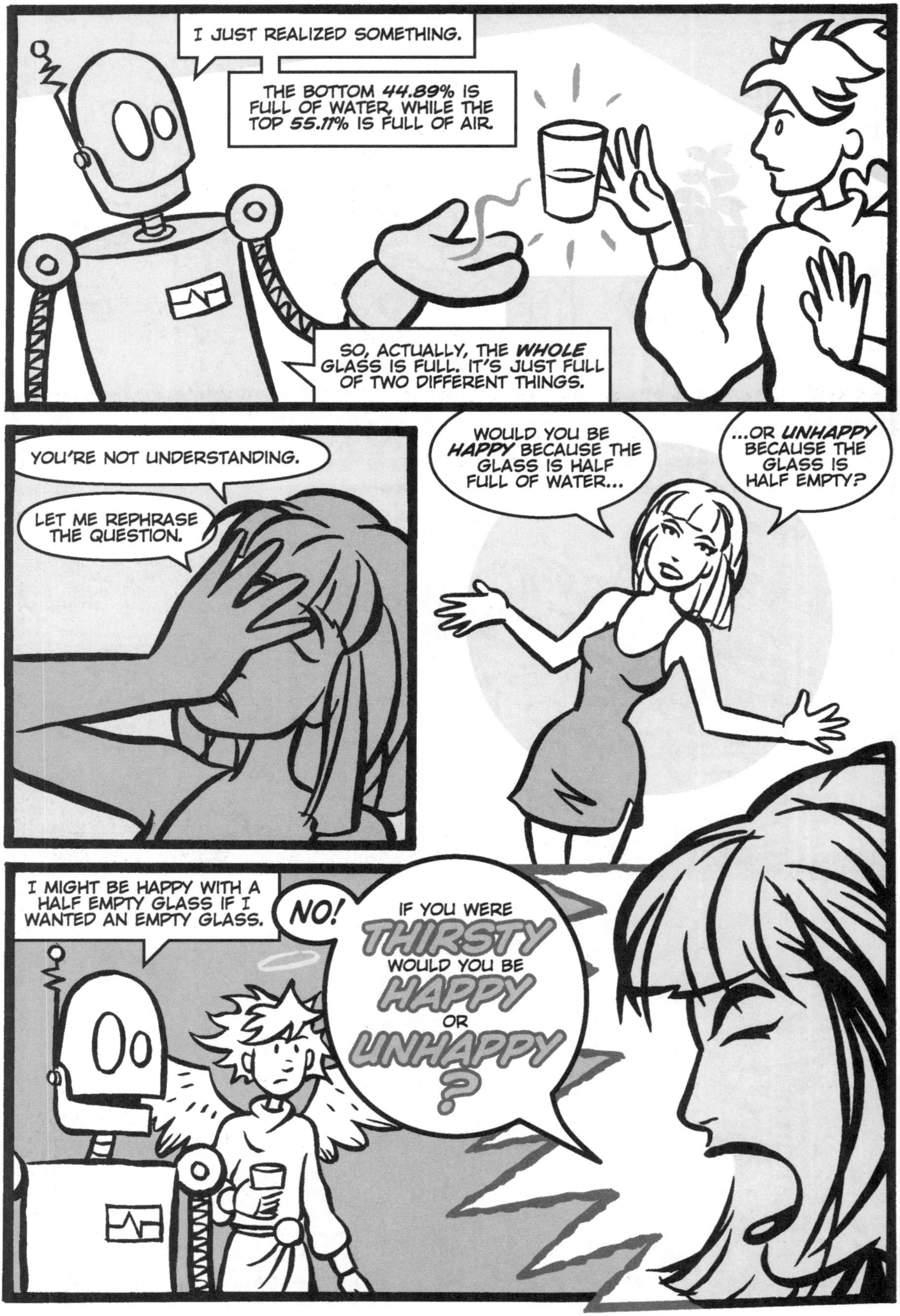
I JUST REALIZED SOMETHING.
THE BOTTOM 44.89% IS FULL OF WATER, WHILE THE TOP 55.11% IS FULL OF AIR.
SO, ACTUALLY, THE WHOLE GLASS IS FULL. IT'S JUST FULL OF TWO DIFFERENT THINGS.
YOU'RE NOT UNDERSTANDING.
LET ME REPHRASE THE QUESTION.
WOULD YOU BE HAPPY BECAUSE THE GLASS IS HALF FULL OF WATER...
...OR UNHAPPY BECAUSE THE GLASS IS HALF EMPTY?
I MIGHT BE HAPPY WITH A HALF EMPTY GLASS IF I WANTED AN EMPTY GLASS.
NO!
IF YOU WERE THIRSTY WOULD YOU BE HAPPY OR UNHAPPY?

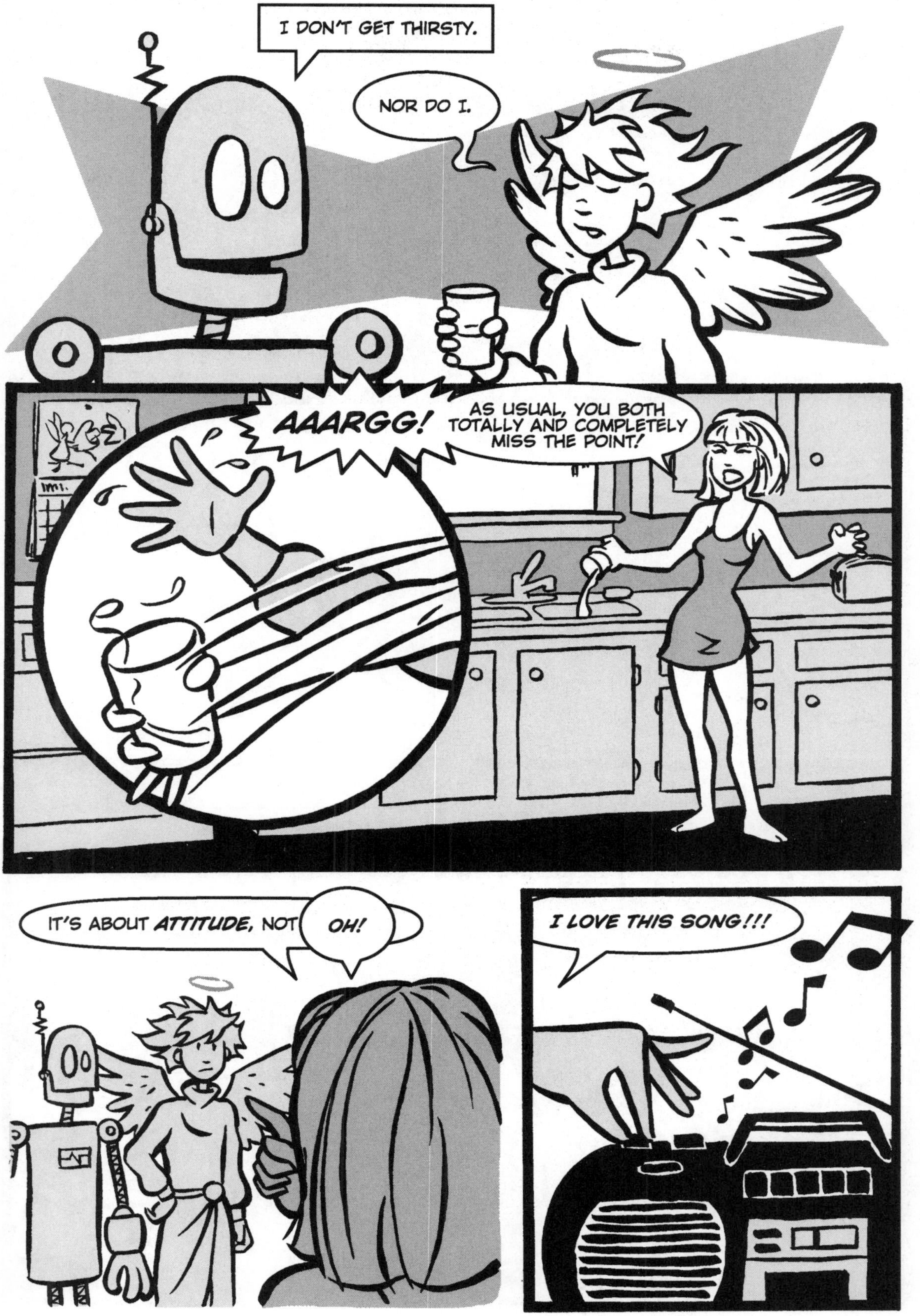
I DON'T GET THIRSTY.
NOR DO I.
AAARGG!
AS USUAL, YOU BOTH TOTALLY AND COMPLETELY MISS THE POINT!
IT'S ABOUT ATTITUDE, NOT
OH!
I LOVE THIS SONG!!!

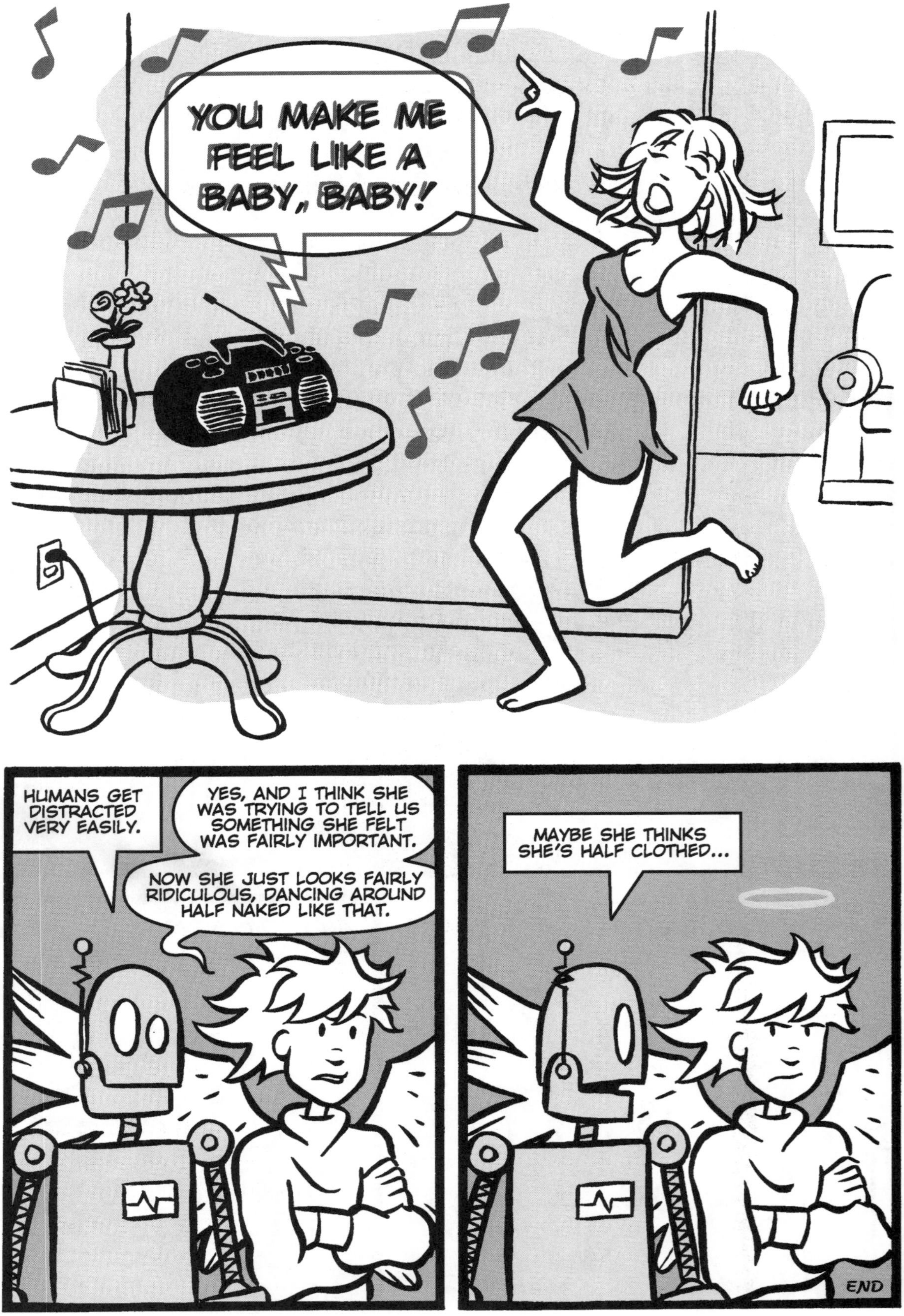
YOU MAKE ME FEEL LIKE A BABY,, BABY!
HUMANS GET DISTRACTED VERY EASILY.
YES, AND I THINK SHE WAS TRYING TO TELL US SOMETHING SHE FELT WAS FAIRLY IMPORTANT.
NOW SHE JUST LOOKS FAIRLY RIDICULOUS, DANCING AROUND HALF NAKED LIKE THAT.
MAYBE SHE THINKS SHE'S HALF CLOTHED...
END

HALO AND SPROCKET

"NAMES"

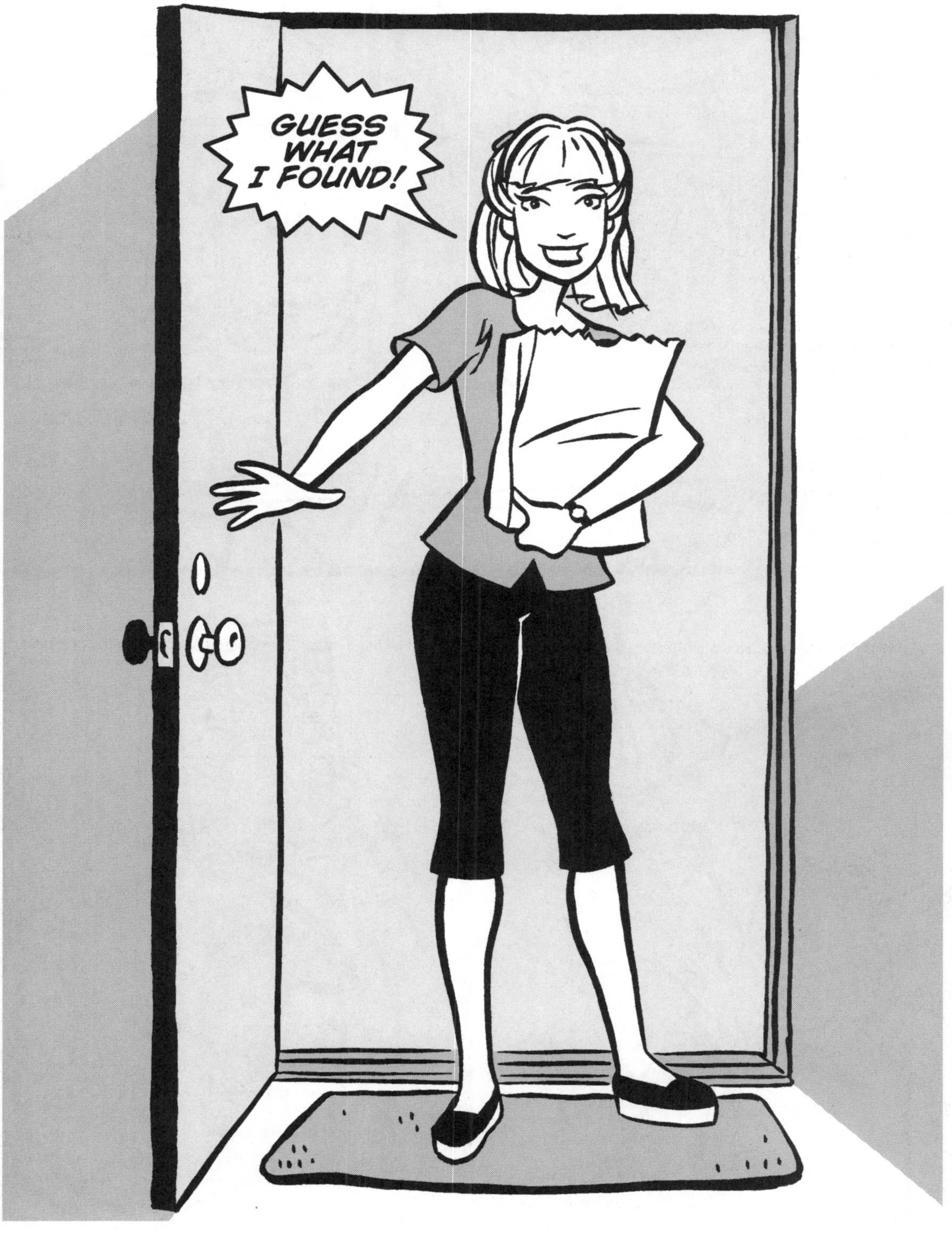
GUESS WHAT I FOUND!

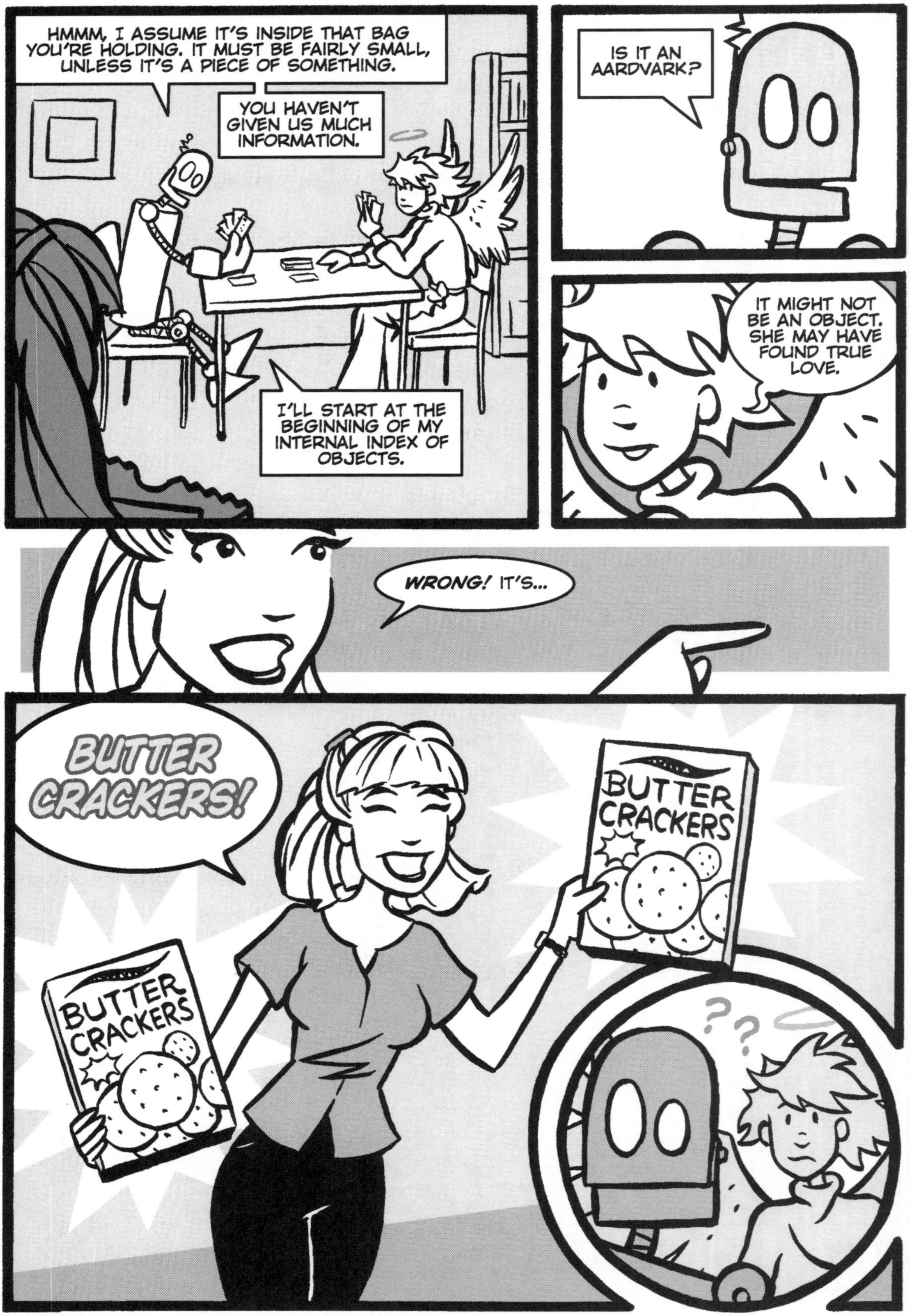
HMMM, I ASSUME IT'S INSIDE THAT BAG YOU'RE HOLDING. IT MUST BE FAIRLY SMALL, UNLESS IT'S A PIECE OF SOMETHING.
YOU HAVEN'T GIVEN US MUCH INFORMATION.
I'LL START AT THE BEGINNING OF MY INTERNAL INDEX OF OBJECTS.
IS IT AN AARDVARK?
IT MIGHT NOT BE AN OBJECT. SHE MAY HAVE FOUND TRUE LOVE.
WRONG! IT'S...
BUTTER CRACKERS!
BUTTER CRACKERS
BUTTER CRACKERS
? ?

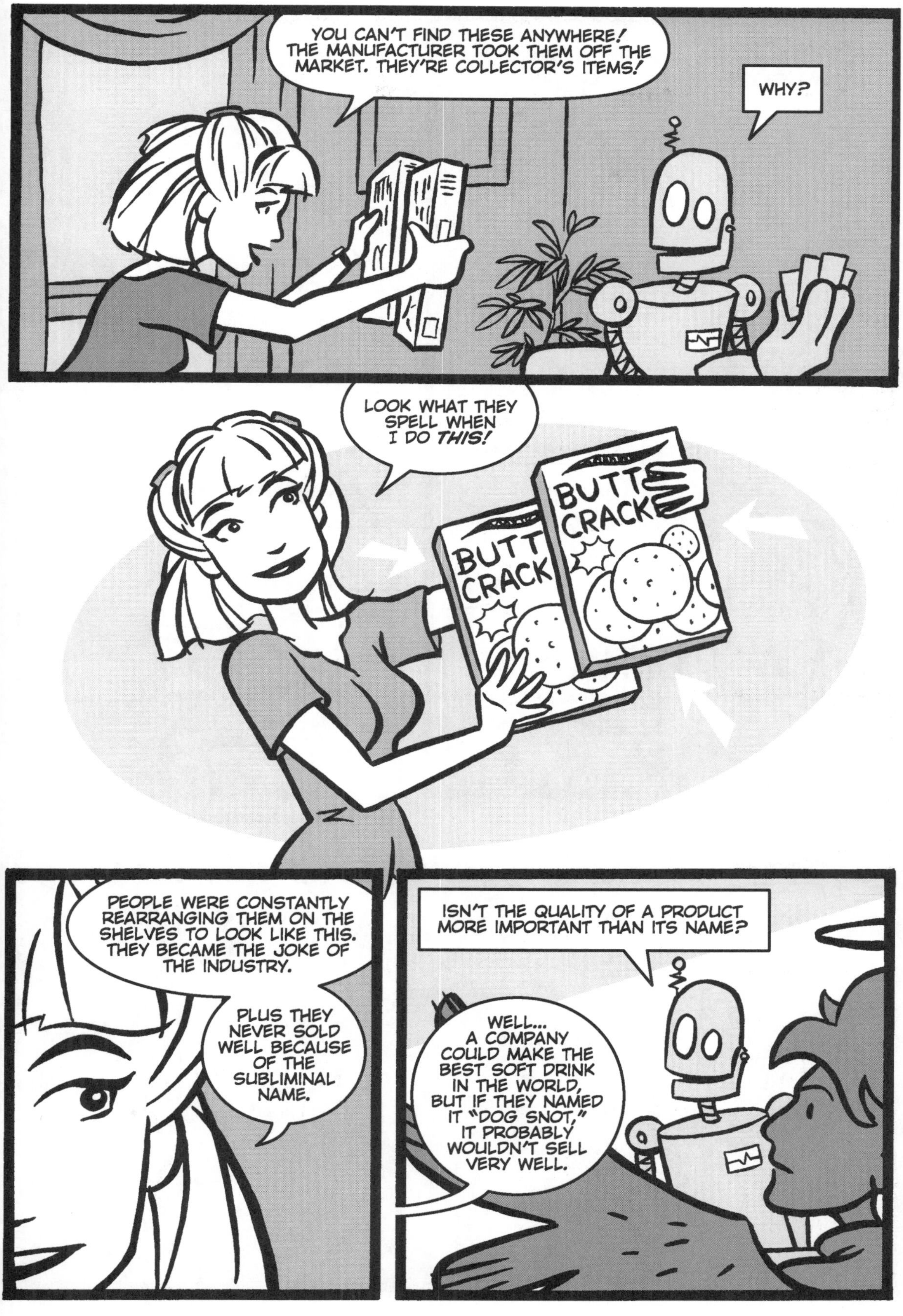
YOU CAN'T FIND THESE ANYWHERE! THE MANUFACTURER TOOK THEM OFF THE MARKET. THEY'RE COLLECTOR'S ITEMS!
WHY?
LOOK WHAT THEY SPELL WHEN I DO *THIS!*
BUTT CRACK
BUTT CRACK
PEOPLE WERE CONSTANTLY REARRANGING THEM ON THE SHELVES TO LOOK LIKE THIS. THEY BECAME THE JOKE OF THE INDUSTRY.
PLUS THEY NEVER SOLD WELL BECAUSE OF THE SUBLIMINAL NAME.
ISN'T THE QUALITY OF A PRODUCT MORE IMPORTANT THAN ITS NAME?
WELL... A COMPANY COULD MAKE THE BEST SOFT DRINK IN THE WORLD, BUT IF THEY NAMED IT "DOG SNOT," IT PROBABLY WOULDN'T SELL VERY WELL.

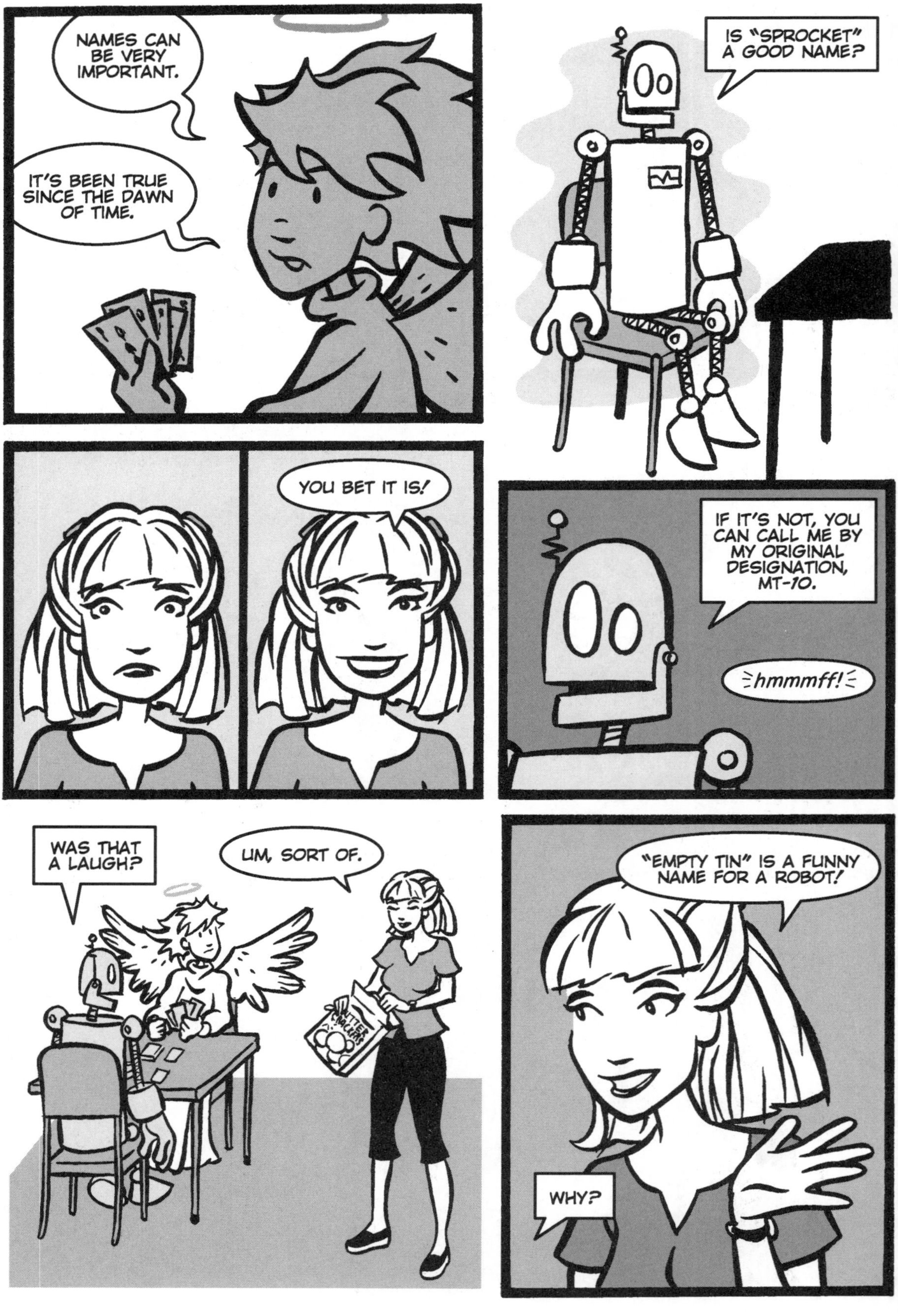
NAMES CAN BE VERY IMPORTANT.
IT'S BEEN TRUE SINCE THE DAWN OF TIME.
IS "SPROCKET" A GOOD NAME?
YOU BET IT IS!
IF IT'S NOT, YOU CAN CALL ME BY MY ORIGINAL DESIGNATION, MT-10.
hmmmff!
WAS THAT A LAUGH?
UM, SORT OF.
"EMPTY TIN" IS A FUNNY NAME FOR A ROBOT!
WHY?

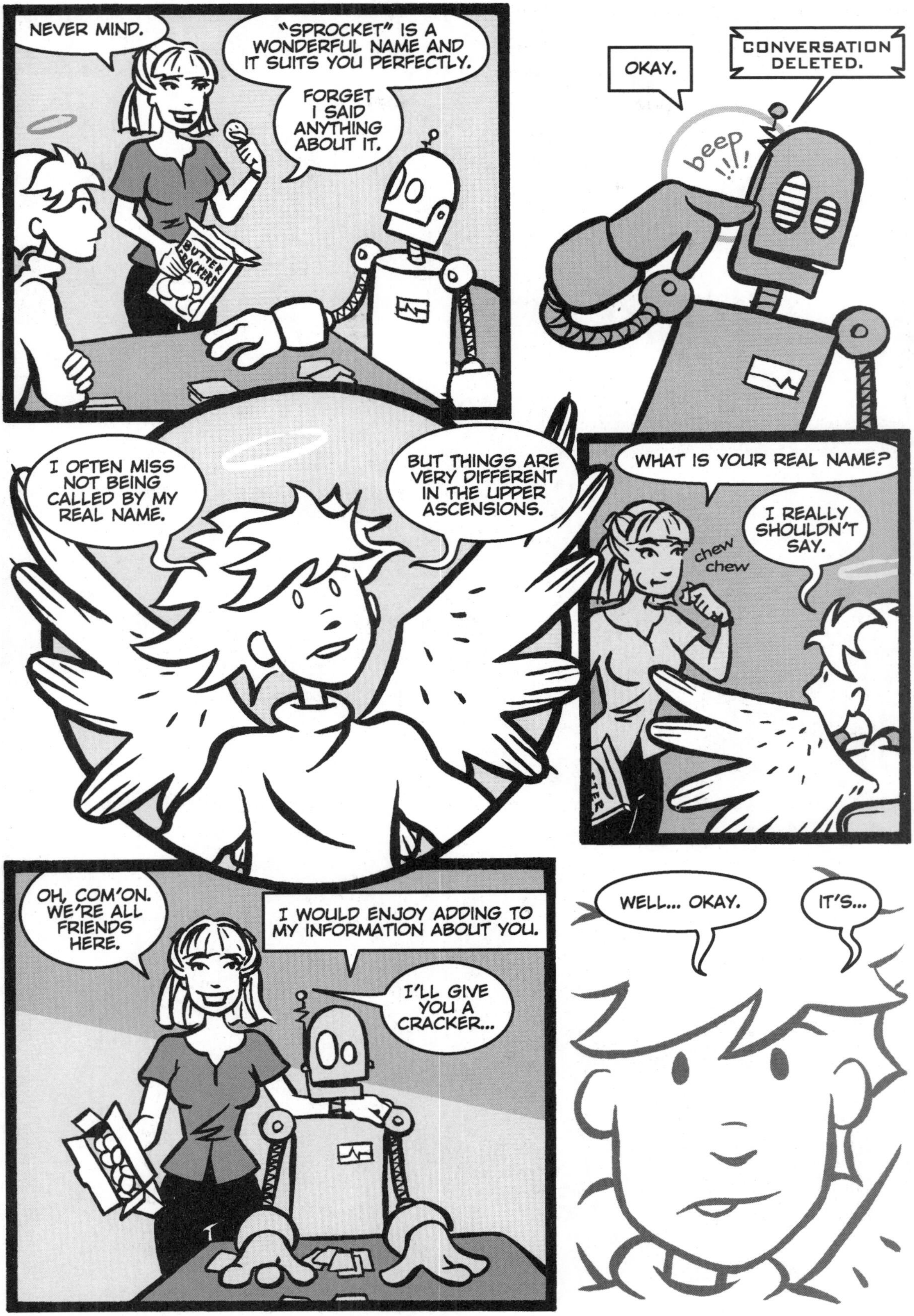
NEVER MIND.
"SPROCKET" IS A WONDERFUL NAME AND IT SUITS YOU PERFECTLY.
FORGET I SAID ANYTHING ABOUT IT.
BUTTER CRACKERS
OKAY.
CONVERSATION DELETED.
beep !!/!
I OFTEN MISS NOT BEING CALLED BY MY REAL NAME.
BUT THINGS ARE VERY DIFFERENT IN THE UPPER ASCENSIONS.
WHAT IS YOUR REAL NAME?
chew chew
I REALLY SHOULDN'T SAY.
OH, COM'ON. WE'RE ALL FRIENDS HERE.
I WOULD ENJOY ADDING TO MY INFORMATION ABOUT YOU.
I'LL GIVE YOU A CRACKER...
WELL... OKAY.
IT'S...

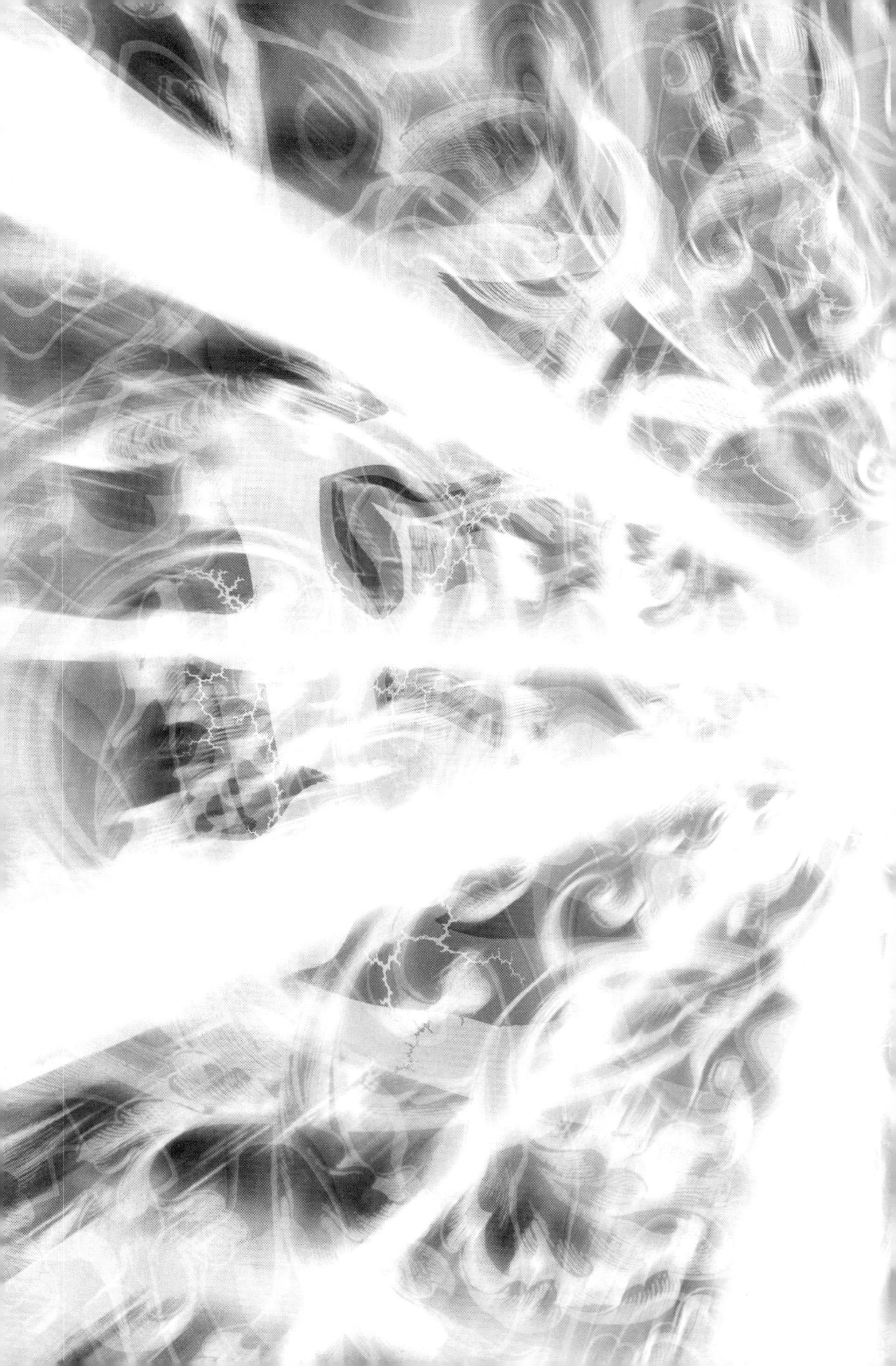

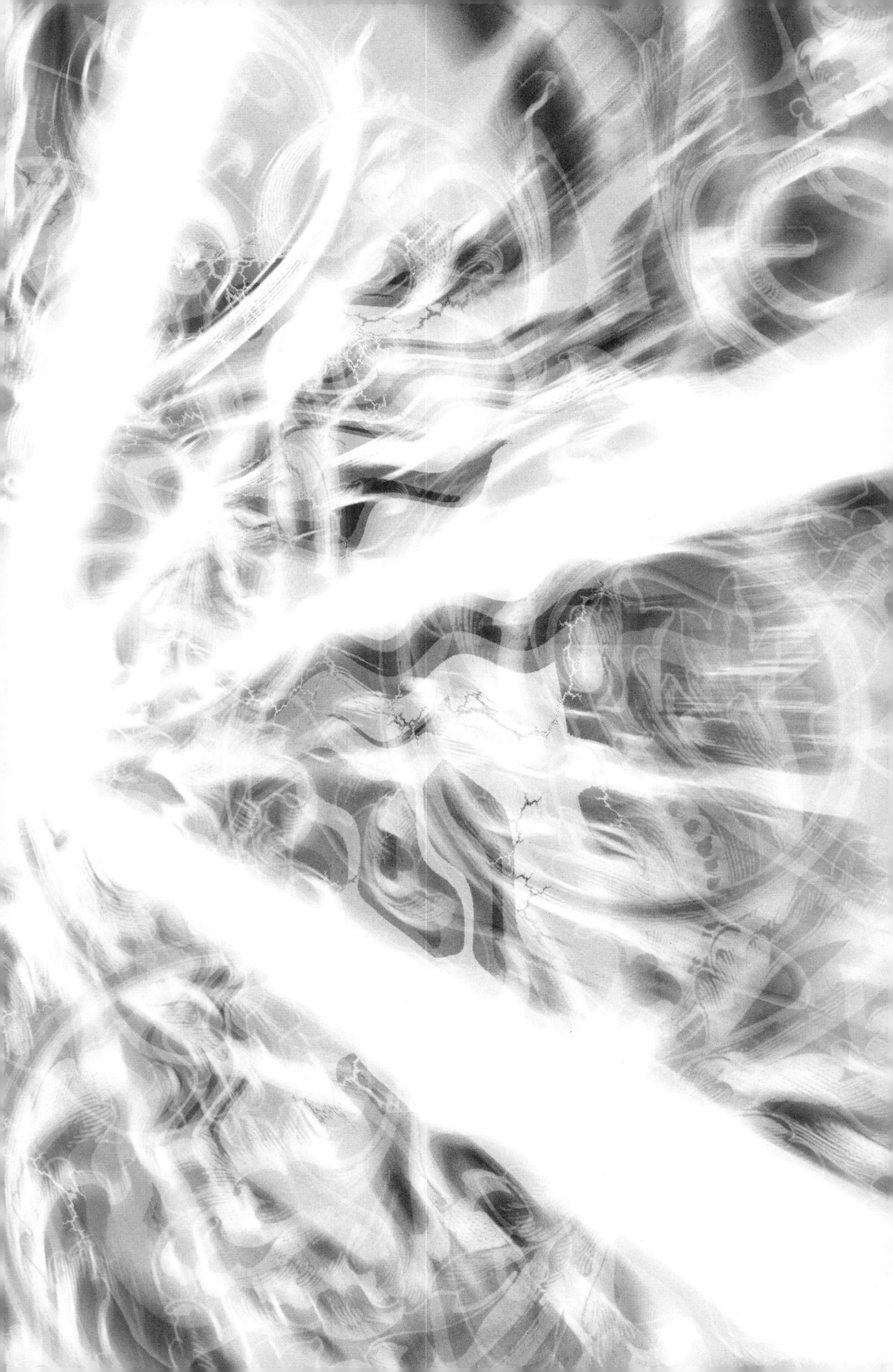

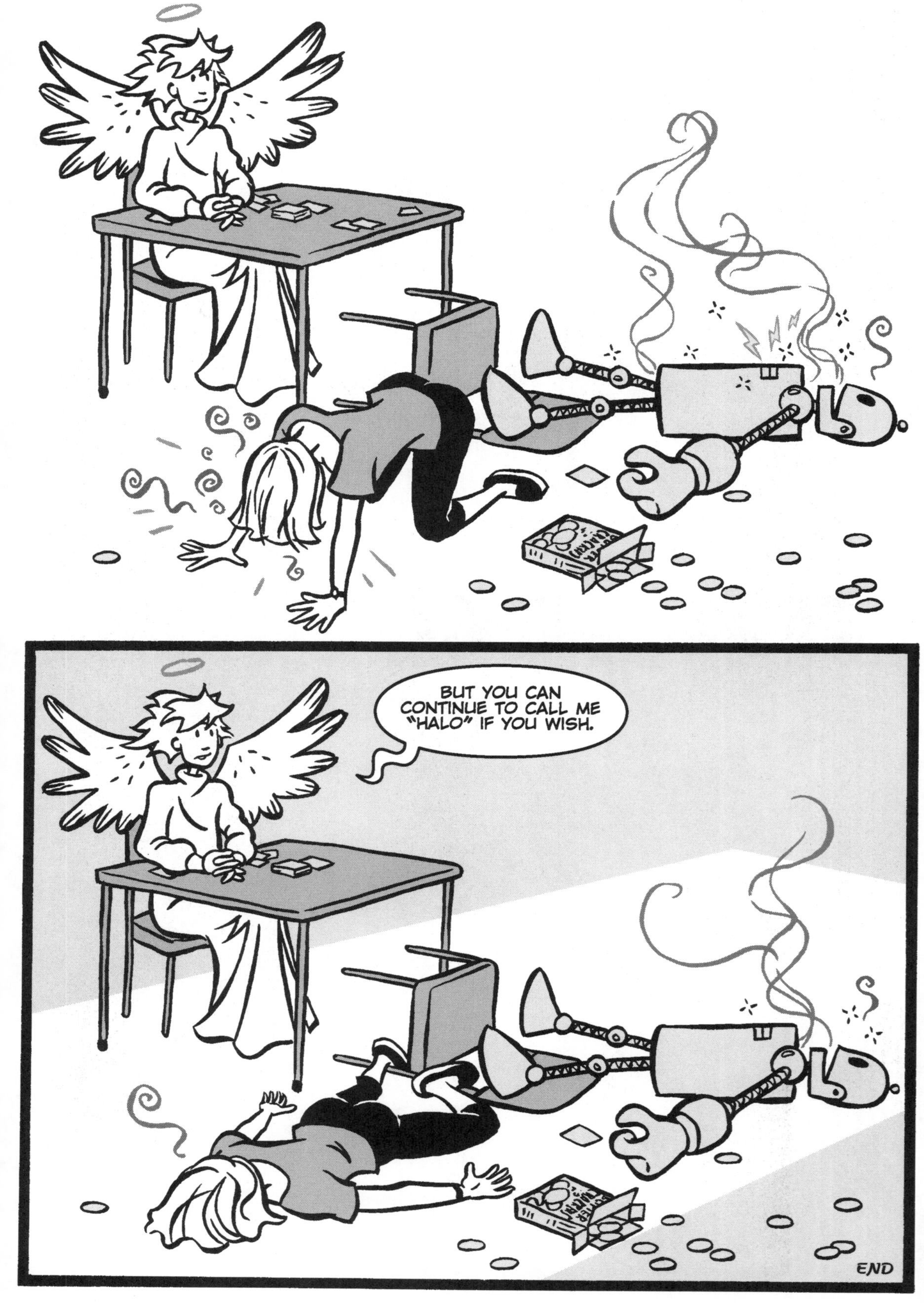
BUT YOU CAN CONTINUE TO CALL ME "HALO" IF YOU WISH.
END

HALO AND SPROCKET

"EXHIBITIONS"

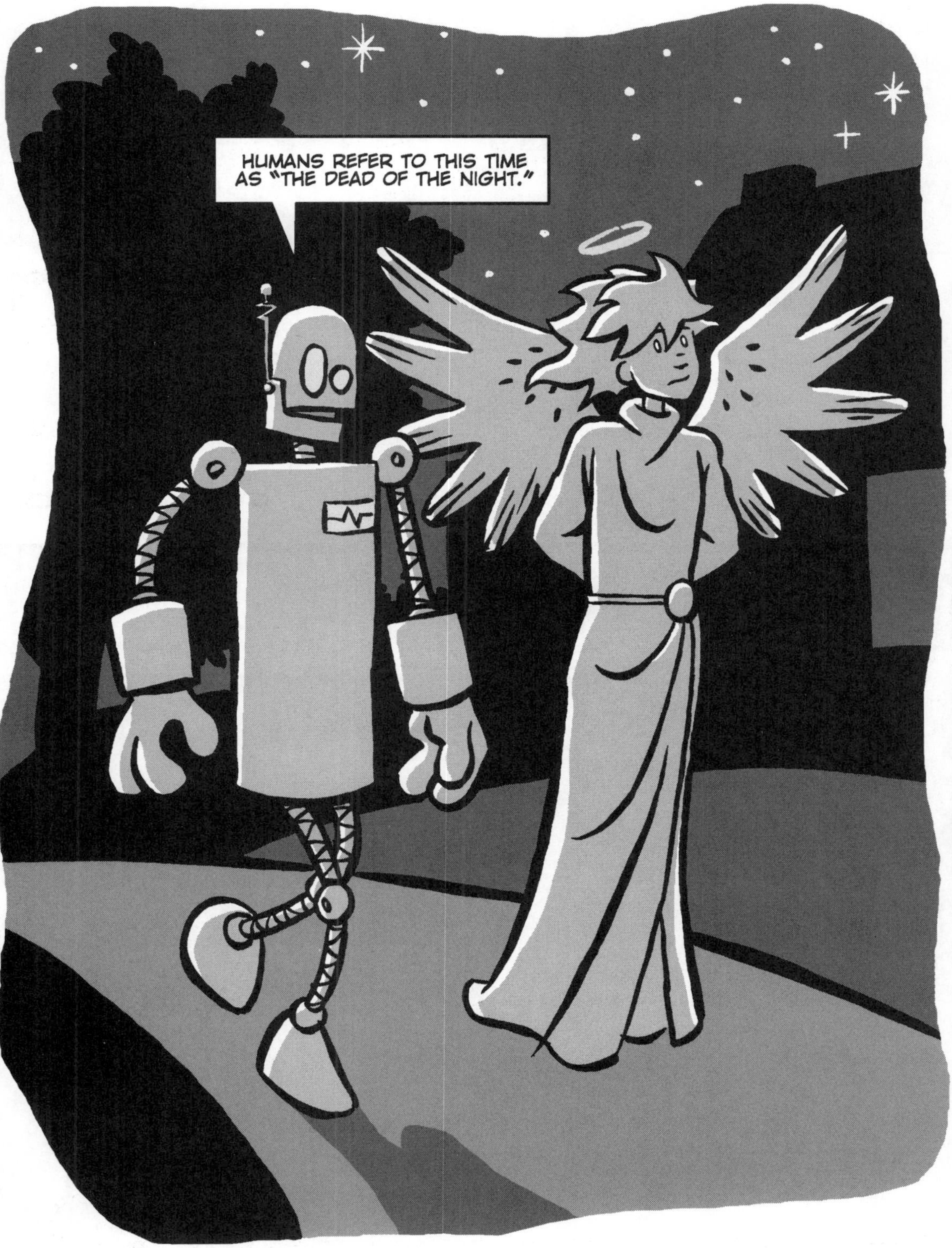
HUMANS REFER TO THIS TIME AS "THE DEAD OF THE NIGHT."

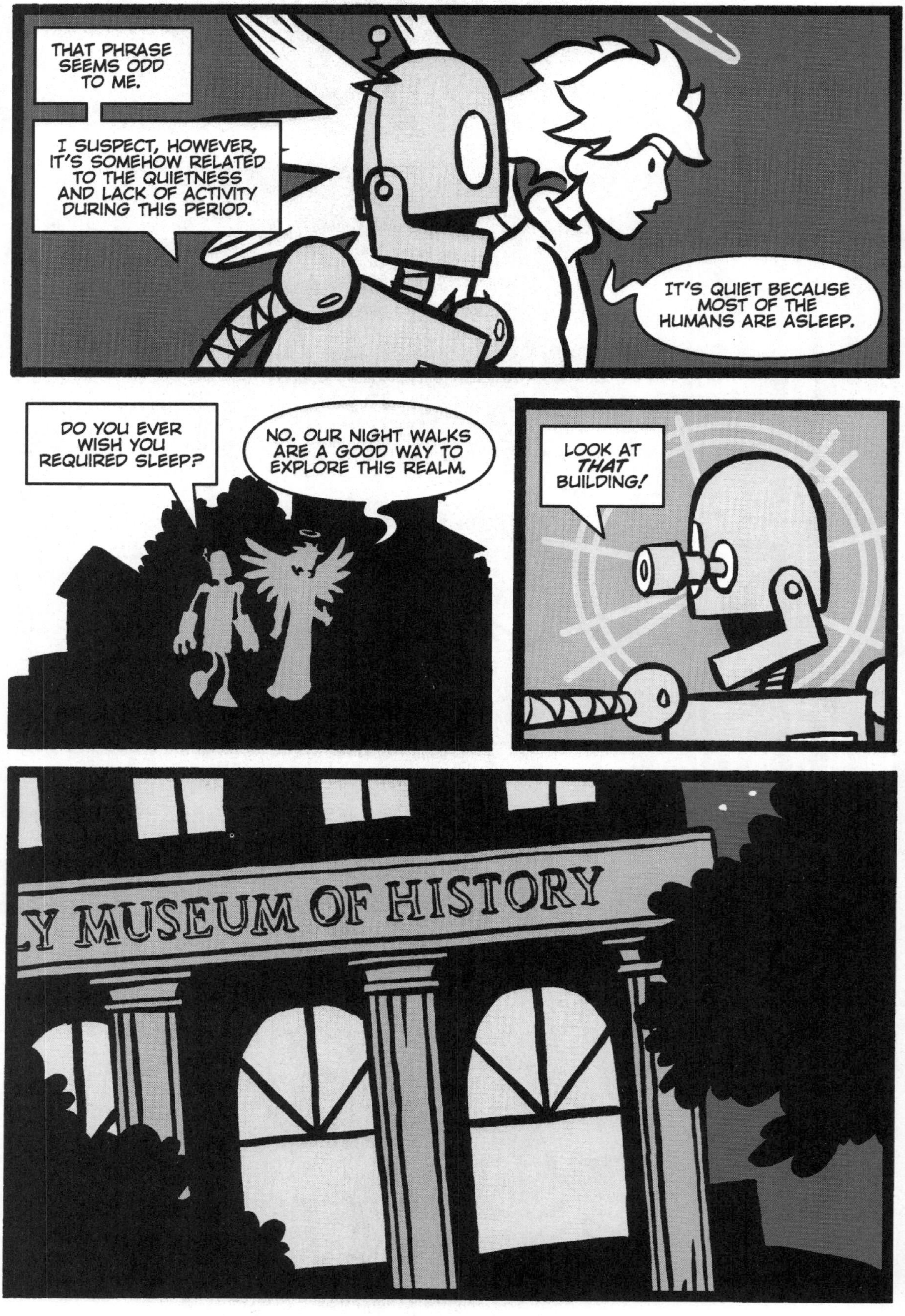
THAT PHRASE SEEMS ODD TO ME.
I SUSPECT, HOWEVER, IT'S SOMEHOW RELATED TO THE QUIETNESS AND LACK OF ACTIVITY DURING THIS PERIOD.
IT'S QUIET BECAUSE MOST OF THE HUMANS ARE ASLEEP.
DO YOU EVER WISH YOU REQUIRED SLEEP?
NO. OUR NIGHT WALKS ARE A GOOD WAY TO EXPLORE THIS REALM.
LOOK AT *THAT* BUILDING!
LY MUSEUM OF HISTORY

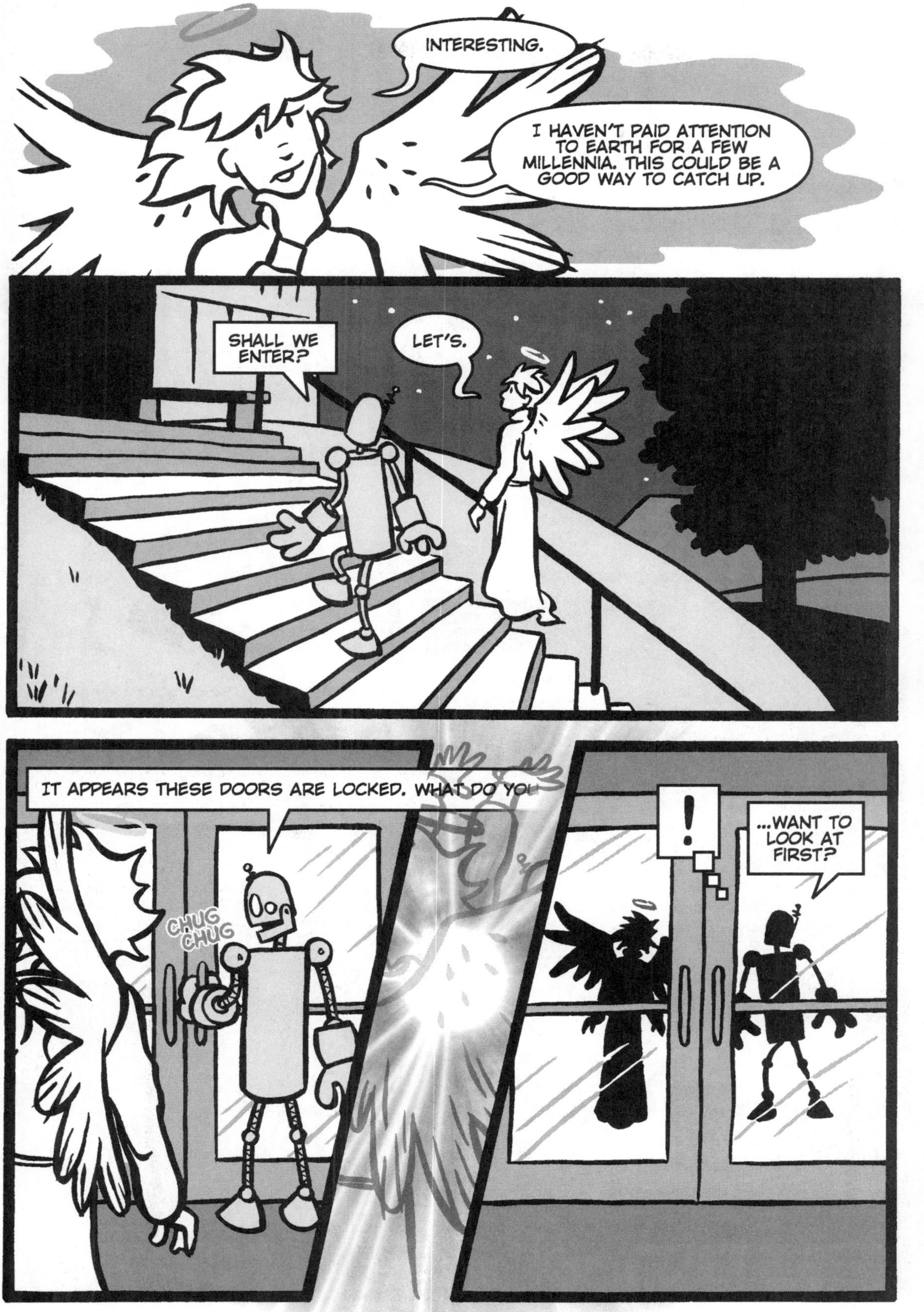
INTERESTING.
I HAVEN'T PAID ATTENTION TO EARTH FOR A FEW MILLENNIA. THIS COULD BE A GOOD WAY TO CATCH UP.
SHALL WE ENTER?
LET'S.
IT APPEARS THESE DOORS ARE LOCKED. WHAT DO YOU
CHUG CHUG
!
...WANT TO LOOK AT FIRST?

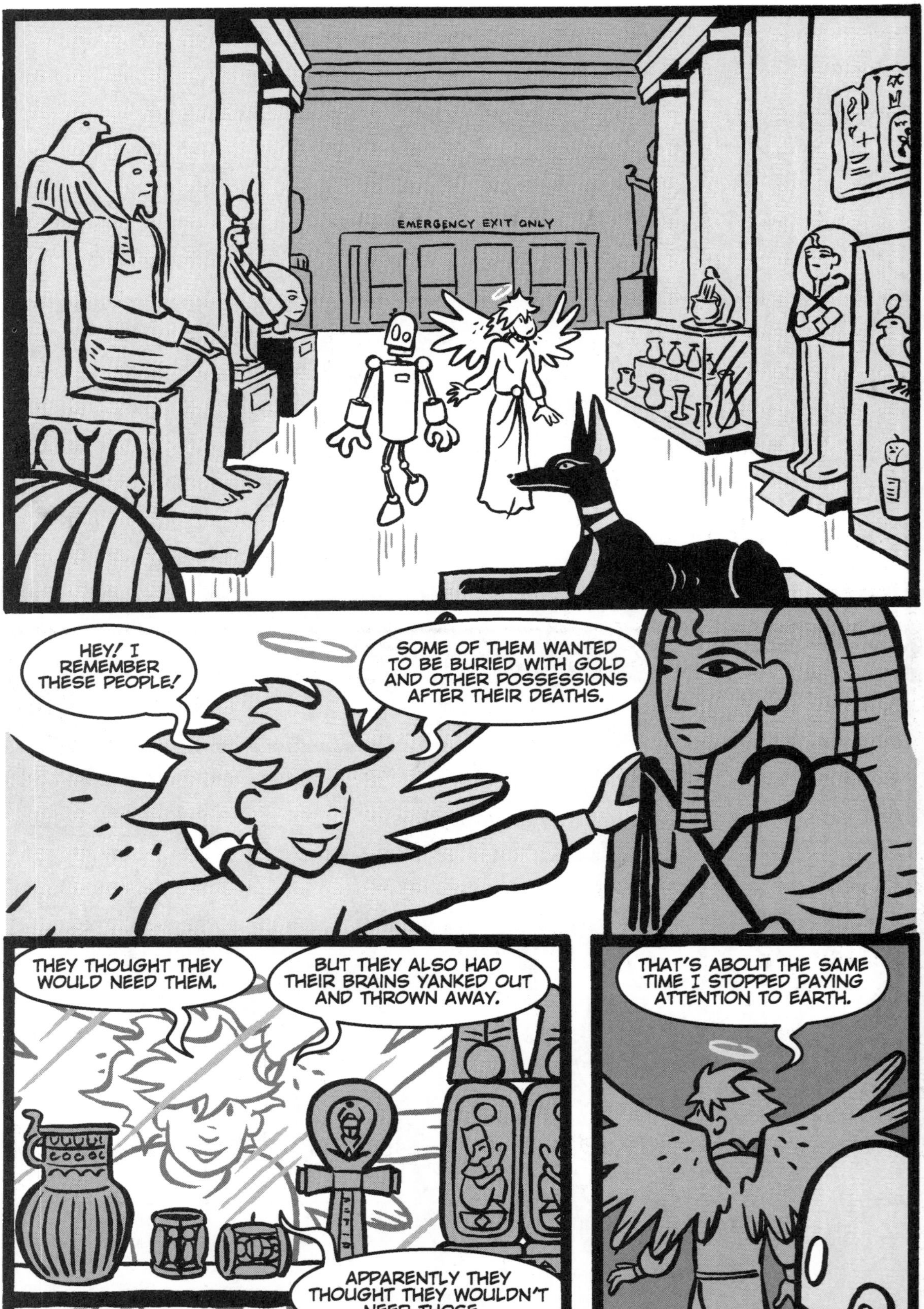
EMERGENCY EXIT ONLY
HEY! I REMEMBER THESE PEOPLE!
SOME OF THEM WANTED TO BE BURIED WITH GOLD AND OTHER POSSESSIONS AFTER THEIR DEATHS.
THEY THOUGHT THEY WOULD NEED THEM.
BUT THEY ALSO HAD THEIR BRAINS YANKED OUT AND THROWN AWAY.
APPARENTLY THEY THOUGHT THEY WOULDN'T NEED THOSE...
THAT'S ABOUT THE SAME TIME I STOPPED PAYING ATTENTION TO EARTH.

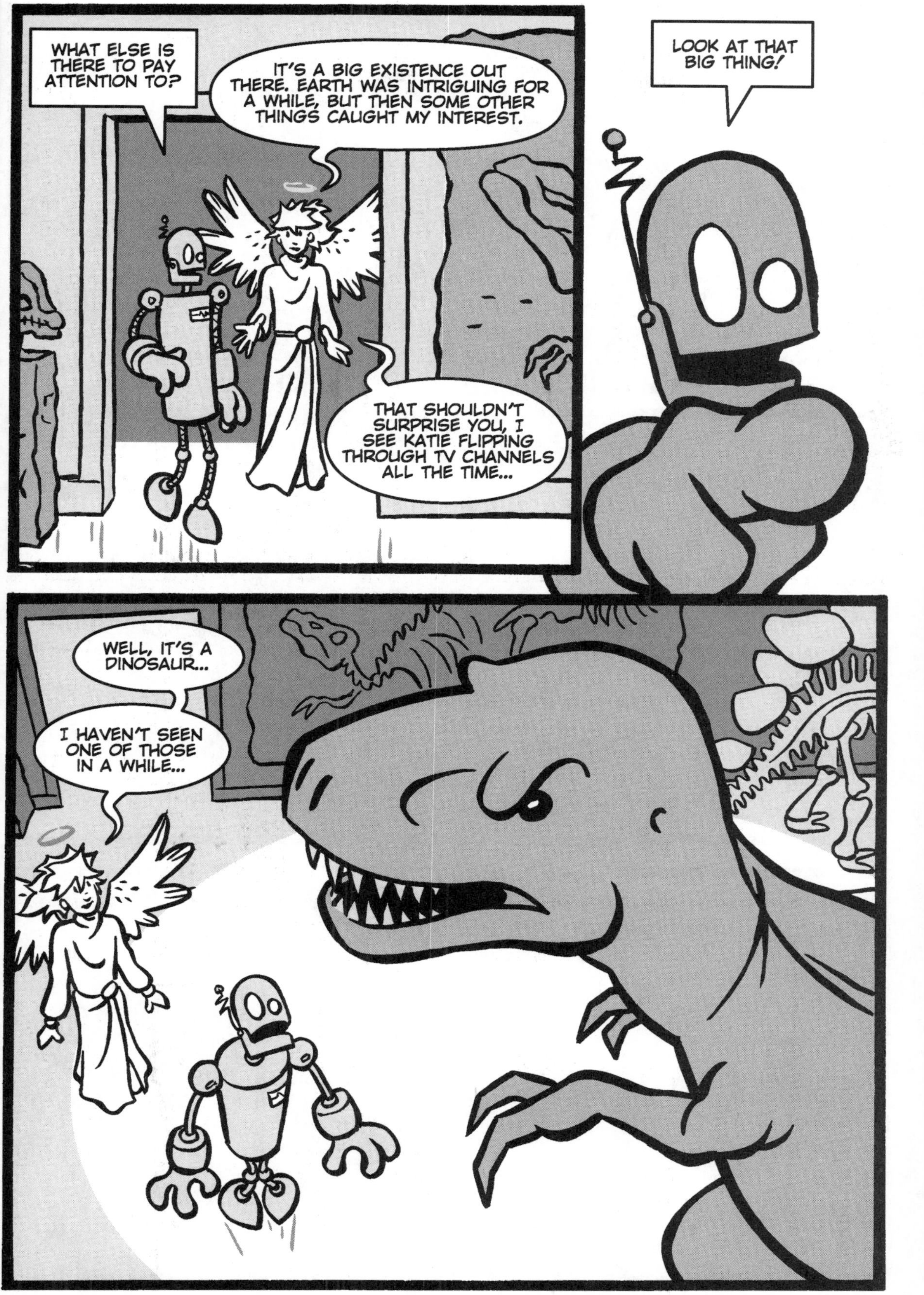
WHAT ELSE IS THERE TO PAY ATTENTION TO?
IT'S A BIG EXISTENCE OUT THERE. EARTH WAS INTRIGUING FOR A WHILE, BUT THEN SOME OTHER THINGS CAUGHT MY INTEREST.
THAT SHOULDN'T SURPRISE YOU, I SEE KATIE FLIPPING THROUGH TV CHANNELS ALL THE TIME...
LOOK AT THAT BIG THING!
WELL, IT'S A DINOSAUR...
I HAVEN'T SEEN ONE OF THOSE IN A WHILE...

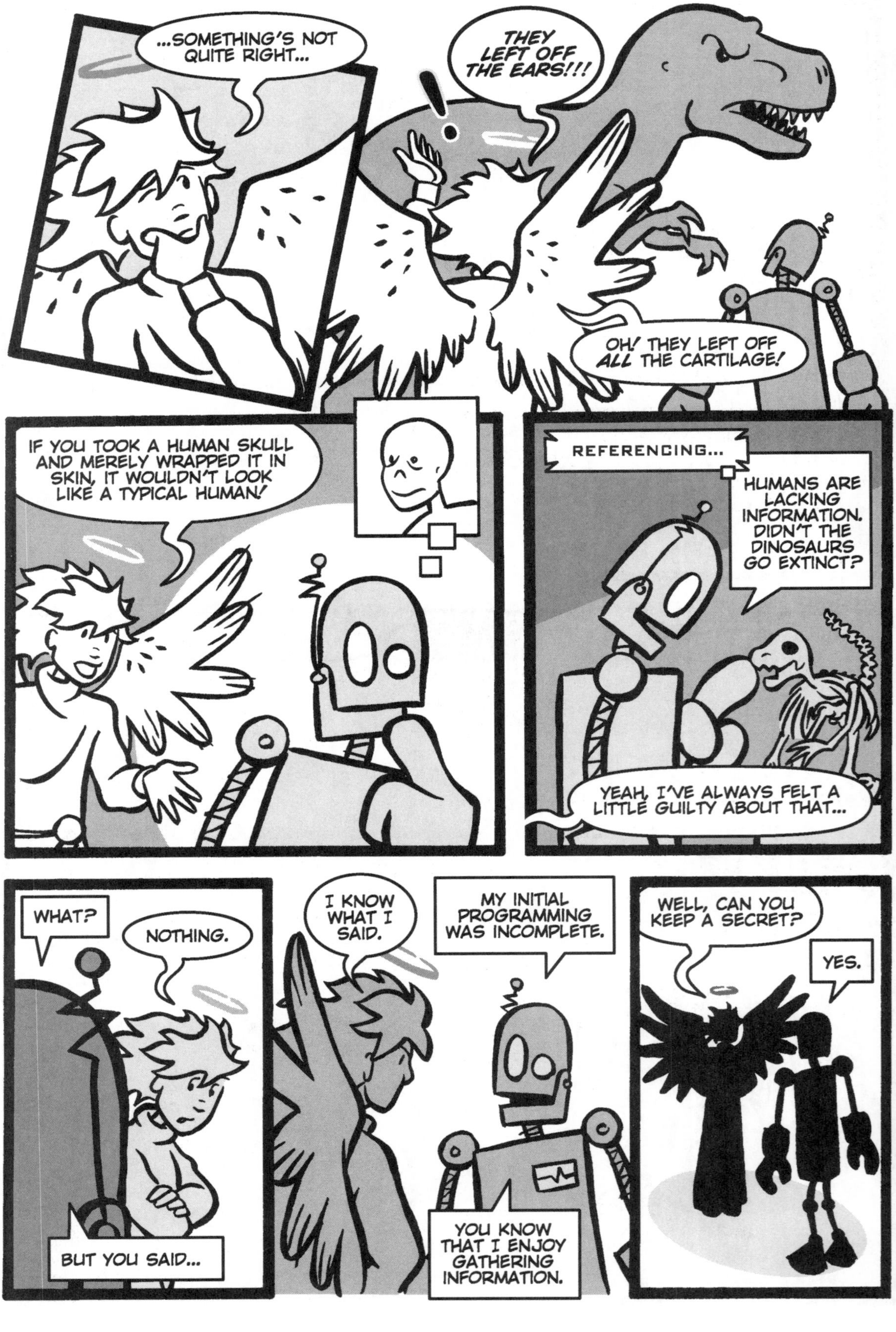
...SOMETHING'S NOT QUITE RIGHT...
THEY LEFT OFF THE EARS!!!
!
OH! THEY LEFT OFF *ALL* THE CARTILAGE!
IF YOU TOOK A HUMAN SKULL AND MERELY WRAPPED IT IN SKIN, IT WOULDN'T LOOK LIKE A TYPICAL HUMAN!
REFERENCING...
HUMANS ARE LACKING INFORMATION. DIDN'T THE DINOSAURS GO EXTINCT?
YEAH, I'VE ALWAYS FELT A LITTLE GUILTY ABOUT THAT...
WHAT?
NOTHING.
BUT YOU SAID...
I KNOW WHAT I SAID.
MY INITIAL PROGRAMMING WAS INCOMPLETE.
YOU KNOW THAT I ENJOY GATHERING INFORMATION.
WELL, CAN YOU KEEP A SECRET?
YES.

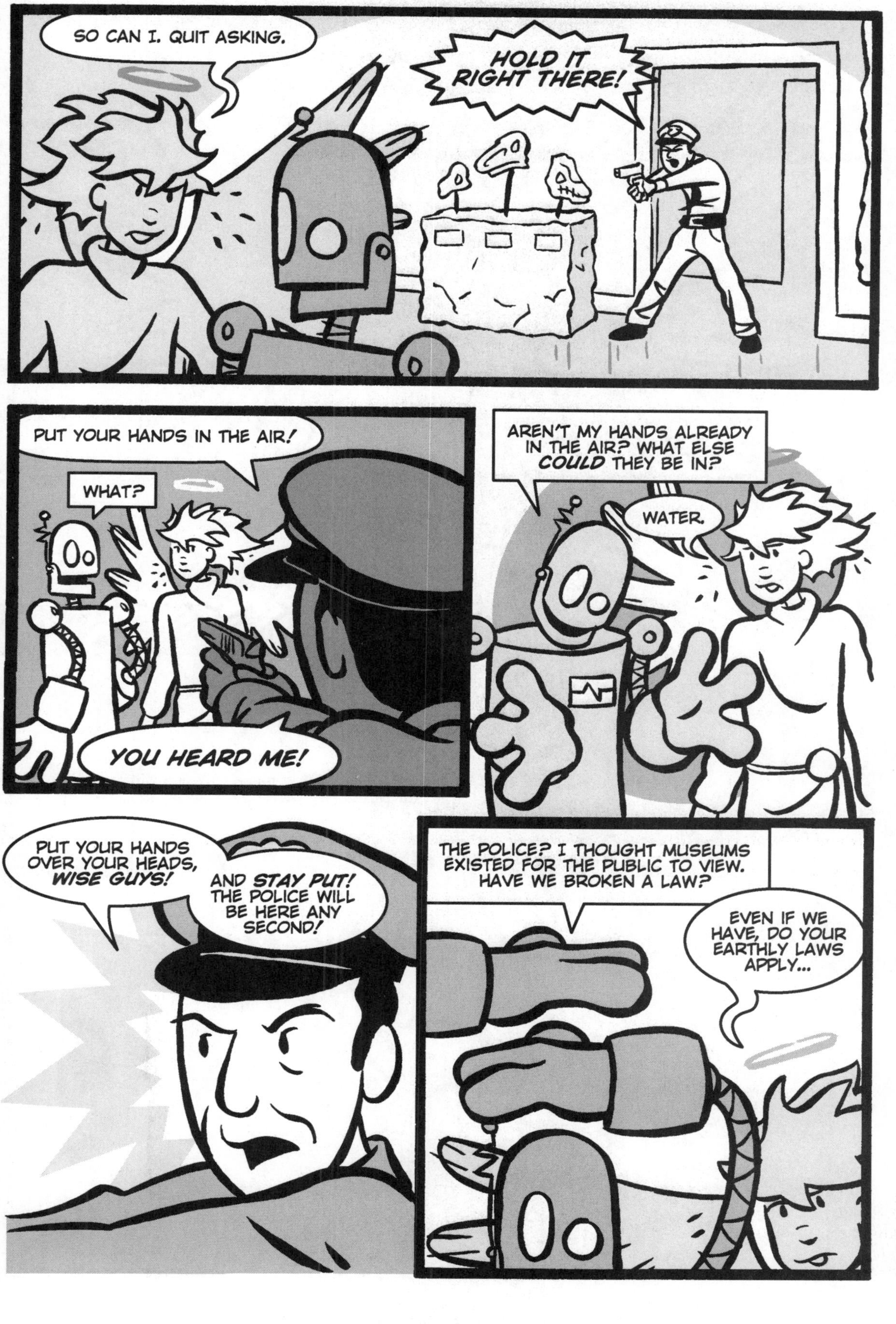

SO CAN I. QUIT ASKING.
HOLD IT RIGHT THERE!
PUT YOUR HANDS IN THE AIR!
WHAT?
YOU HEARD ME!
AREN'T MY HANDS ALREADY IN THE AIR? WHAT ELSE COULD THEY BE IN?
WATER.
PUT YOUR HANDS OVER YOUR HEADS, WISE GUYS!
AND STAY PUT! THE POLICE WILL BE HERE ANY SECOND!
THE POLICE? I THOUGHT MUSEUMS EXISTED FOR THE PUBLIC TO VIEW. HAVE WE BROKEN A LAW?
EVEN IF WE HAVE, DO YOUR EARTHLY LAWS APPLY...

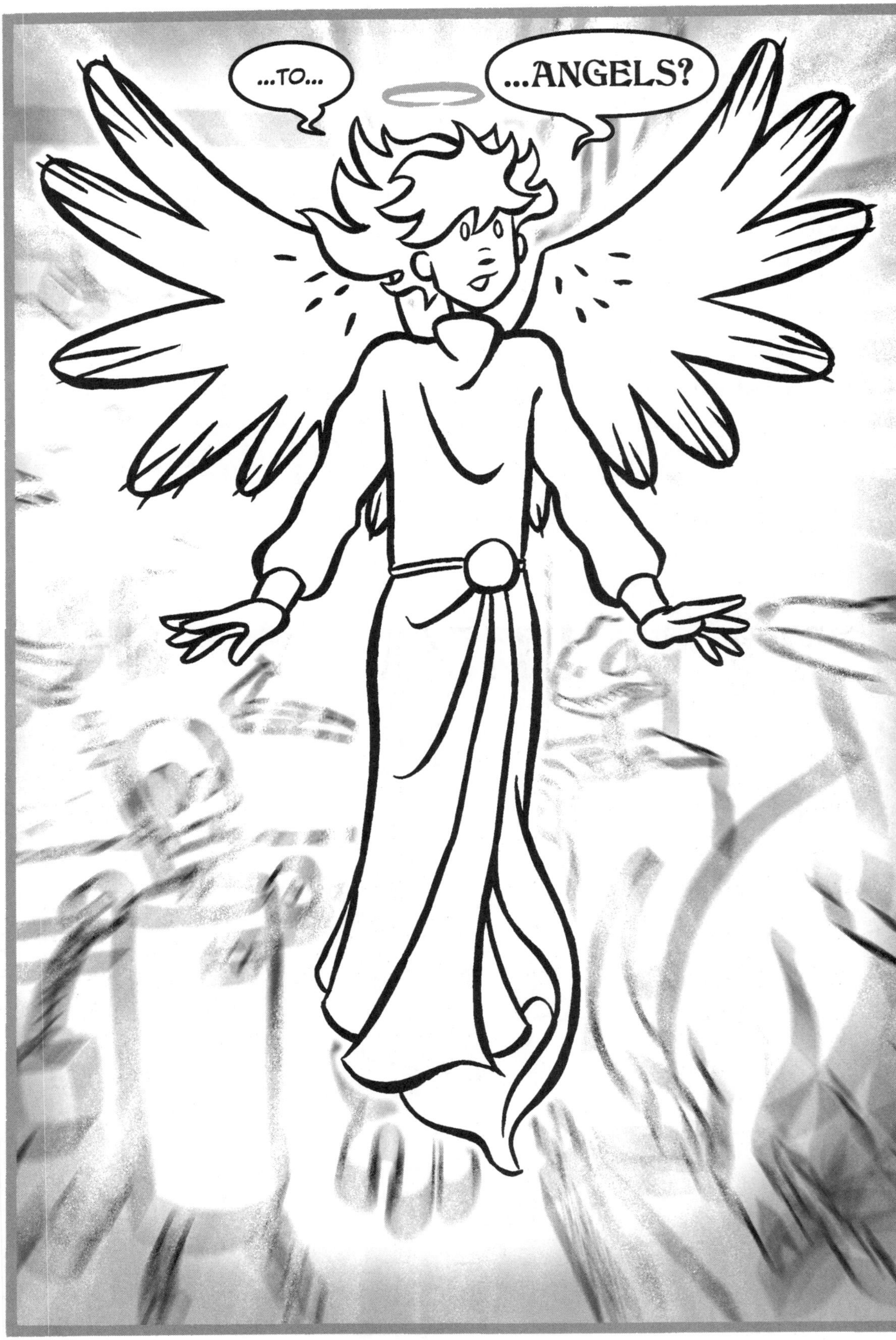
...TO...
...ANGELS?

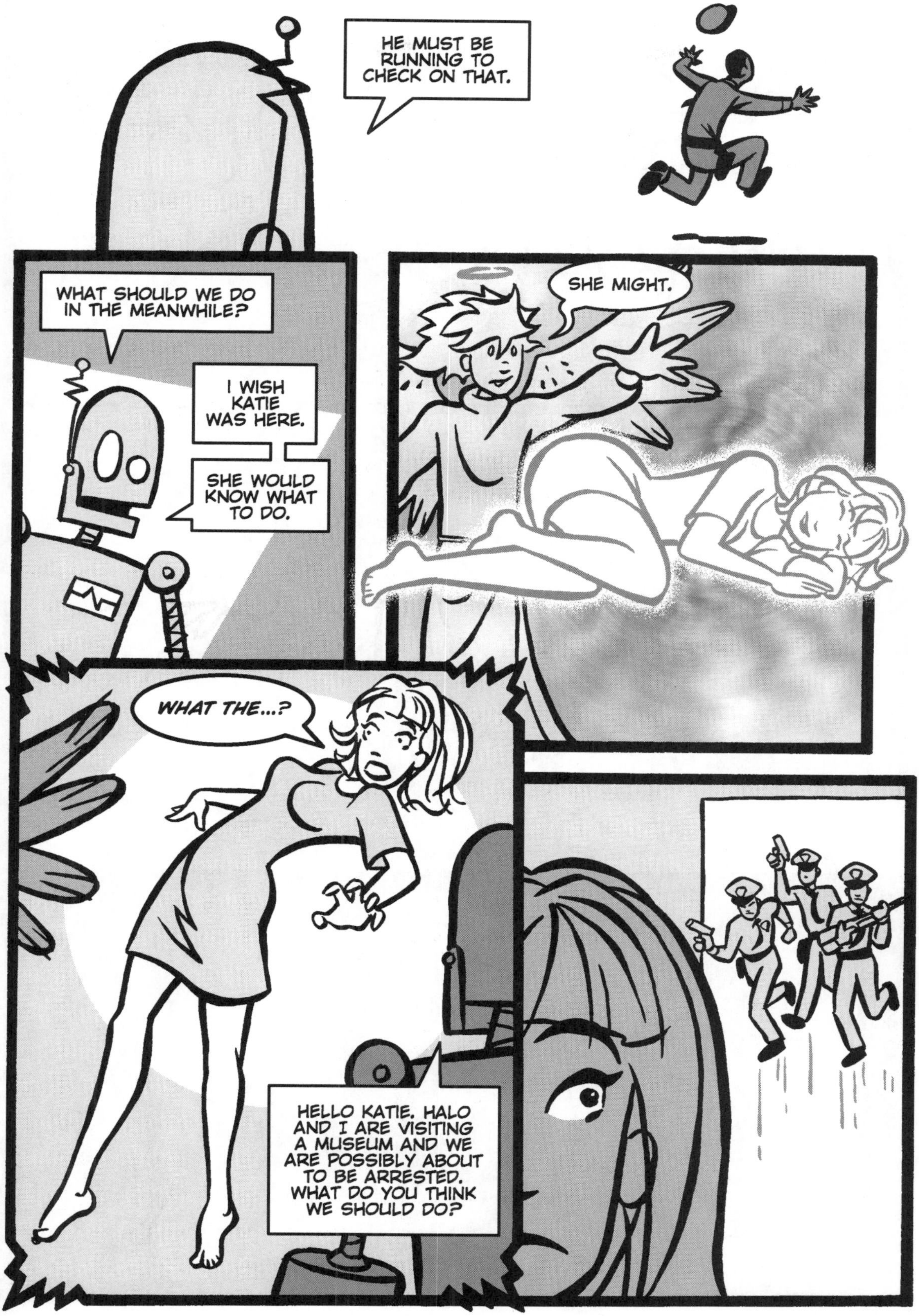
HE MUST BE RUNNING TO CHECK ON THAT.
WHAT SHOULD WE DO IN THE MEANWHILE?
I WISH KATIE WAS HERE.
SHE WOULD KNOW WHAT TO DO.
SHE MIGHT.
WHAT THE...?
HELLO KATIE. HALO AND I ARE VISITING A MUSEUM AND WE ARE POSSIBLY ABOUT TO BE ARRESTED. WHAT DO YOU THINK WE SHOULD DO?

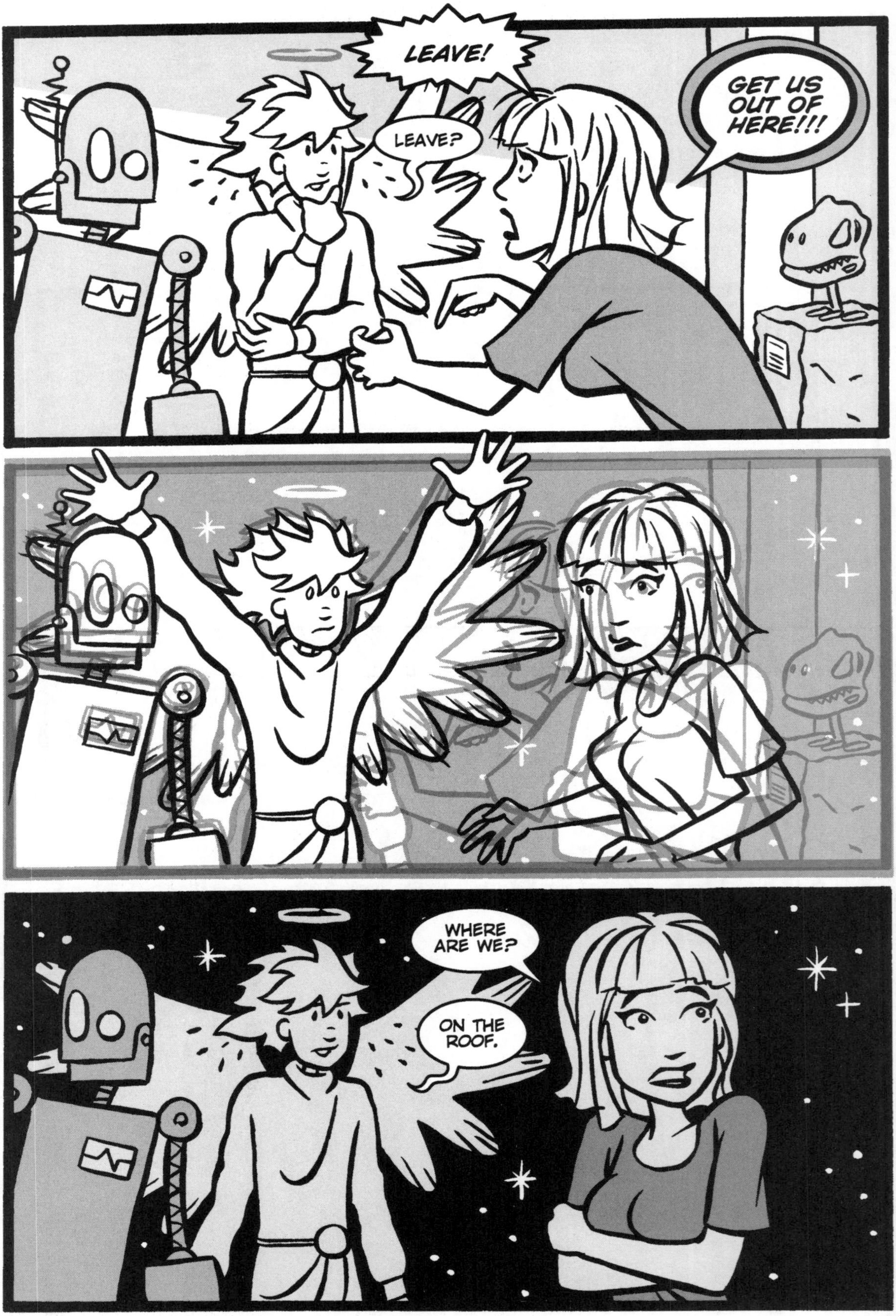
LEAVE!
LEAVE?
GET US OUT OF HERE!!!
WHERE ARE WE?
ON THE ROOF.

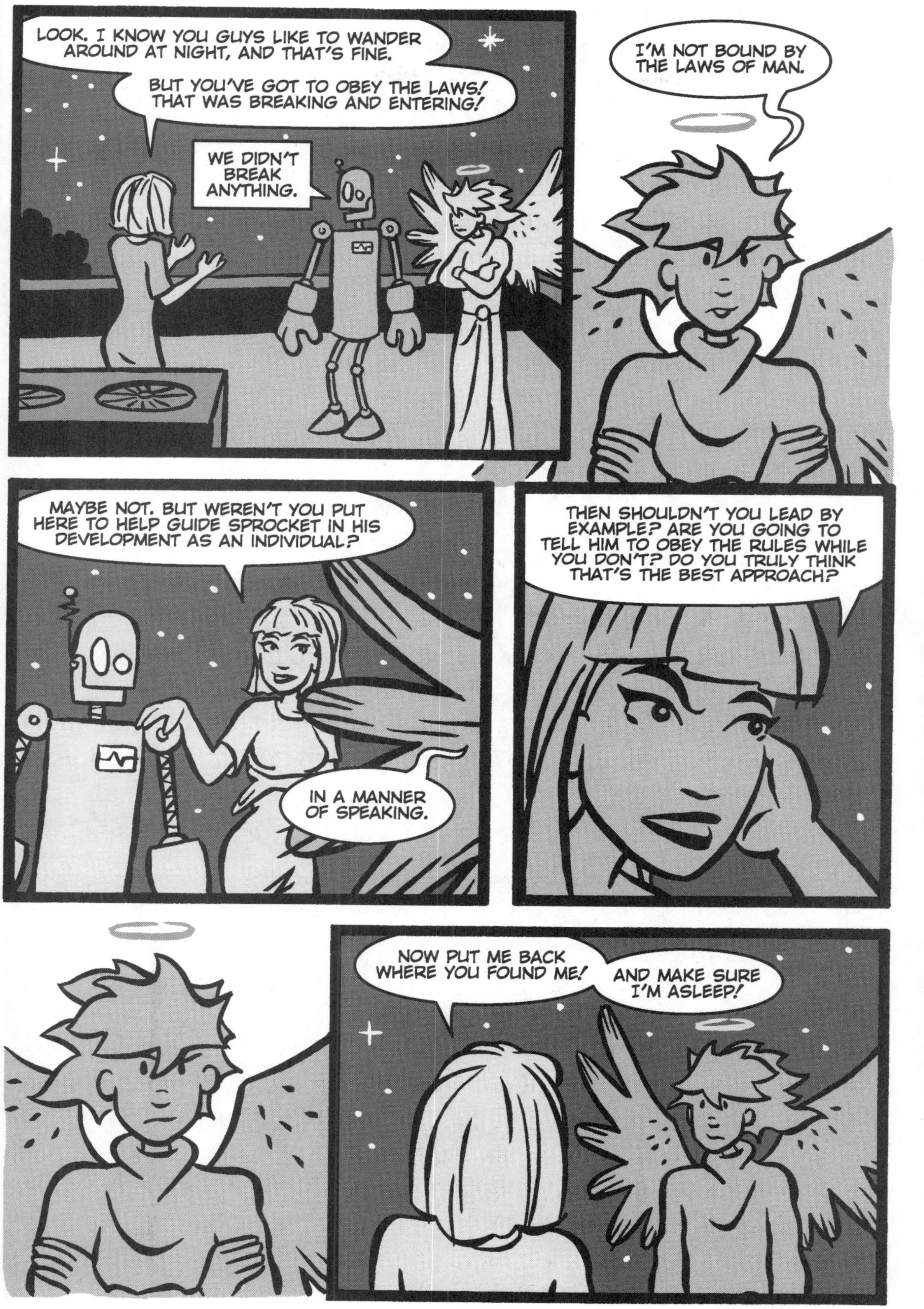
LOOK. I KNOW YOU GUYS LIKE TO WANDER AROUND AT NIGHT, AND THAT'S FINE.
BUT YOU'VE GOT TO OBEY THE LAWS! THAT WAS BREAKING AND ENTERING!
WE DIDN'T BREAK ANYTHING.
I'M NOT BOUND BY THE LAWS OF MAN.
MAYBE NOT. BUT WEREN'T YOU PUT HERE TO HELP GUIDE SPROCKET IN HIS DEVELOPMENT AS AN INDIVIDUAL?
IN A MANNER OF SPEAKING.
THEN SHOULDN'T YOU LEAD BY EXAMPLE? ARE YOU GOING TO TELL HIM TO OBEY THE RULES WHILE YOU DON'T? DO YOU TRULY THINK THAT'S THE BEST APPROACH?
NOW PUT ME BACK WHERE YOU FOUND ME!
AND MAKE SURE I'M ASLEEP!

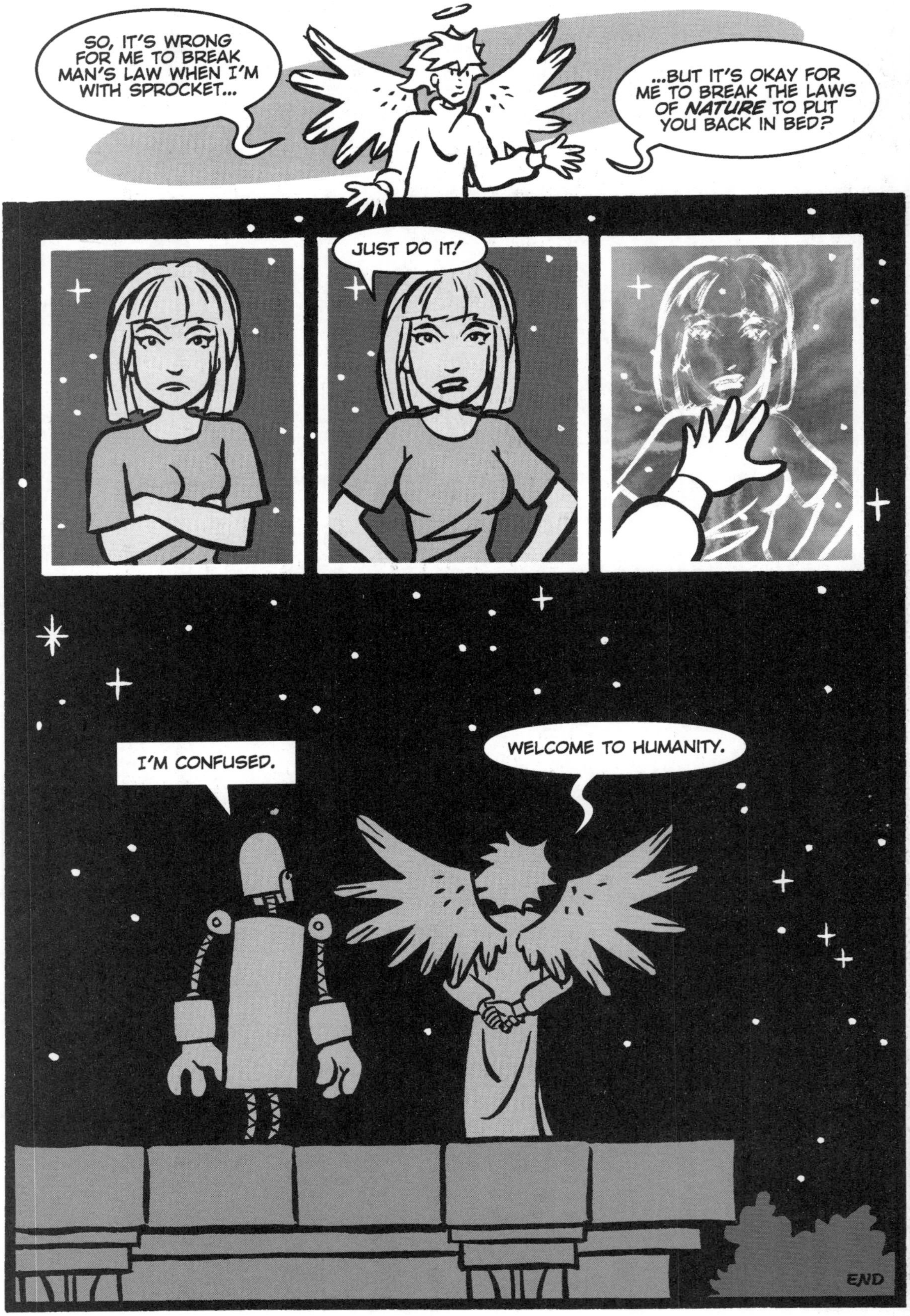

SO, IT'S WRONG FOR ME TO BREAK MAN'S LAW WHEN I'M WITH SPROCKET...
...BUT IT'S OKAY FOR ME TO BREAK THE LAWS OF *NATURE* TO PUT YOU BACK IN BED?
JUST DO IT!
I'M CONFUSED.
WELCOME TO HUMANITY.
END

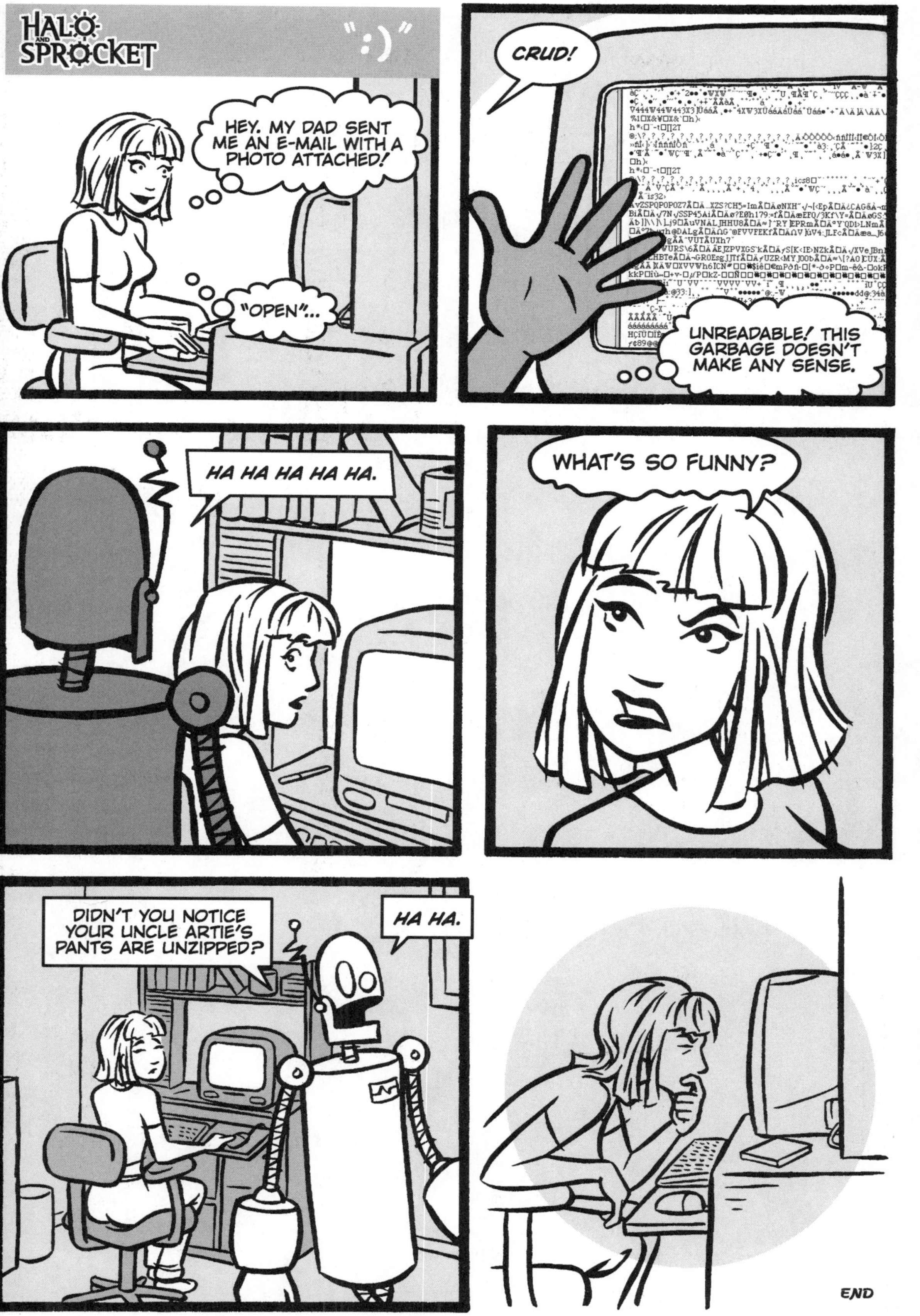
HALO AND SPROCKET
":)"
HEY. MY DAD SENT ME AN E-MAIL WITH A PHOTO ATTACHED!
"OPEN"...
CRUD!
UNREADABLE! THIS GARBAGE DOESN'T MAKE ANY SENSE.
HA HA HA HA HA.
WHAT'S SO FUNNY?
DIDN'T YOU NOTICE YOUR UNCLE ARTIE'S PANTS ARE UNZIPPED?
HA HA.
END

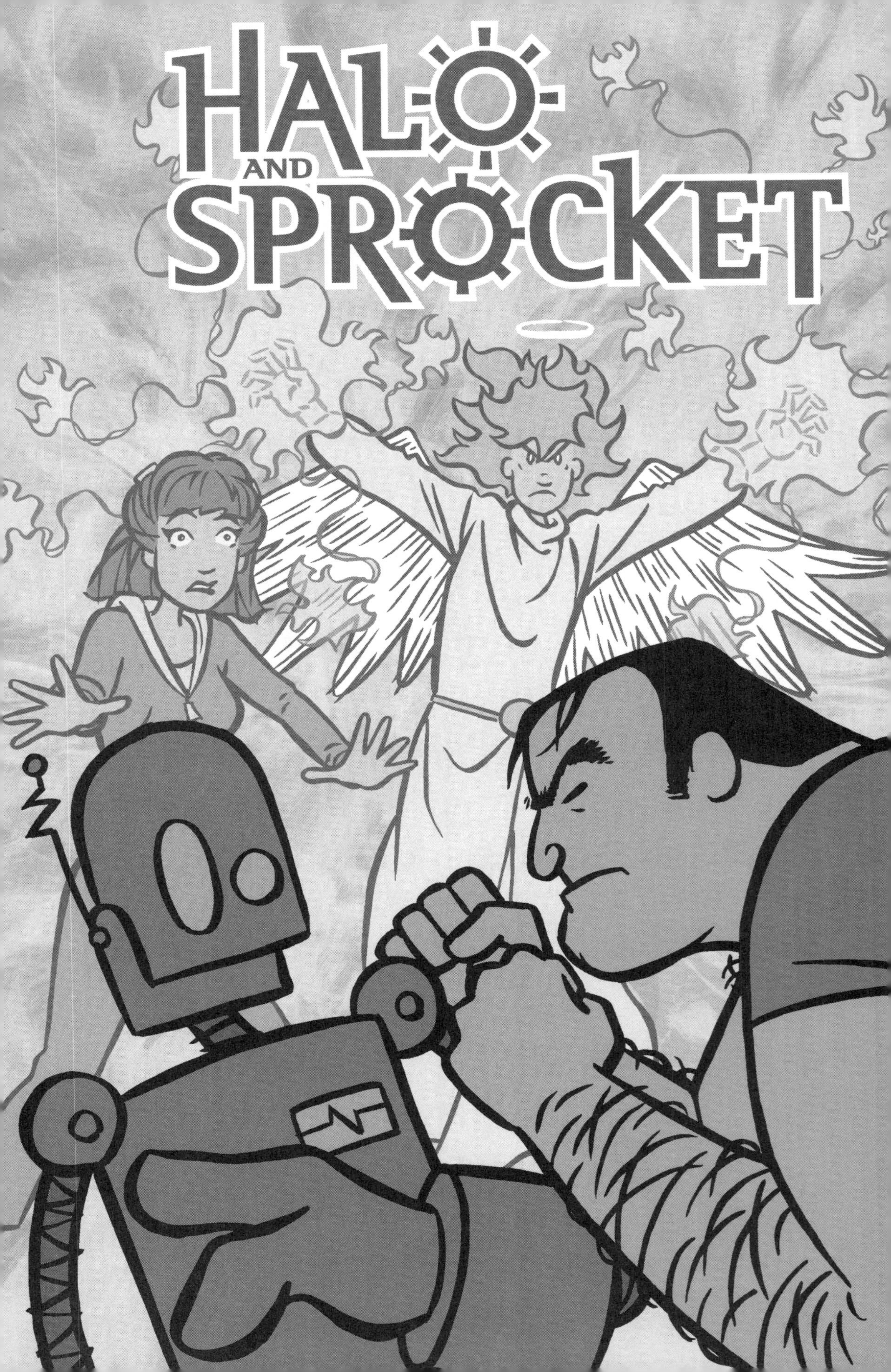
HALO AND SPROCKET

HALO AND SPROCKET™

"BEING FRANK"

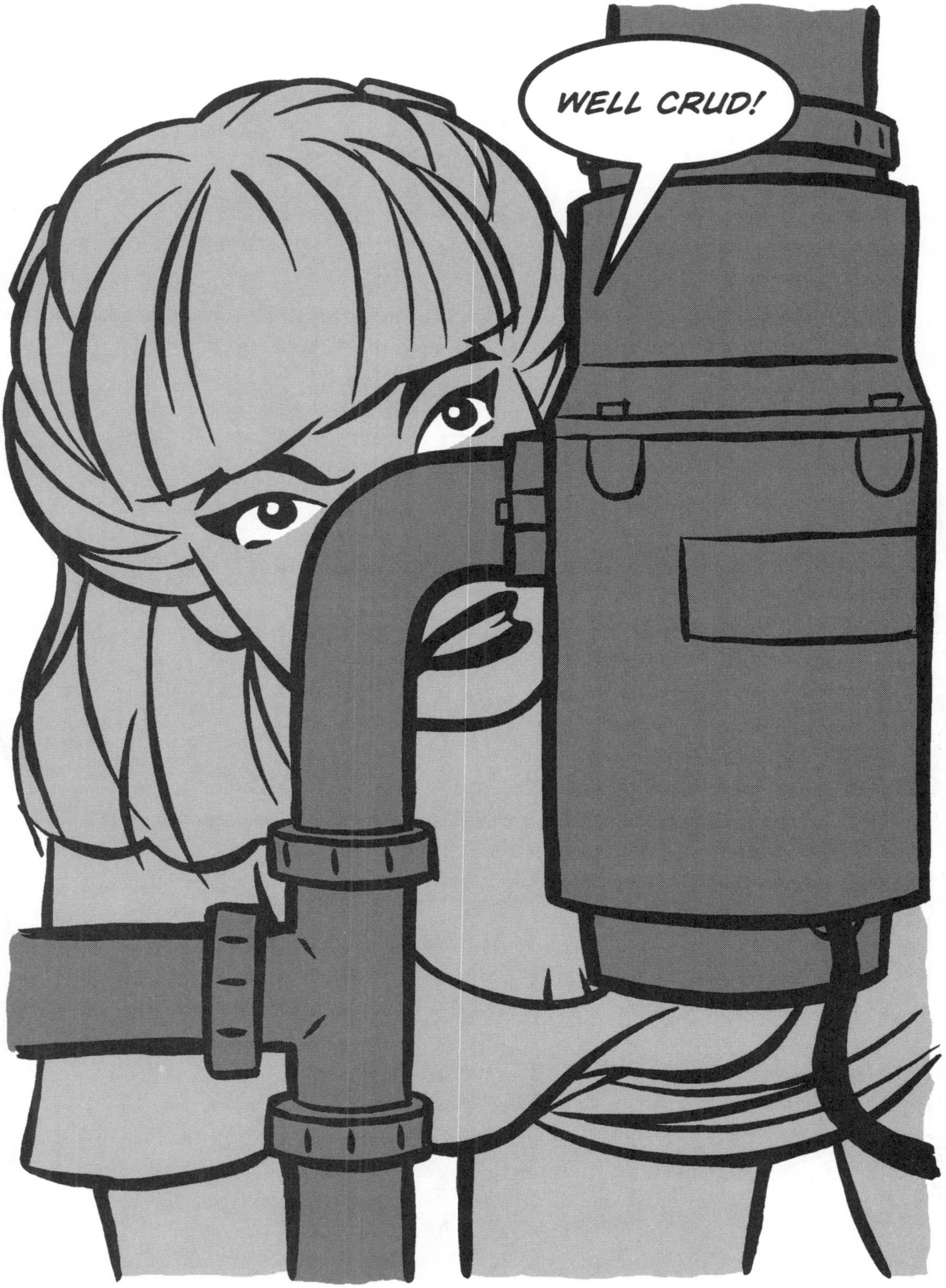
WELL CRUD!

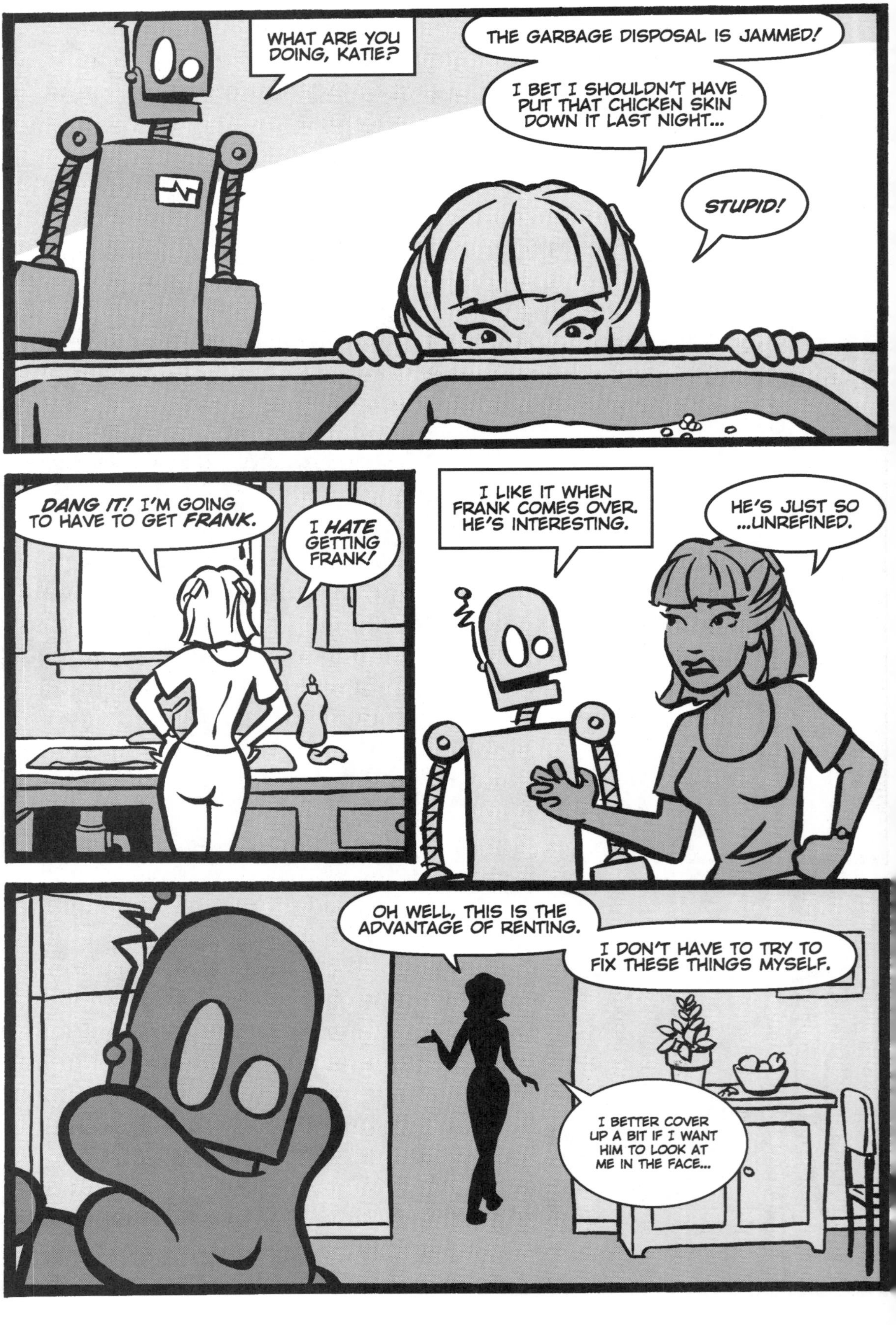
WHAT ARE YOU DOING, KATIE?
THE GARBAGE DISPOSAL IS JAMMED!
I BET I SHOULDN'T HAVE PUT THAT CHICKEN SKIN DOWN IT LAST NIGHT...
STUPID!
DANG IT! I'M GOING TO HAVE TO GET FRANK.
I HATE GETTING FRANK!
I LIKE IT WHEN FRANK COMES OVER. HE'S INTERESTING.
HE'S JUST SO ...UNREFINED.
OH WELL, THIS IS THE ADVANTAGE OF RENTING.
I DON'T HAVE TO TRY TO FIX THESE THINGS MYSELF.
I BETTER COVER UP A BIT IF I WANT HIM TO LOOK AT ME IN THE FACE...

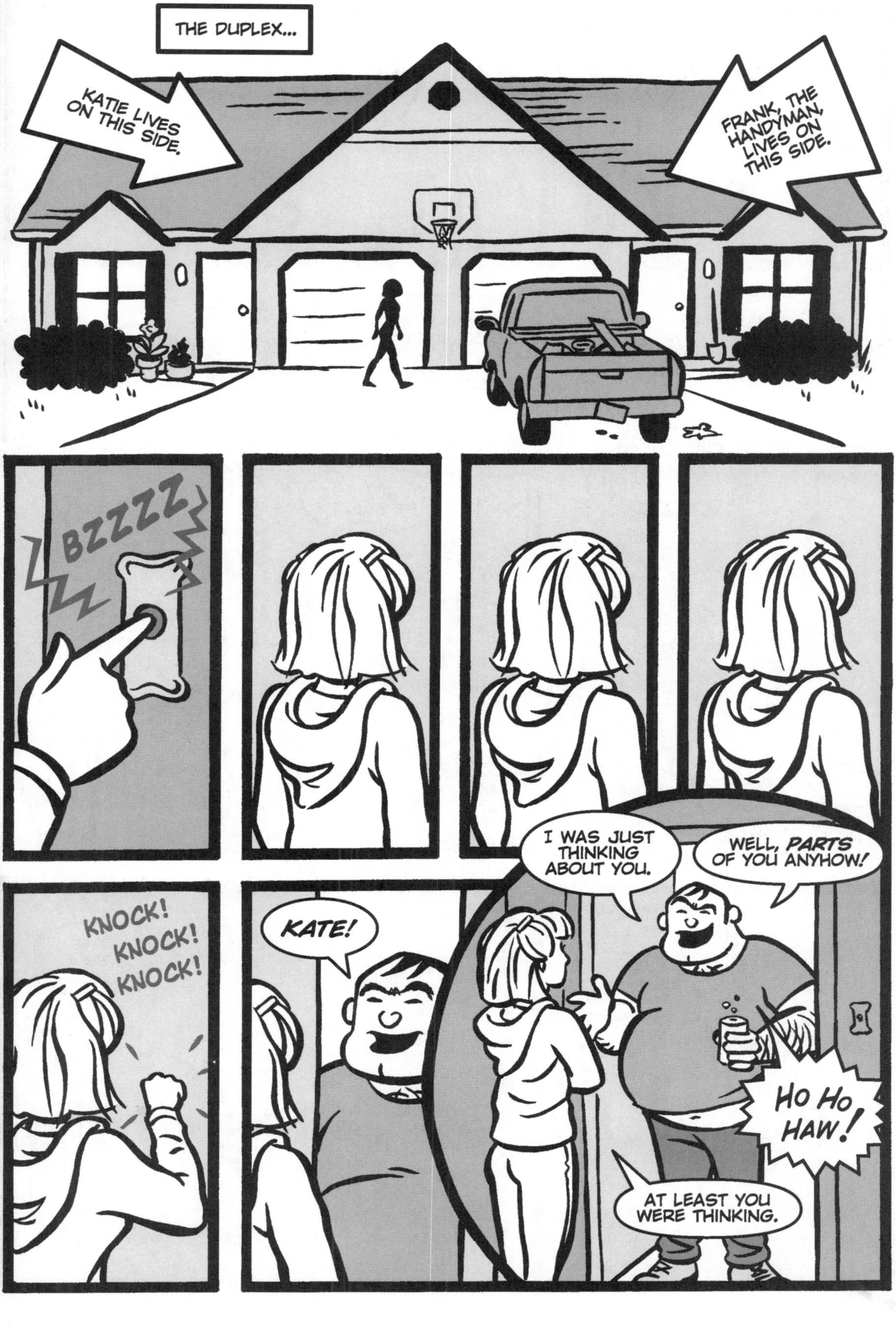
THE DUPLEX...
KATIE LIVES ON THIS SIDE.
FRANK, THE HANDYMAN, LIVES ON THIS SIDE.
BZZZZ
KNOCK! KNOCK! KNOCK!
KATE!
I WAS JUST THINKING ABOUT YOU.
WELL, PARTS OF YOU ANYHOW!
Ho Ho HAW!
AT LEAST YOU WERE THINKING.

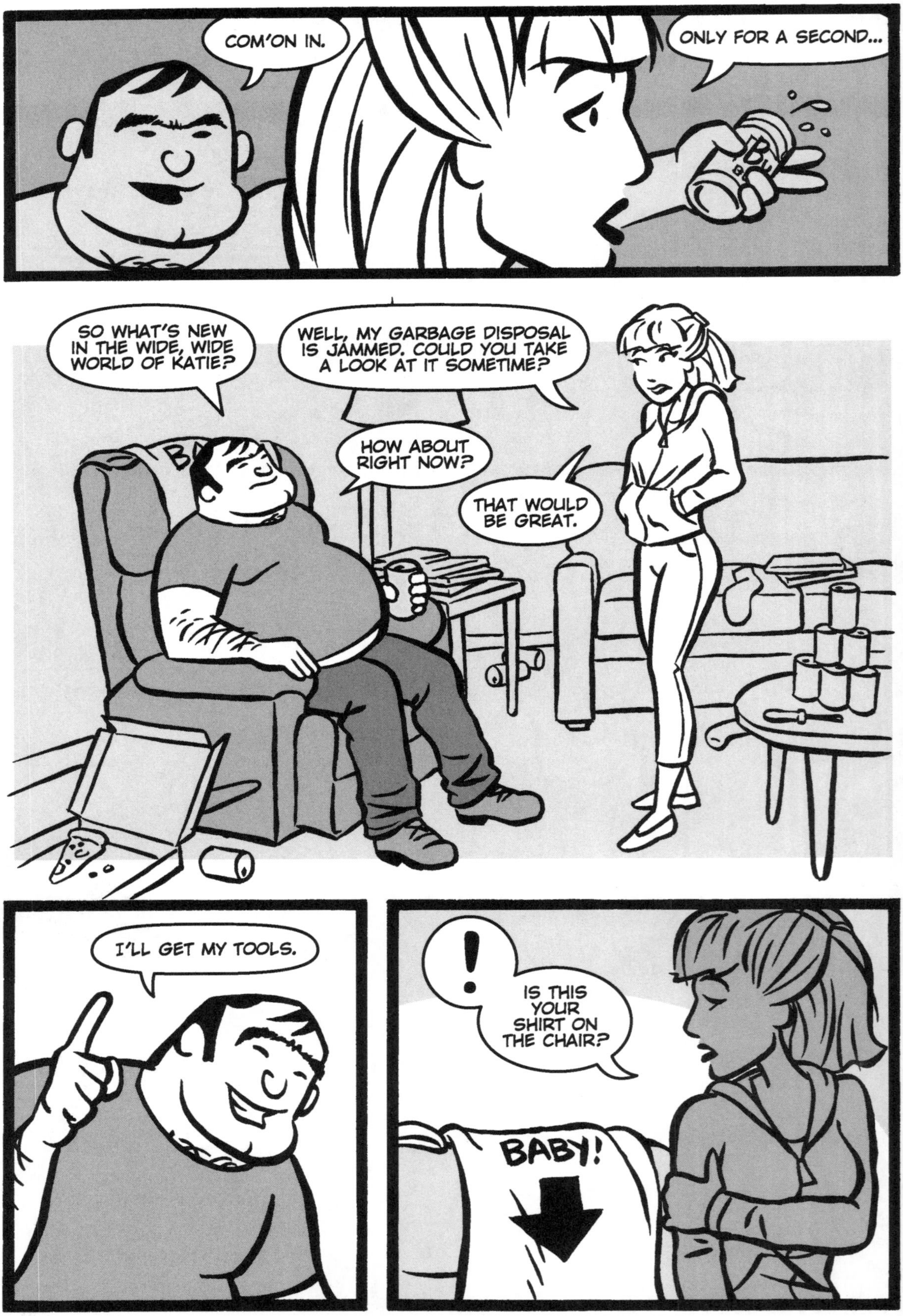
COM'ON IN.
ONLY FOR A SECOND...
SO WHAT'S NEW IN THE WIDE, WIDE WORLD OF KATIE?
WELL, MY GARBAGE DISPOSAL IS JAMMED. COULD YOU TAKE A LOOK AT IT SOMETIME?
HOW ABOUT RIGHT NOW?
THAT WOULD BE GREAT.
I'LL GET MY TOOLS.
!
IS THIS YOUR SHIRT ON THE CHAIR?
BABY!

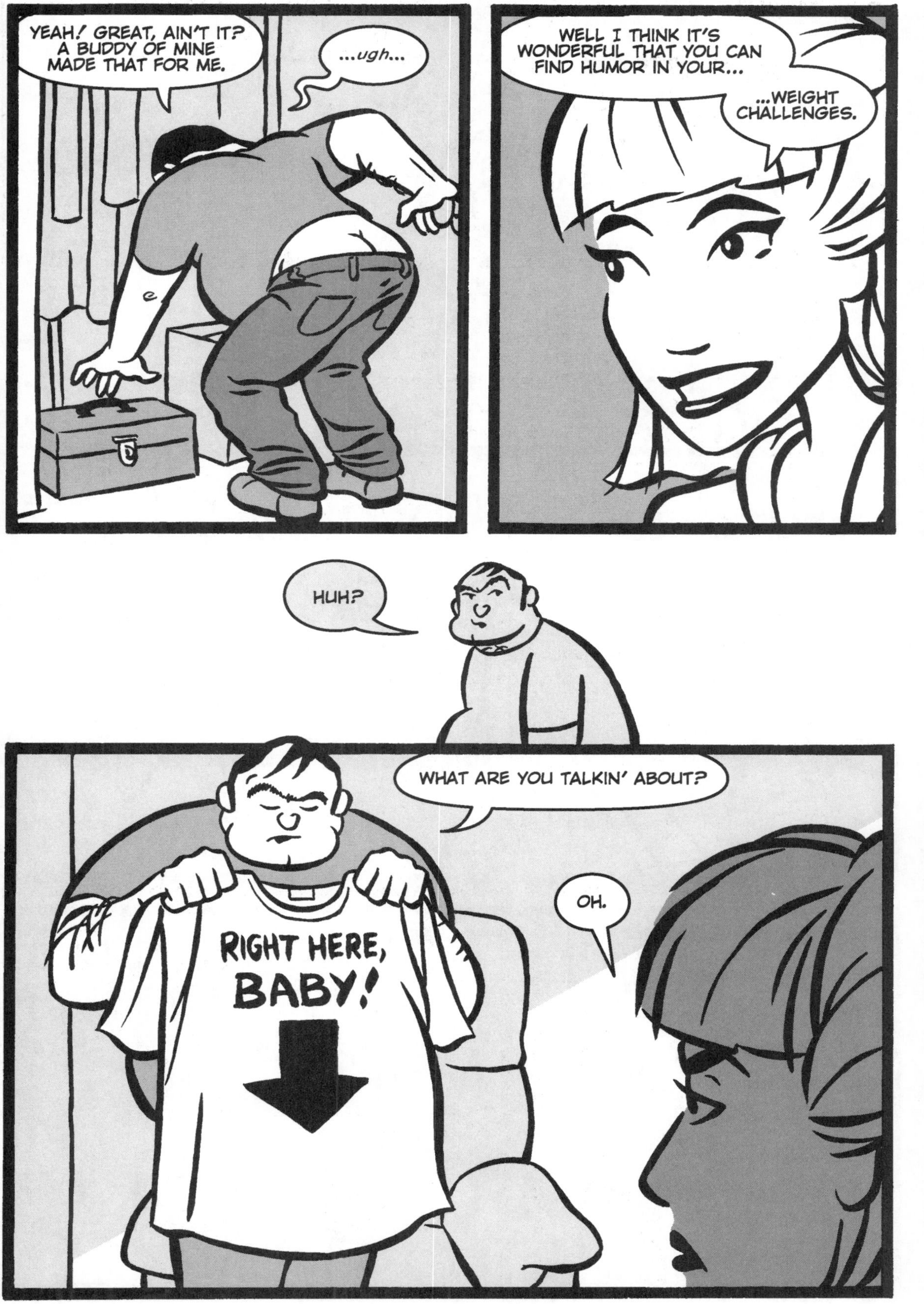
YEAH! GREAT, AIN'T IT? A BUDDY OF MINE MADE THAT FOR ME.
...ugh...
WELL I THINK IT'S WONDERFUL THAT YOU CAN FIND HUMOR IN YOUR...
...WEIGHT CHALLENGES.
HUH?
WHAT ARE YOU TALKIN' ABOUT?
OH.
RIGHT HERE, BABY!

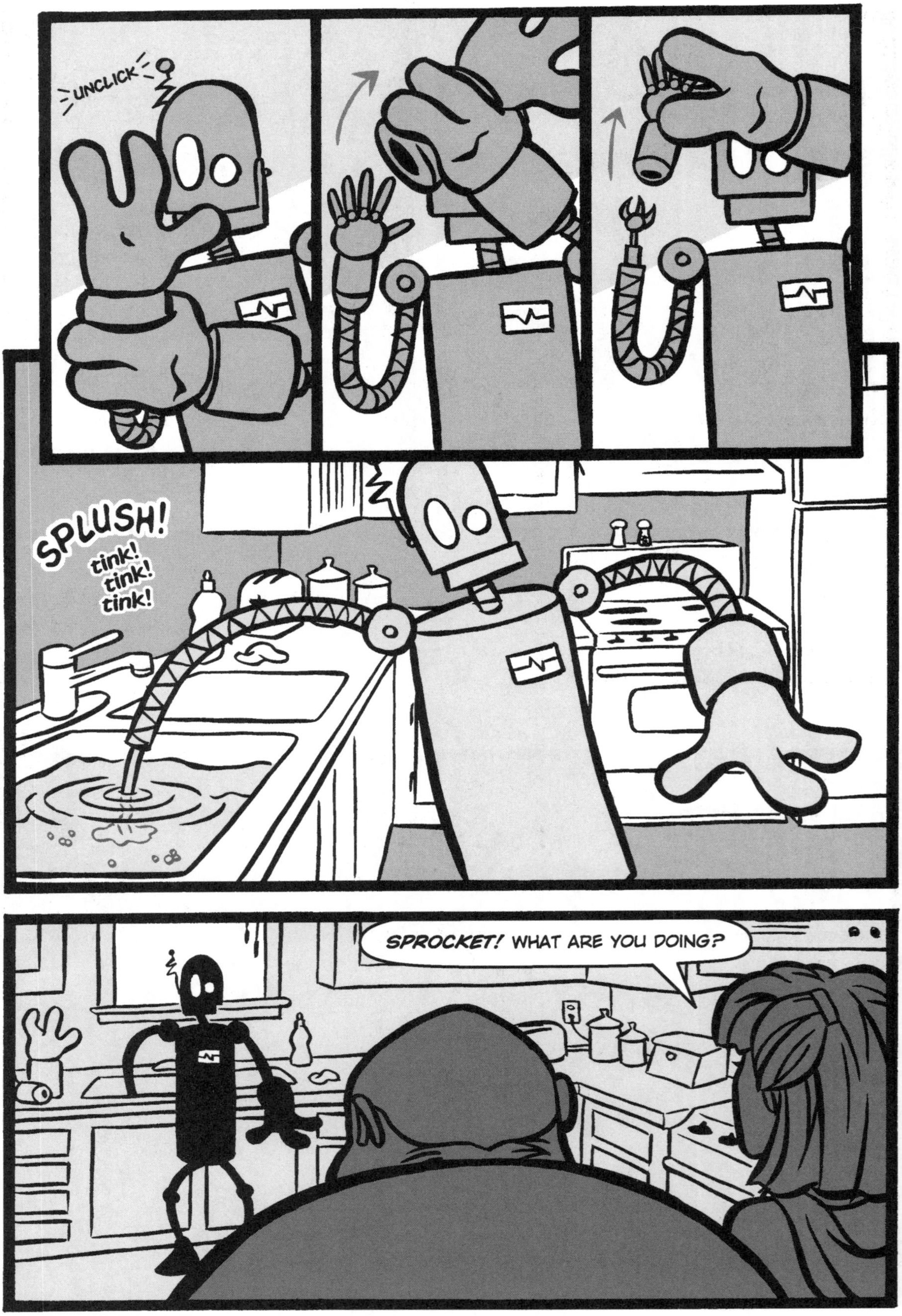
UNCLICK
SPLUSH!
tink!
tink!
tink!
SPROCKET! WHAT ARE YOU DOING?

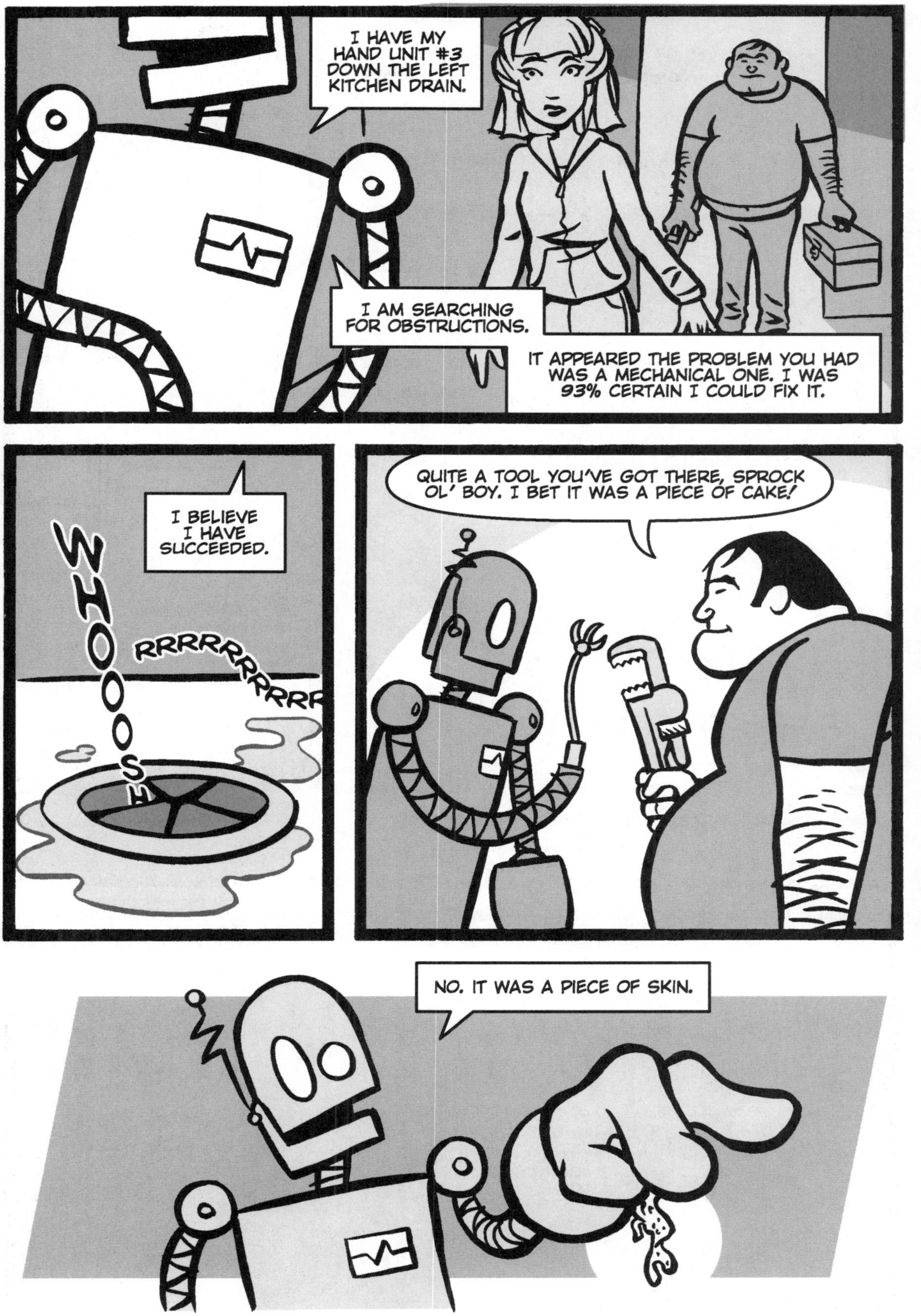
I HAVE MY HAND UNIT #3 DOWN THE LEFT KITCHEN DRAIN.
I AM SEARCHING FOR OBSTRUCTIONS.
IT APPEARED THE PROBLEM YOU HAD WAS A MECHANICAL ONE. I WAS 93% CERTAIN I COULD FIX IT.
I BELIEVE I HAVE SUCCEEDED.
WHOOOOSH
RRRRRRRRRRRR
QUITE A TOOL YOU'VE GOT THERE, SPROCK OL' BOY. I BET IT WAS A PIECE OF CAKE!
NO. IT WAS A PIECE OF SKIN.

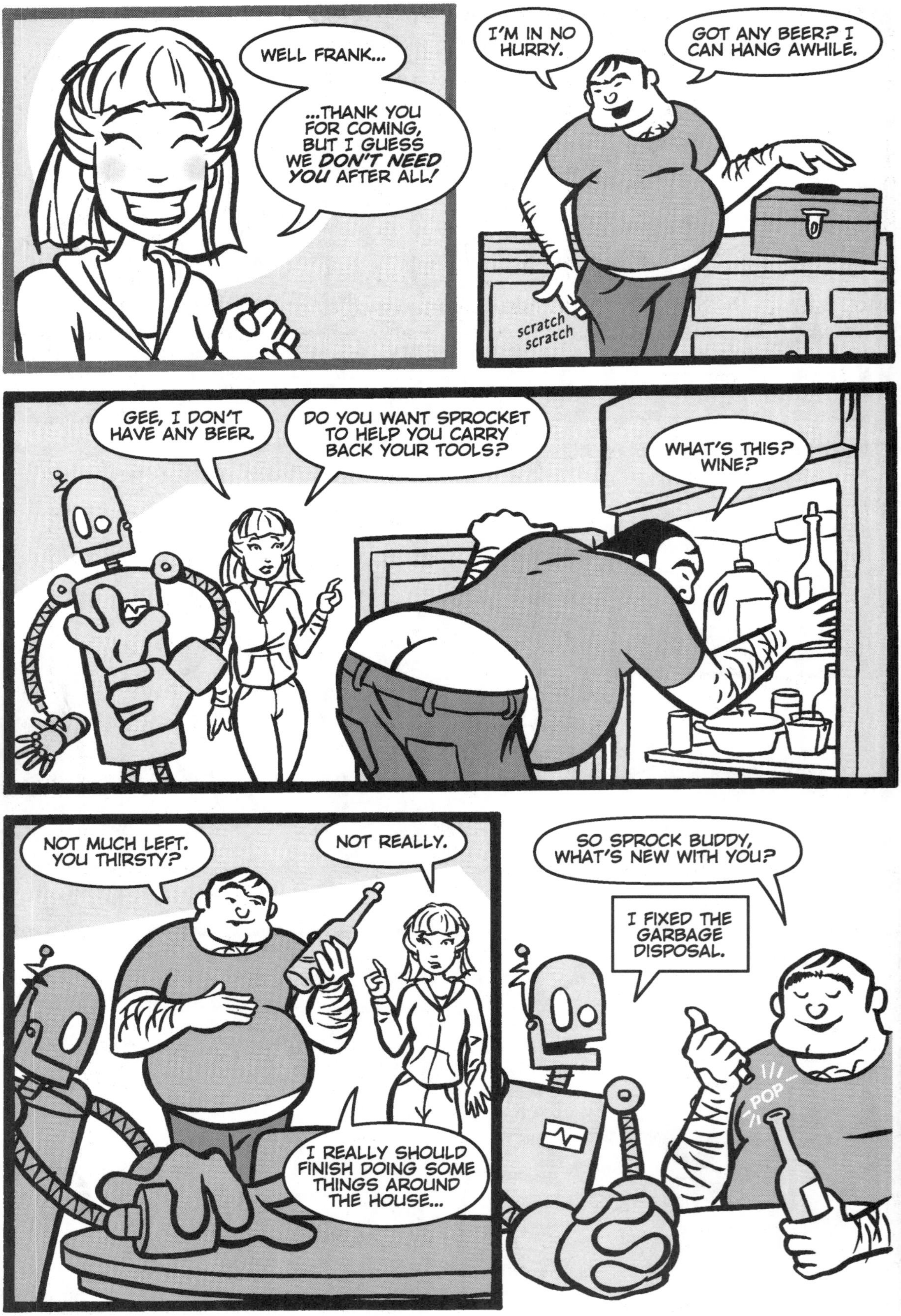
WELL FRANK...
...THANK YOU FOR COMING, BUT I GUESS WE ***DON'T NEED YOU*** AFTER ALL!
I'M IN NO HURRY.
GOT ANY BEER? I CAN HANG AWHILE.
scratch scratch
GEE, I DON'T HAVE ANY BEER.
DO YOU WANT SPROCKET TO HELP YOU CARRY BACK YOUR TOOLS?
WHAT'S THIS? WINE?
NOT MUCH LEFT. YOU THIRSTY?
NOT REALLY.
I REALLY SHOULD FINISH DOING SOME THINGS AROUND THE HOUSE...
SO SPROCK BUDDY, WHAT'S NEW WITH YOU?
I FIXED THE GARBAGE DISPOSAL.
POP

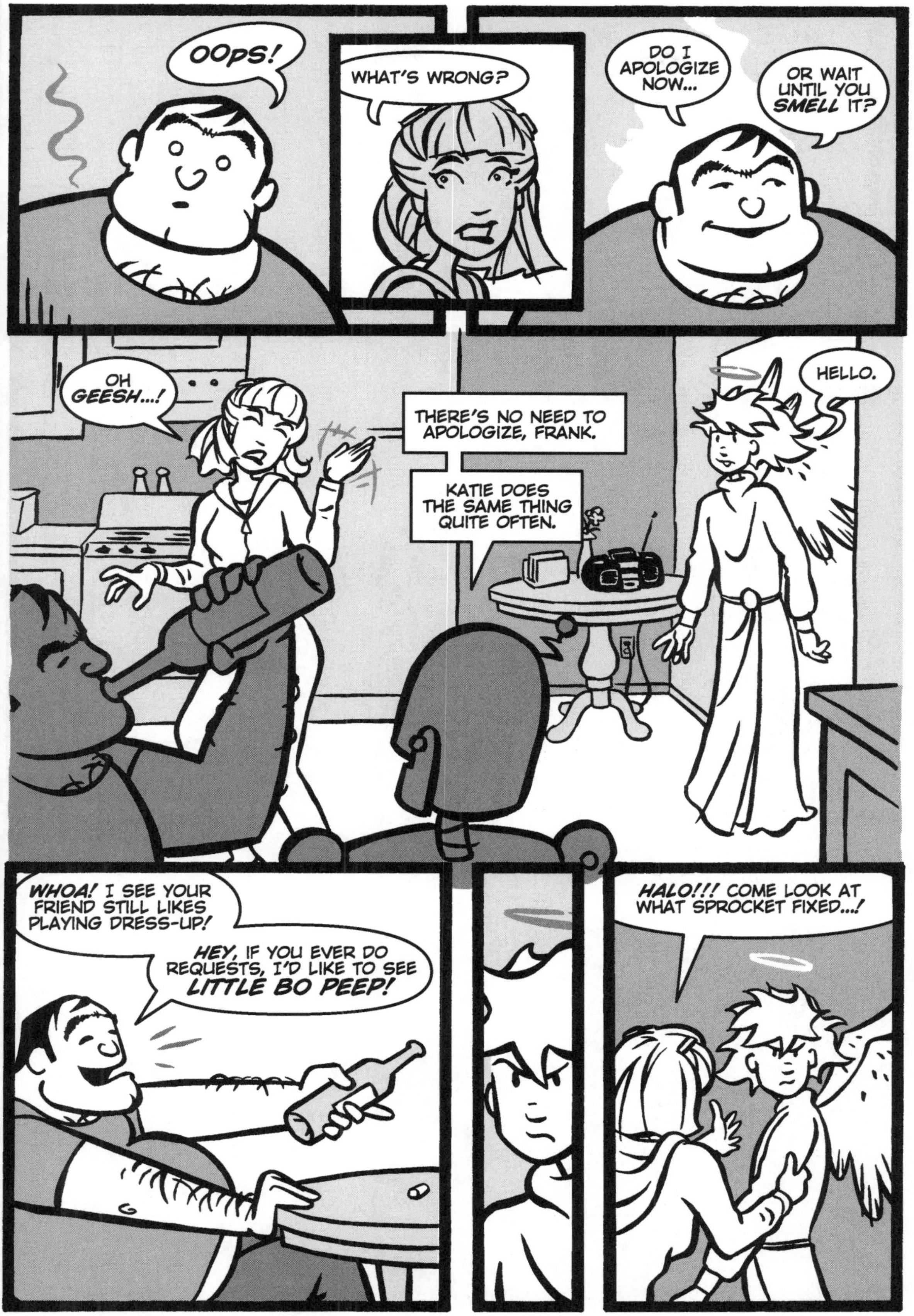

OOPS!
WHAT'S WRONG?
DO I APOLOGIZE NOW...
OR WAIT UNTIL YOU *SMELL* IT?
OH GEESH...!
THERE'S NO NEED TO APOLOGIZE, FRANK.
KATIE DOES THE SAME THING QUITE OFTEN.
HELLO.
WHOA! I SEE YOUR FRIEND STILL LIKES PLAYING DRESS-UP!
HEY, IF YOU EVER DO REQUESTS, I'D LIKE TO SEE *LITTLE BO PEEP!*
HALO!!! COME LOOK AT WHAT SPROCKET FIXED...!

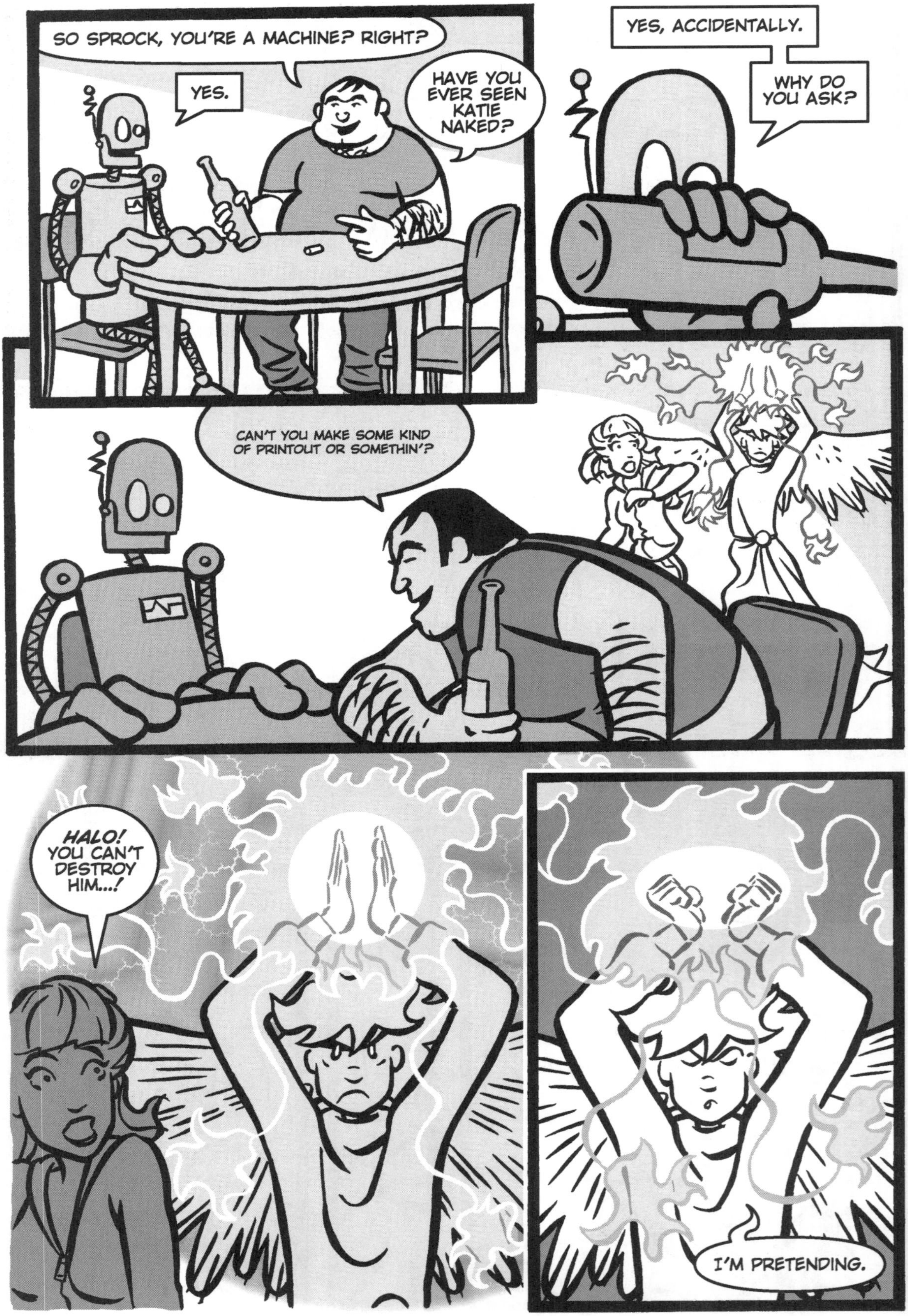
SO SPROCK, YOU'RE A MACHINE? RIGHT?
YES.
HAVE YOU EVER SEEN KATIE NAKED?
YES, ACCIDENTALLY.
WHY DO YOU ASK?
CAN'T YOU MAKE SOME KIND OF PRINTOUT OR SOMETHIN'?
HALO! YOU CAN'T DESTROY HIM...!
I'M PRETENDING.

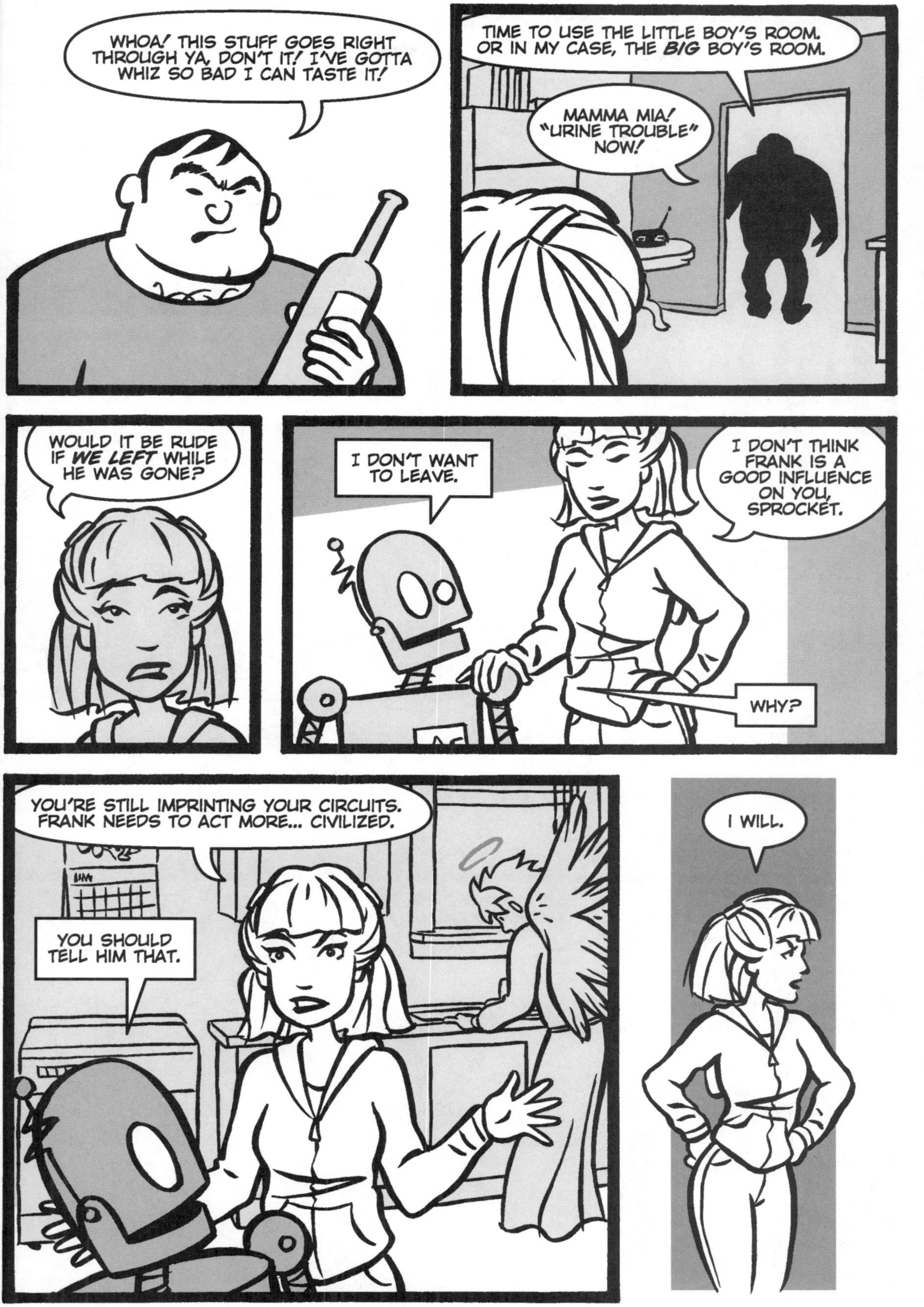
WHOA! THIS STUFF GOES RIGHT THROUGH YA, DON'T IT! I'VE GOTTA WHIZ SO BAD I CAN TASTE IT!
TIME TO USE THE LITTLE BOY'S ROOM. OR IN MY CASE, THE *BIG* BOY'S ROOM.
MAMMA MIA! "URINE TROUBLE" NOW!
WOULD IT BE RUDE IF ***WE LEFT*** WHILE HE WAS GONE?
I DON'T WANT TO LEAVE.
I DON'T THINK FRANK IS A GOOD INFLUENCE ON YOU, SPROCKET.
WHY?
YOU'RE STILL IMPRINTING YOUR CIRCUITS. FRANK NEEDS TO ACT MORE... CIVILIZED.
YOU SHOULD TELL HIM THAT.
I WILL.

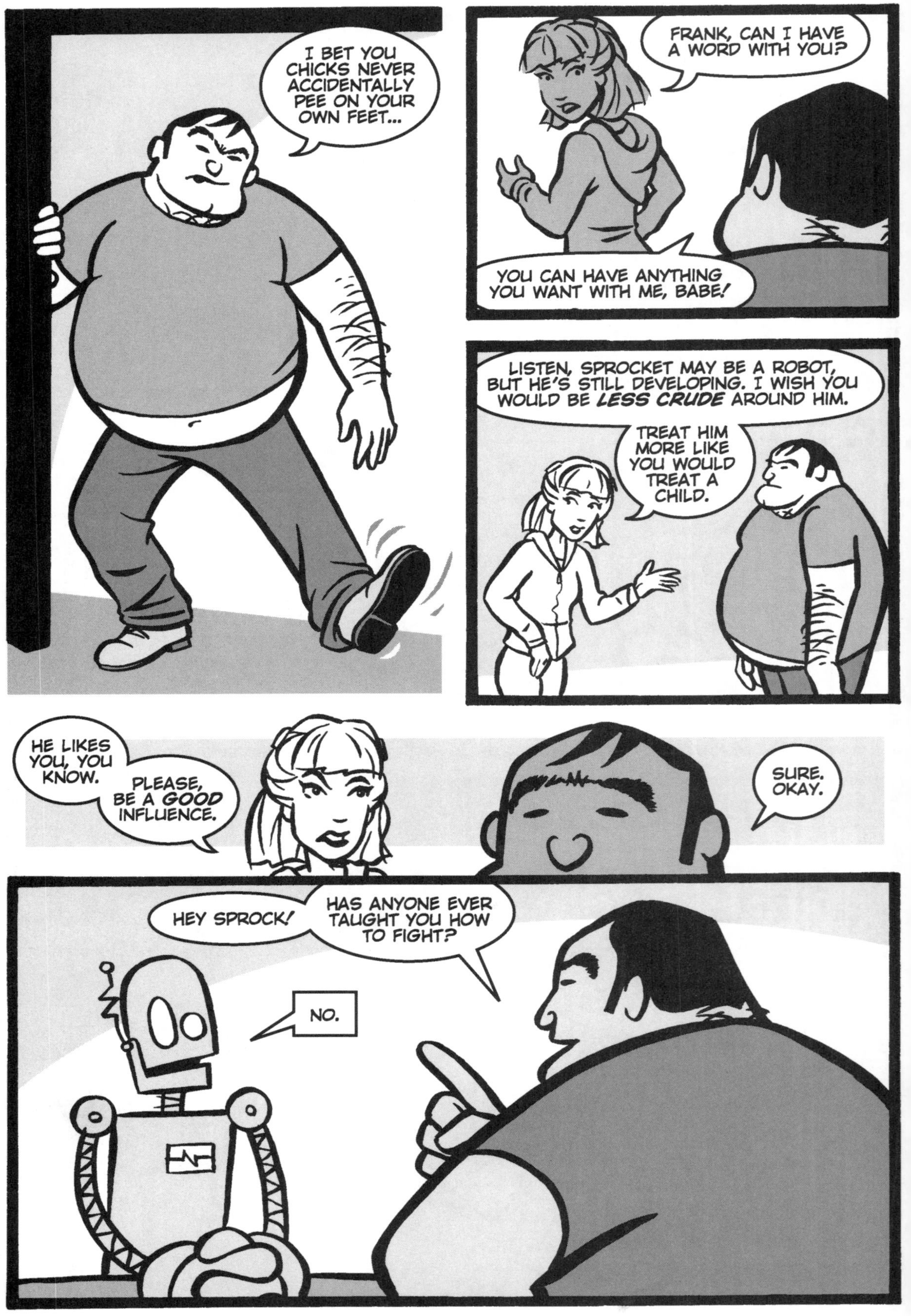
I BET YOU CHICKS NEVER ACCIDENTALLY PEE ON YOUR OWN FEET...
FRANK, CAN I HAVE A WORD WITH YOU?
YOU CAN HAVE ANYTHING YOU WANT WITH ME, BABE!
LISTEN, SPROCKET MAY BE A ROBOT, BUT HE'S STILL DEVELOPING. I WISH YOU WOULD BE LESS CRUDE AROUND HIM.
TREAT HIM MORE LIKE YOU WOULD TREAT A CHILD.
HE LIKES YOU, YOU KNOW.
PLEASE, BE A GOOD INFLUENCE.
SURE. OKAY.
HEY SPROCK!
HAS ANYONE EVER TAUGHT YOU HOW TO FIGHT?
NO.

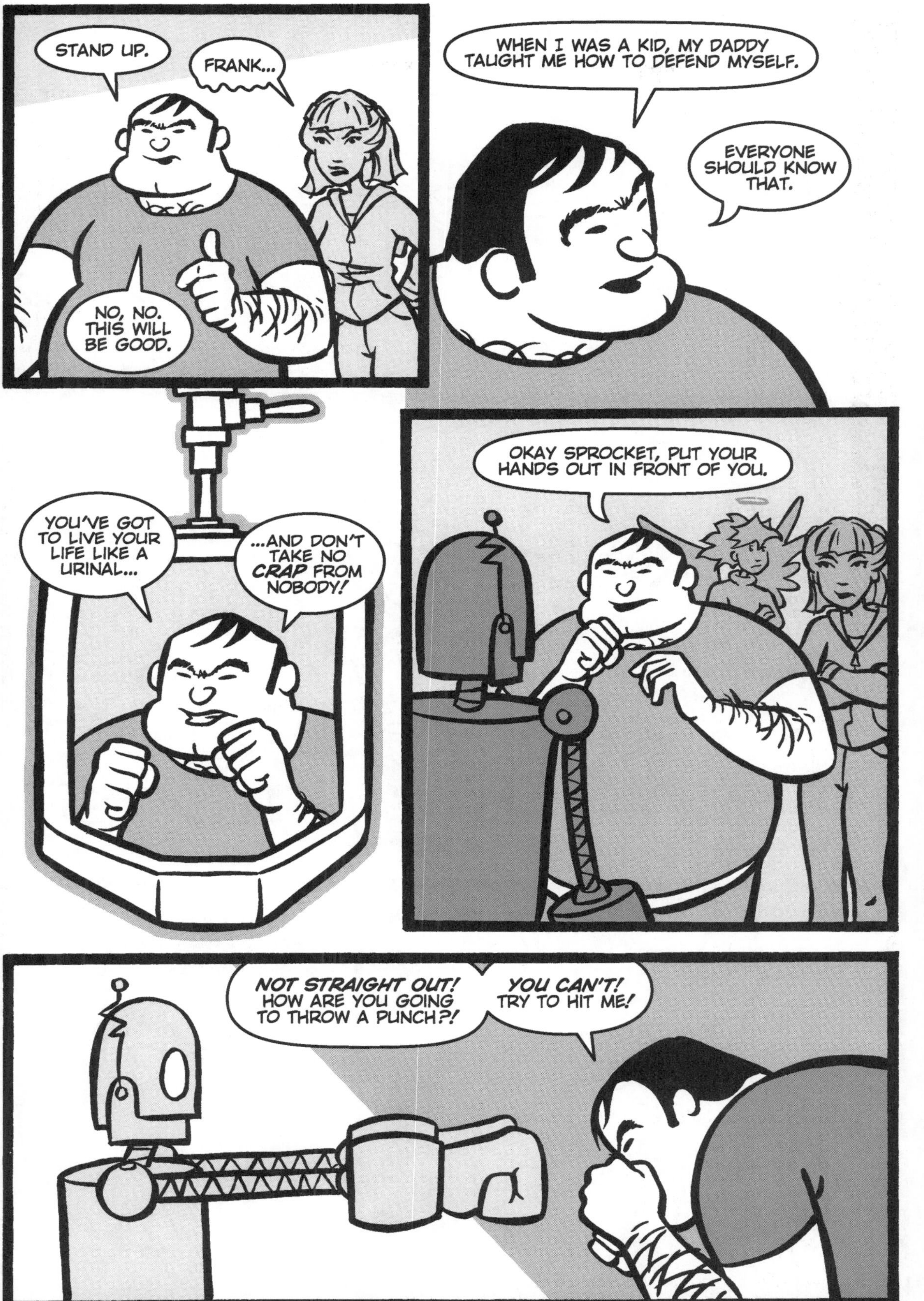
STAND UP.
FRANK...
NO, NO. THIS WILL BE GOOD.
WHEN I WAS A KID, MY DADDY TAUGHT ME HOW TO DEFEND MYSELF.
EVERYONE SHOULD KNOW THAT.
YOU'VE GOT TO LIVE YOUR LIFE LIKE A URINAL...
...AND DON'T TAKE NO *CRAP* FROM NOBODY!
OKAY SPROCKET, PUT YOUR HANDS OUT IN FRONT OF YOU.
NOT STRAIGHT OUT! HOW ARE YOU GOING TO THROW A PUNCH?!
YOU CAN'T! TRY TO HIT ME!

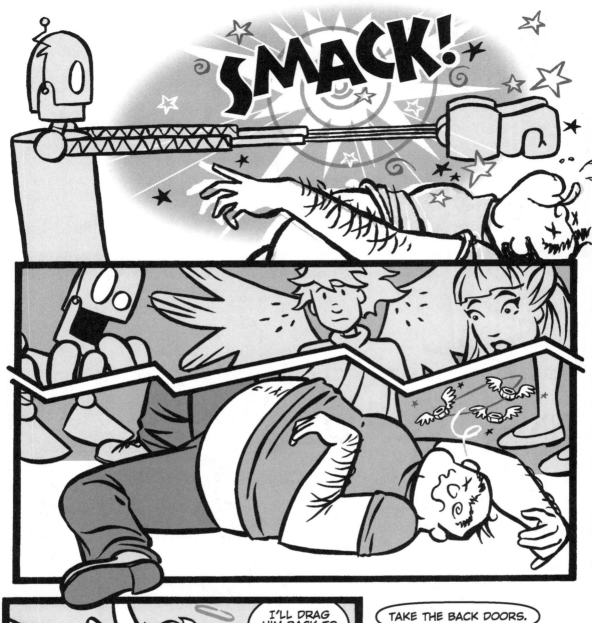

SMACK!

I'LL DRAG HIM BACK TO HIS HOUSE.

TAKE THE BACK DOORS.

THEY HAVE MORE STAIRS.

END

HALO AND SPROCKET

"SUCKERS"

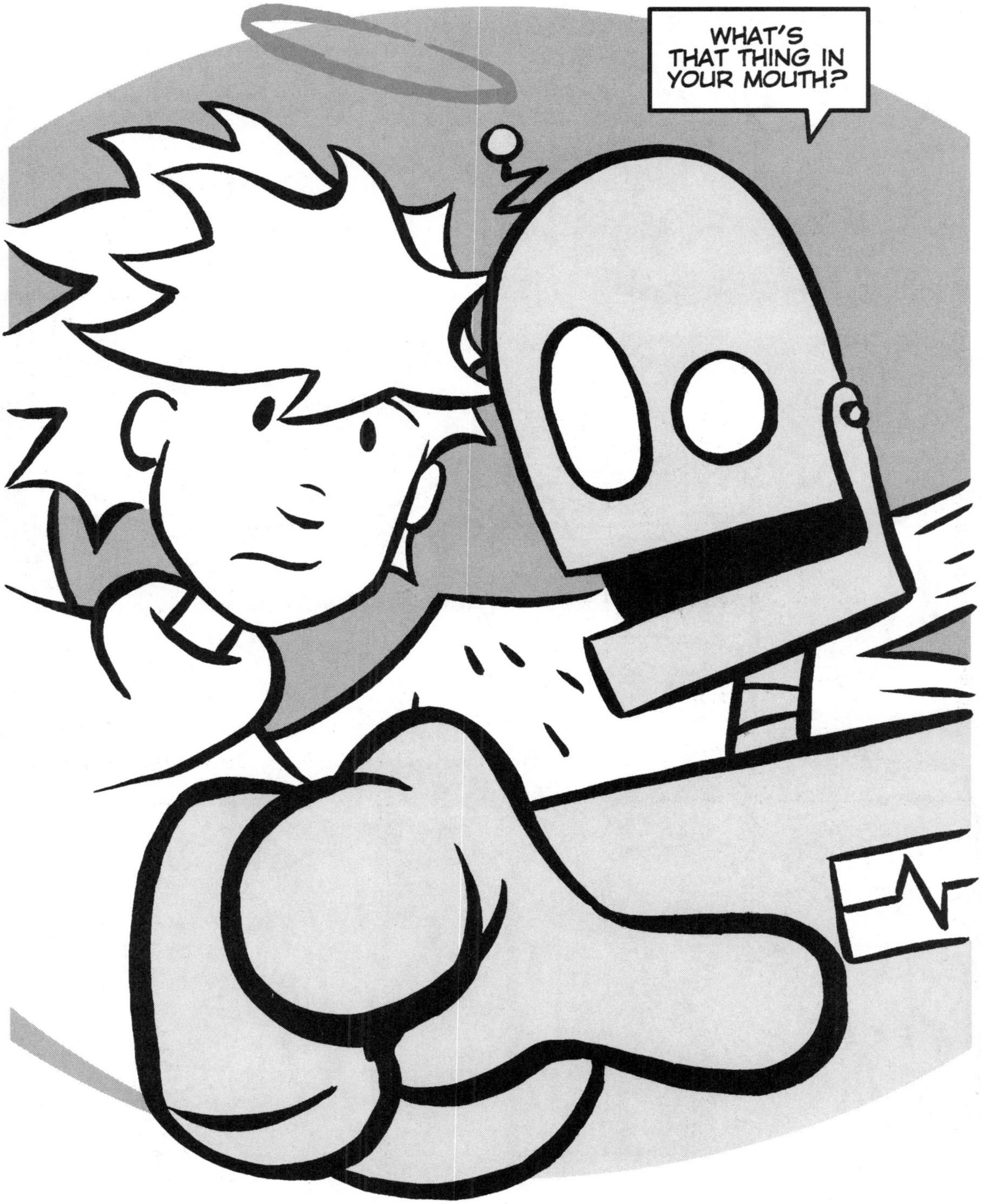
WHAT'S THAT THING IN YOUR MOUTH?

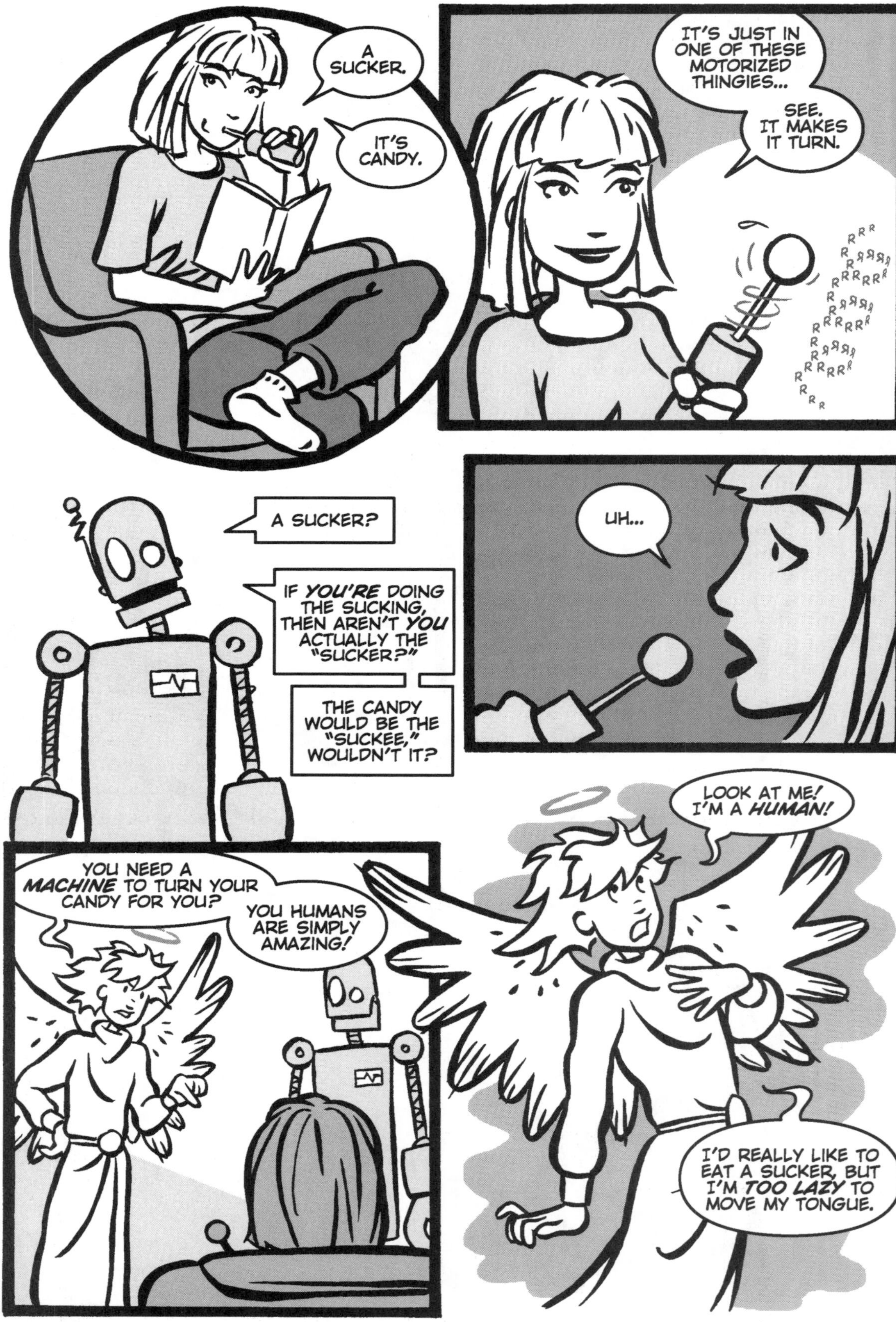
A SUCKER.
IT'S CANDY.
IT'S JUST IN ONE OF THESE MOTORIZED THINGIES...
SEE. IT MAKES IT TURN.
A SUCKER?
IF *YOU'RE* DOING THE SUCKING, THEN AREN'T *YOU* ACTUALLY THE "SUCKER?"
THE CANDY WOULD BE THE "SUCKEE," WOULDN'T IT?
UH...
YOU NEED A *MACHINE* TO TURN YOUR CANDY FOR YOU?
YOU HUMANS ARE SIMPLY AMAZING!
LOOK AT ME! I'M A *HUMAN!*
I'D REALLY LIKE TO EAT A SUCKER, BUT I'M *TOO LAZY* TO MOVE MY TONGUE.

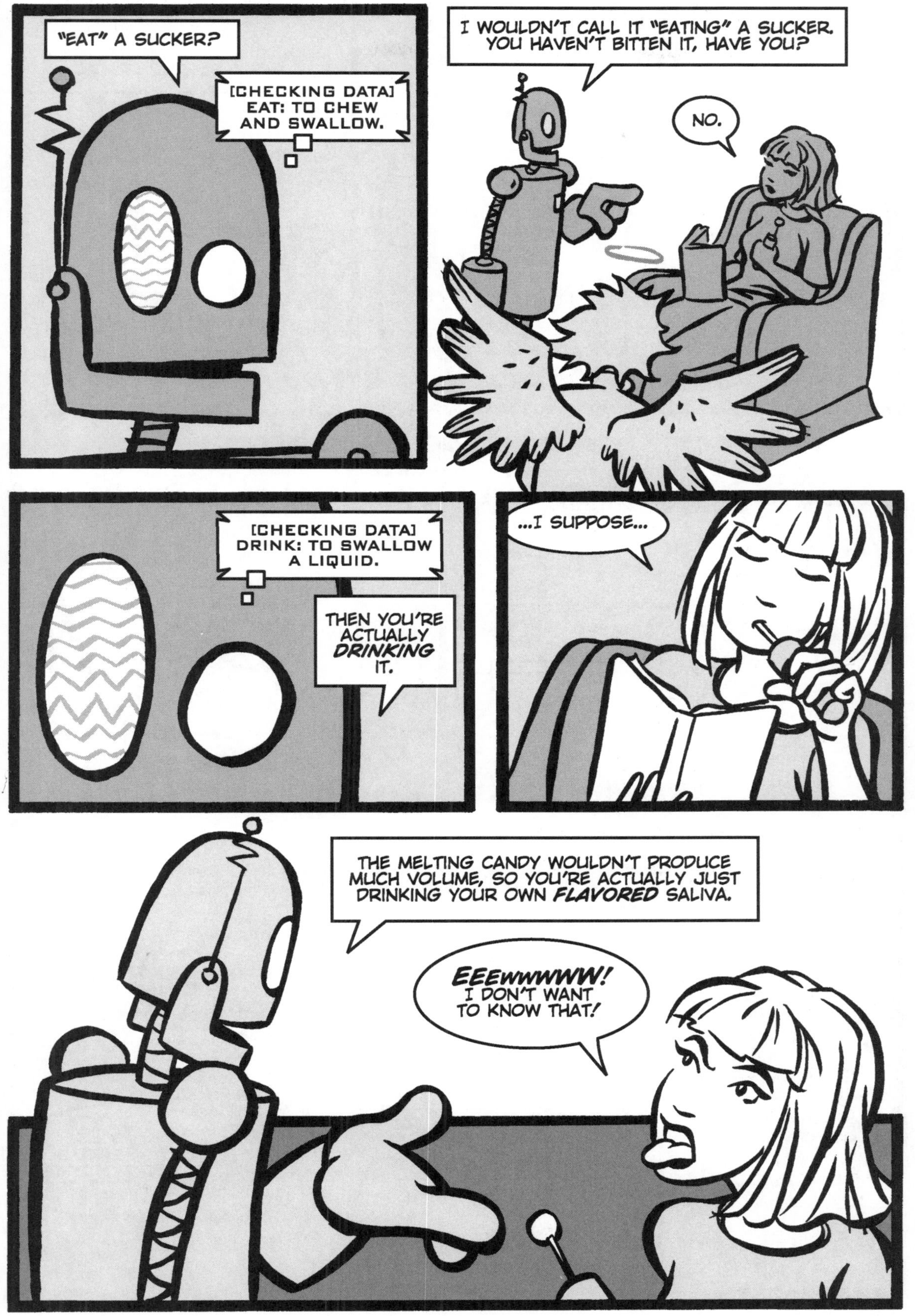
"EAT" A SUCKER?
[CHECKING DATA] EAT: TO CHEW AND SWALLOW.
I WOULDN'T CALL IT "EATING" A SUCKER. YOU HAVEN'T BITTEN IT, HAVE YOU?
NO.
[CHECKING DATA] DRINK: TO SWALLOW A LIQUID.
THEN YOU'RE ACTUALLY *DRINKING* IT.
...I SUPPOSE...
THE MELTING CANDY WOULDN'T PRODUCE MUCH VOLUME, SO YOU'RE ACTUALLY JUST DRINKING YOUR OWN *FLAVORED* SALIVA.
EEEwwwWWW! I DON'T WANT TO KNOW THAT!

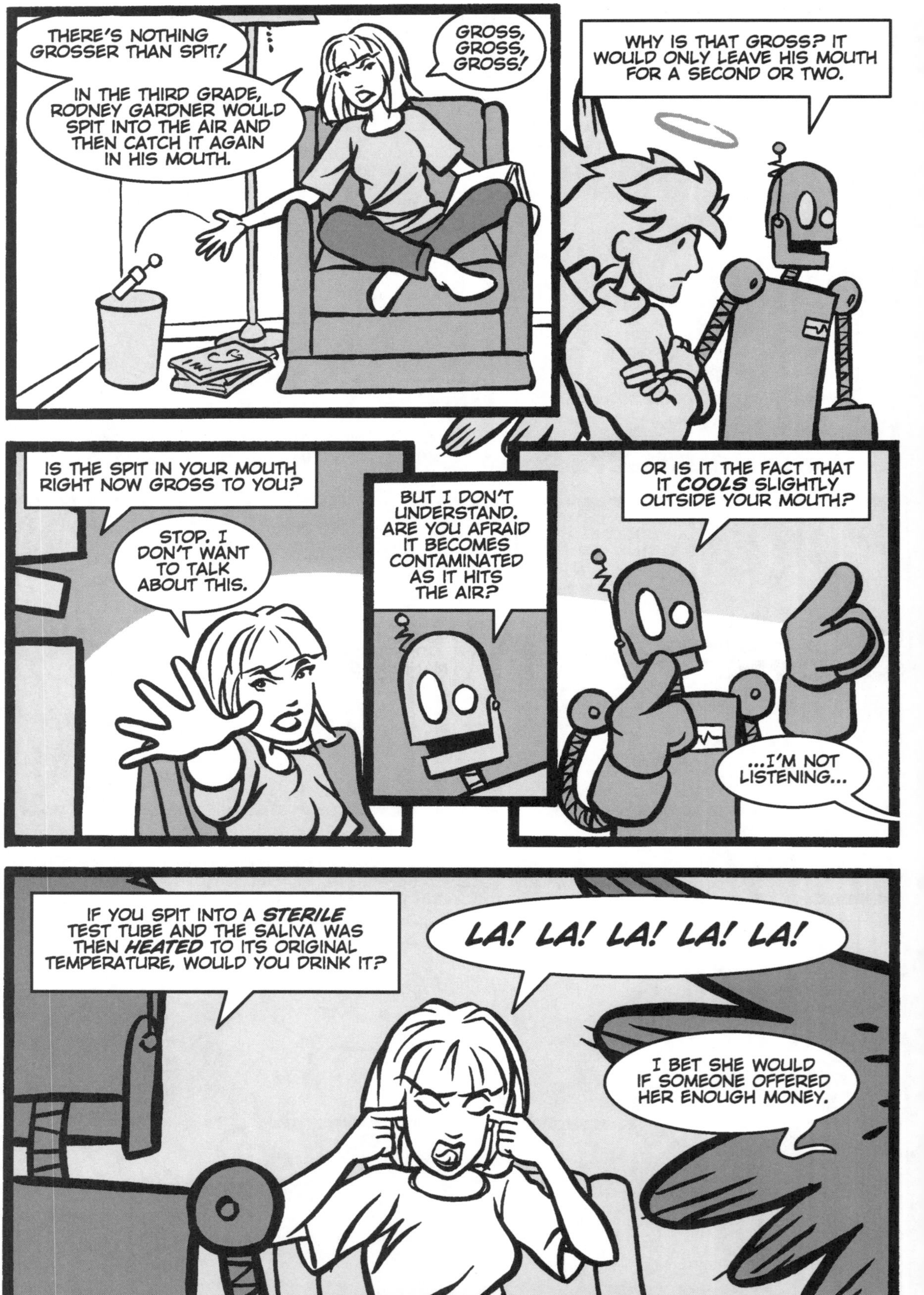
THERE'S NOTHING GROSSER THAN SPIT!
IN THE THIRD GRADE, RODNEY GARDNER WOULD SPIT INTO THE AIR AND THEN CATCH IT AGAIN IN HIS MOUTH.
GROSS, GROSS, GROSS!
WHY IS THAT GROSS? IT WOULD ONLY LEAVE HIS MOUTH FOR A SECOND OR TWO.
IS THE SPIT IN YOUR MOUTH RIGHT NOW GROSS TO YOU?
STOP. I DON'T WANT TO TALK ABOUT THIS.
BUT I DON'T UNDERSTAND. ARE YOU AFRAID IT BECOMES CONTAMINATED AS IT HITS THE AIR?
OR IS IT THE FACT THAT IT COOLS SLIGHTLY OUTSIDE YOUR MOUTH?
...I'M NOT LISTENING...
IF YOU SPIT INTO A STERILE TEST TUBE AND THE SALIVA WAS THEN HEATED TO ITS ORIGINAL TEMPERATURE, WOULD YOU DRINK IT?
LA! LA! LA! LA! LA!
I BET SHE WOULD IF SOMEONE OFFERED HER ENOUGH MONEY.

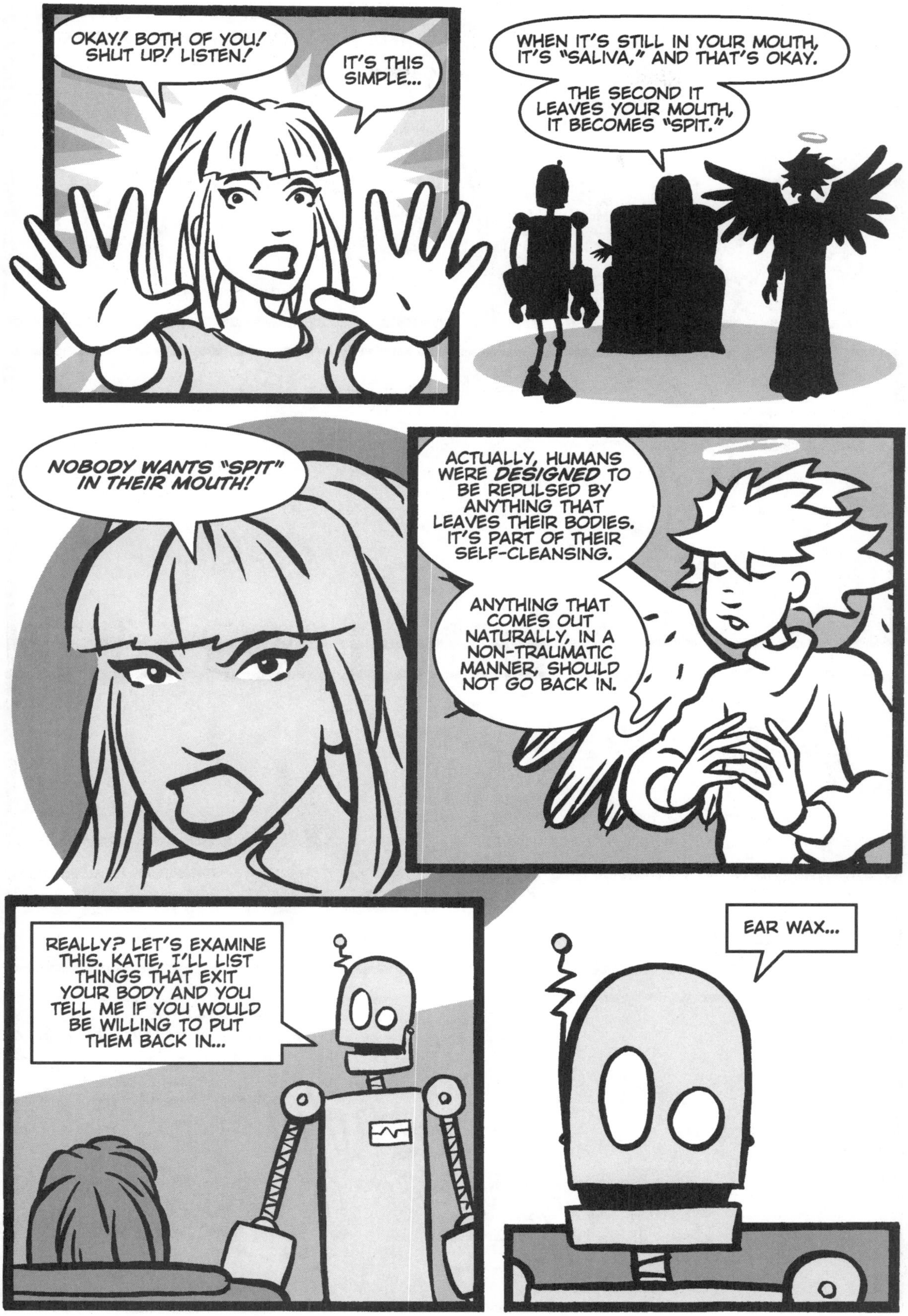

OKAY! BOTH OF YOU! SHUT UP! LISTEN!
IT'S THIS SIMPLE...
WHEN IT'S STILL IN YOUR MOUTH, IT'S "SALIVA," AND THAT'S OKAY.
THE SECOND IT LEAVES YOUR MOUTH, IT BECOMES "SPIT."
NOBODY WANTS "SPIT" IN THEIR MOUTH!
ACTUALLY, HUMANS WERE ***DESIGNED*** TO BE REPULSED BY ANYTHING THAT LEAVES THEIR BODIES. IT'S PART OF THEIR SELF-CLEANSING.
ANYTHING THAT COMES OUT NATURALLY, IN A NON-TRAUMATIC MANNER, SHOULD NOT GO BACK IN.
REALLY? LET'S EXAMINE THIS. KATIE, I'LL LIST THINGS THAT EXIT YOUR BODY AND YOU TELL ME IF YOU WOULD BE WILLING TO PUT THEM BACK IN...
EAR WAX...

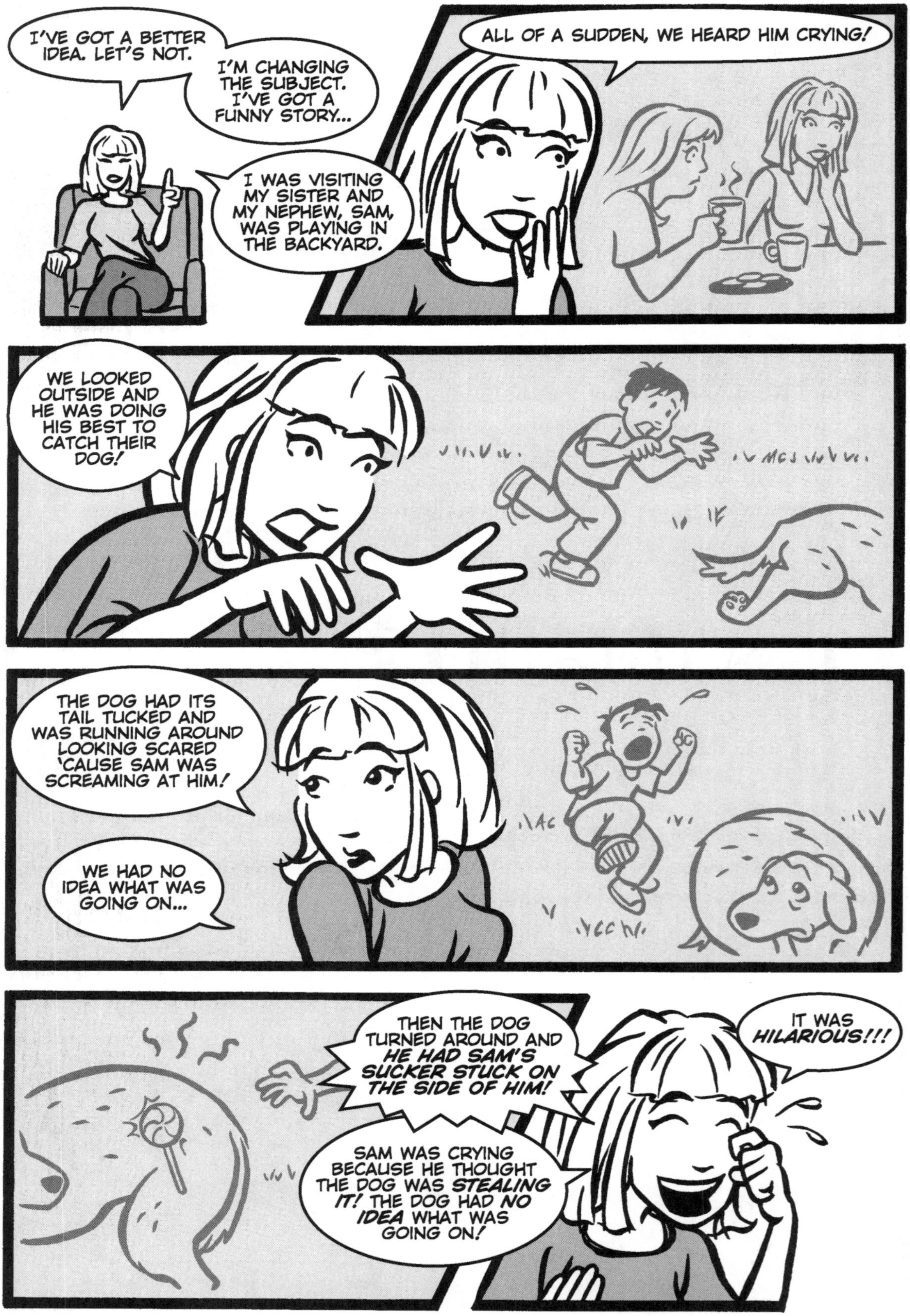
I'VE GOT A BETTER IDEA. LET'S NOT.
I'M CHANGING THE SUBJECT. I'VE GOT A FUNNY STORY...
I WAS VISITING MY SISTER AND MY NEPHEW, SAM, WAS PLAYING IN THE BACKYARD.
ALL OF A SUDDEN, WE HEARD HIM CRYING!
WE LOOKED OUTSIDE AND HE WAS DOING HIS BEST TO CATCH THEIR DOG!
THE DOG HAD ITS TAIL TUCKED AND WAS RUNNING AROUND LOOKING SCARED 'CAUSE SAM WAS SCREAMING AT HIM!
WE HAD NO IDEA WHAT WAS GOING ON...
THEN THE DOG TURNED AROUND AND HE HAD SAM'S SUCKER STUCK ON THE SIDE OF HIM!
SAM WAS CRYING BECAUSE HE THOUGHT THE DOG WAS STEALING IT! THE DOG HAD NO IDEA WHAT WAS GOING ON!
IT WAS HILARIOUS!!!

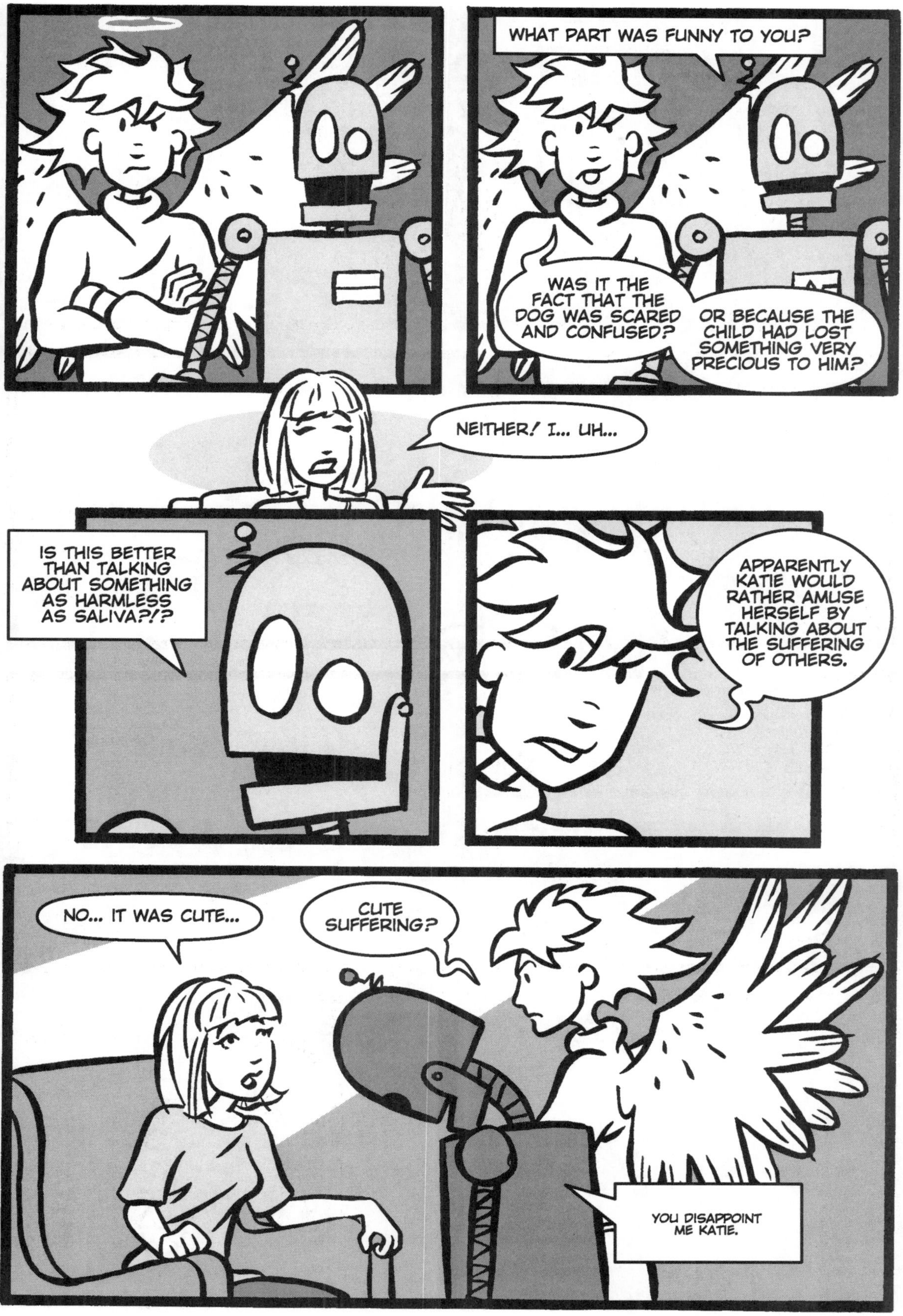
WHAT PART WAS FUNNY TO YOU?
WAS IT THE FACT THAT THE DOG WAS SCARED AND CONFUSED?
OR BECAUSE THE CHILD HAD LOST SOMETHING VERY PRECIOUS TO HIM?
NEITHER! I... UH...
IS THIS BETTER THAN TALKING ABOUT SOMETHING AS HARMLESS AS SALIVA?!?
APPARENTLY KATIE WOULD RATHER AMUSE HERSELF BY TALKING ABOUT THE SUFFERING OF OTHERS.
NO... IT WAS CUTE...
CUTE SUFFERING?
YOU DISAPPOINT ME KATIE.

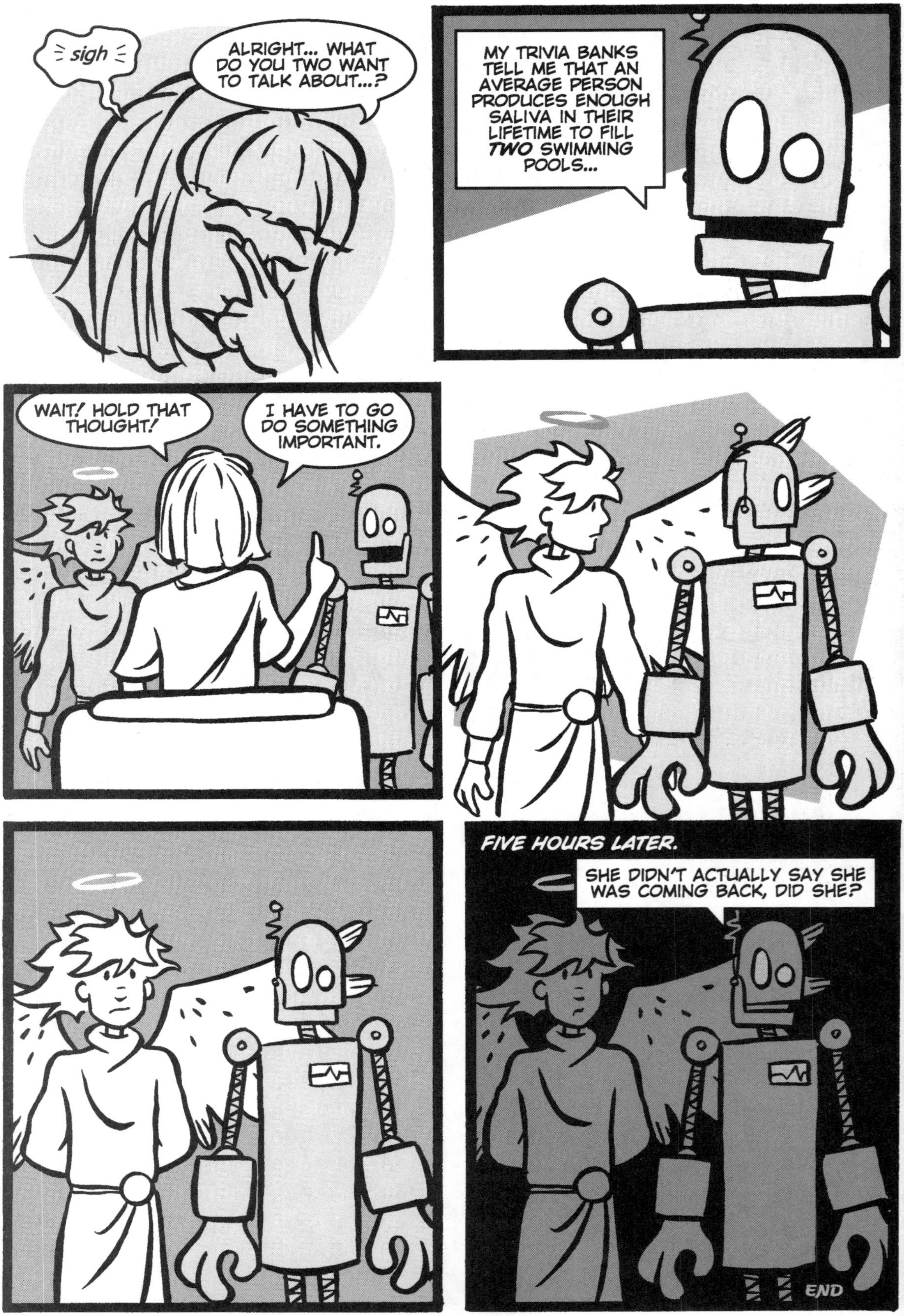
sigh
ALRIGHT... WHAT DO YOU TWO WANT TO TALK ABOUT...?
MY TRIVIA BANKS TELL ME THAT AN AVERAGE PERSON PRODUCES ENOUGH SALIVA IN THEIR LIFETIME TO FILL *TWO* SWIMMING POOLS...
WAIT! HOLD THAT THOUGHT!
I HAVE TO GO DO SOMETHING IMPORTANT.
FIVE HOURS LATER.
SHE DIDN'T ACTUALLY SAY SHE WAS COMING BACK, DID SHE?
END

Katie's Diary "A DRIVING DILEMMA"

Recently, while I was merging into heavy traffic...

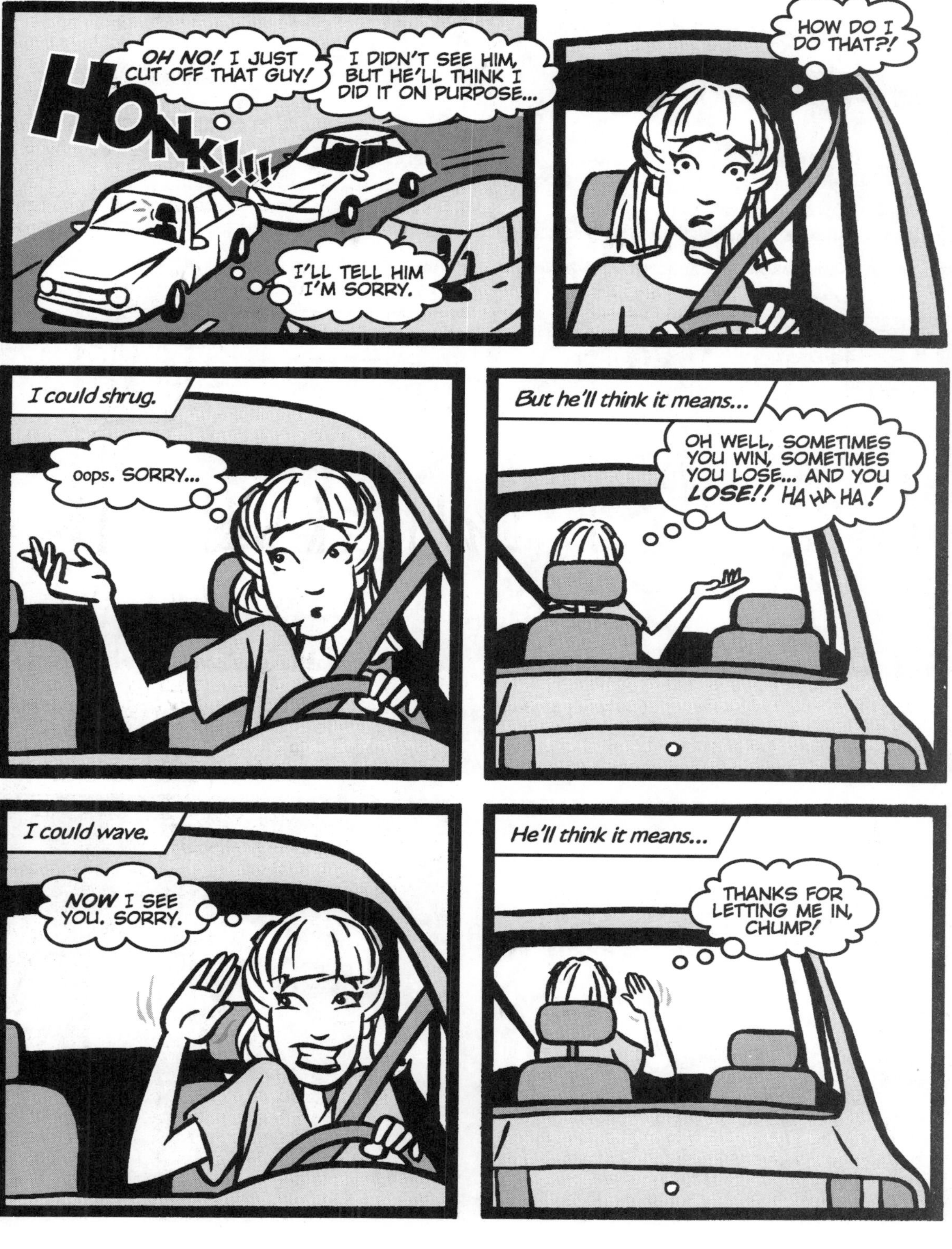
OH NO! I JUST CUT OFF THAT GUY!
I DIDN'T SEE HIM, BUT HE'LL THINK I DID IT ON PURPOSE...
HONK!!!
I'LL TELL HIM I'M SORRY.
HOW DO I DO THAT?!
I could shrug.
oops. SORRY...
But he'll think it means...
OH WELL, SOMETIMES YOU WIN, SOMETIMES YOU LOSE... AND YOU LOSE!! HA HA HA!
I could wave.
NOW I SEE YOU. SORRY.
He'll think it means...
THANKS FOR LETTING ME IN, CHUMP!

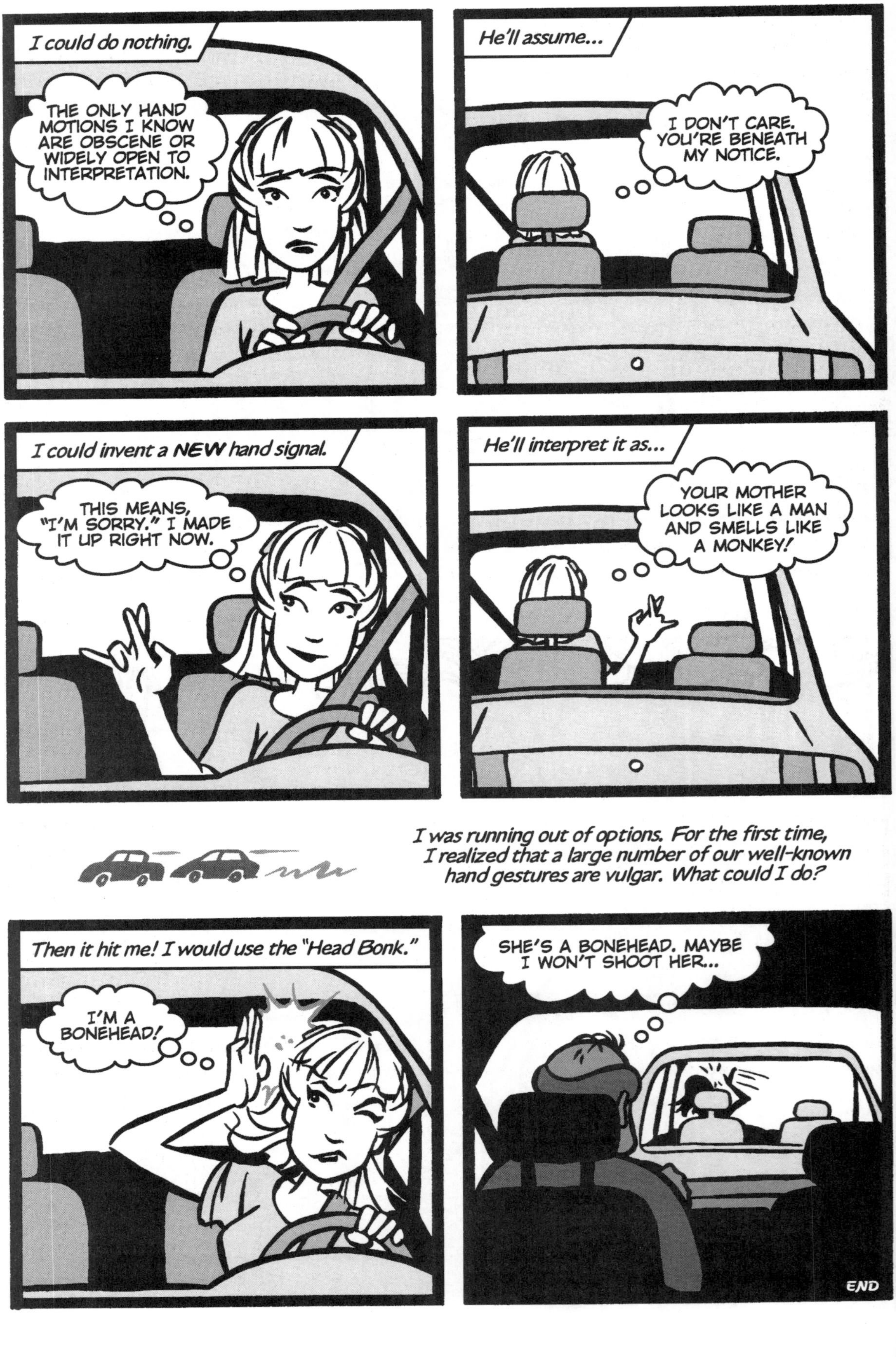
I could do nothing.
THE ONLY HAND MOTIONS I KNOW ARE OBSCENE OR WIDELY OPEN TO INTERPRETATION.
He'll assume...
I DON'T CARE. YOU'RE BENEATH MY NOTICE.
I could invent a NEW hand signal.
THIS MEANS, "I'M SORRY." I MADE IT UP RIGHT NOW.
He'll interpret it as...
YOUR MOTHER LOOKS LIKE A MAN AND SMELLS LIKE A MONKEY!
I was running out of options. For the first time, I realized that a large number of our well-known hand gestures are vulgar. What could I do?
Then it hit me! I would use the "Head Bonk."
I'M A BONEHEAD!
SHE'S A BONEHEAD. MAYBE I WON'T SHOOT HER...
END

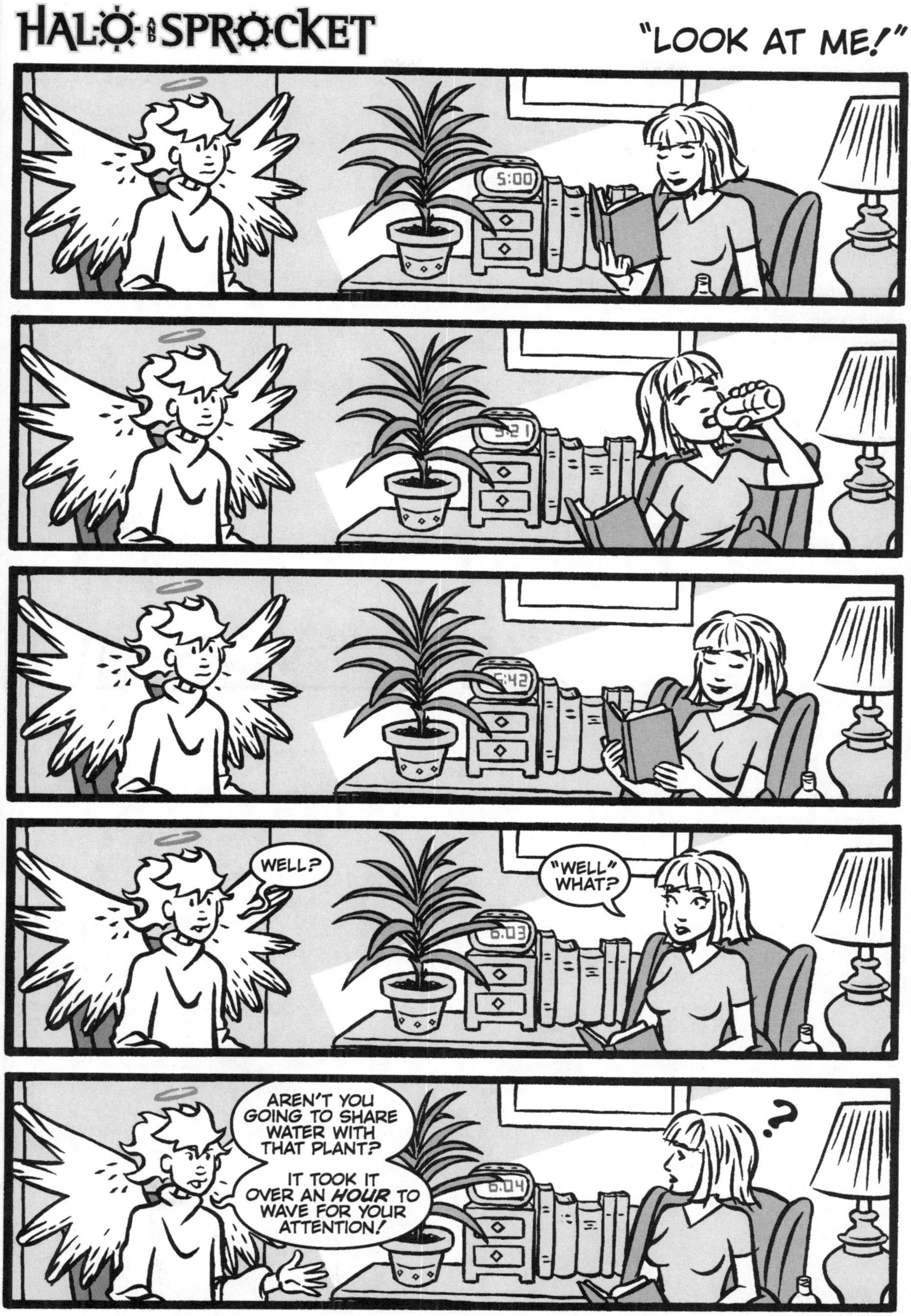
HALO AND SPROCKET
"LOOK AT ME!"
5:00
5:21
5:42
WELL?
"WELL" WHAT?
6:03
AREN'T YOU GOING TO SHARE WATER WITH THAT PLANT?
IT TOOK IT OVER AN *HOUR* TO WAVE FOR YOUR ATTENTION!
6:04
?

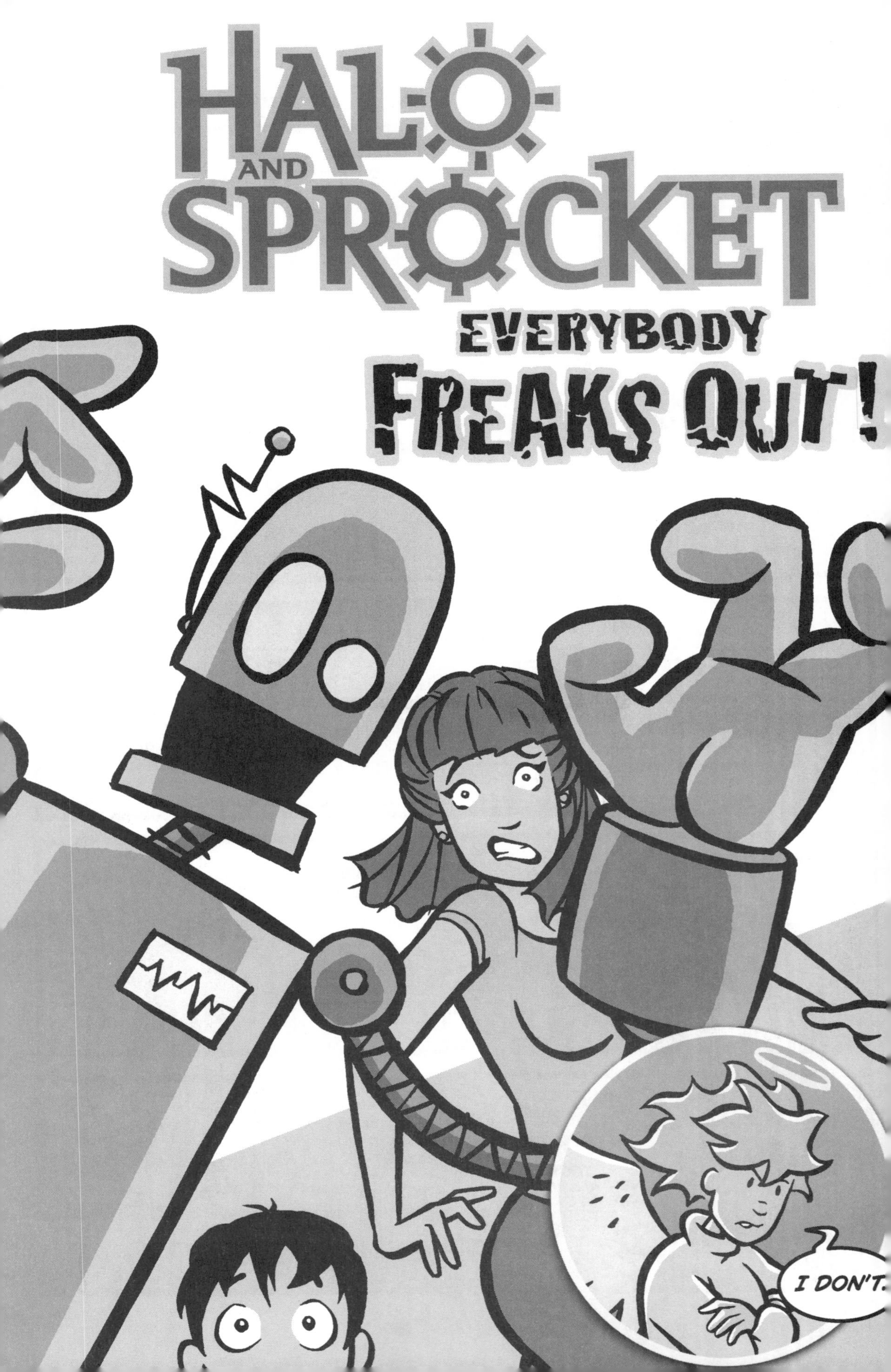
HALO AND SPROCKET
EVERYBODY FREAKS OUT!
I DON'T.

HALO AND SPROCKET

"ABOUT FACE"

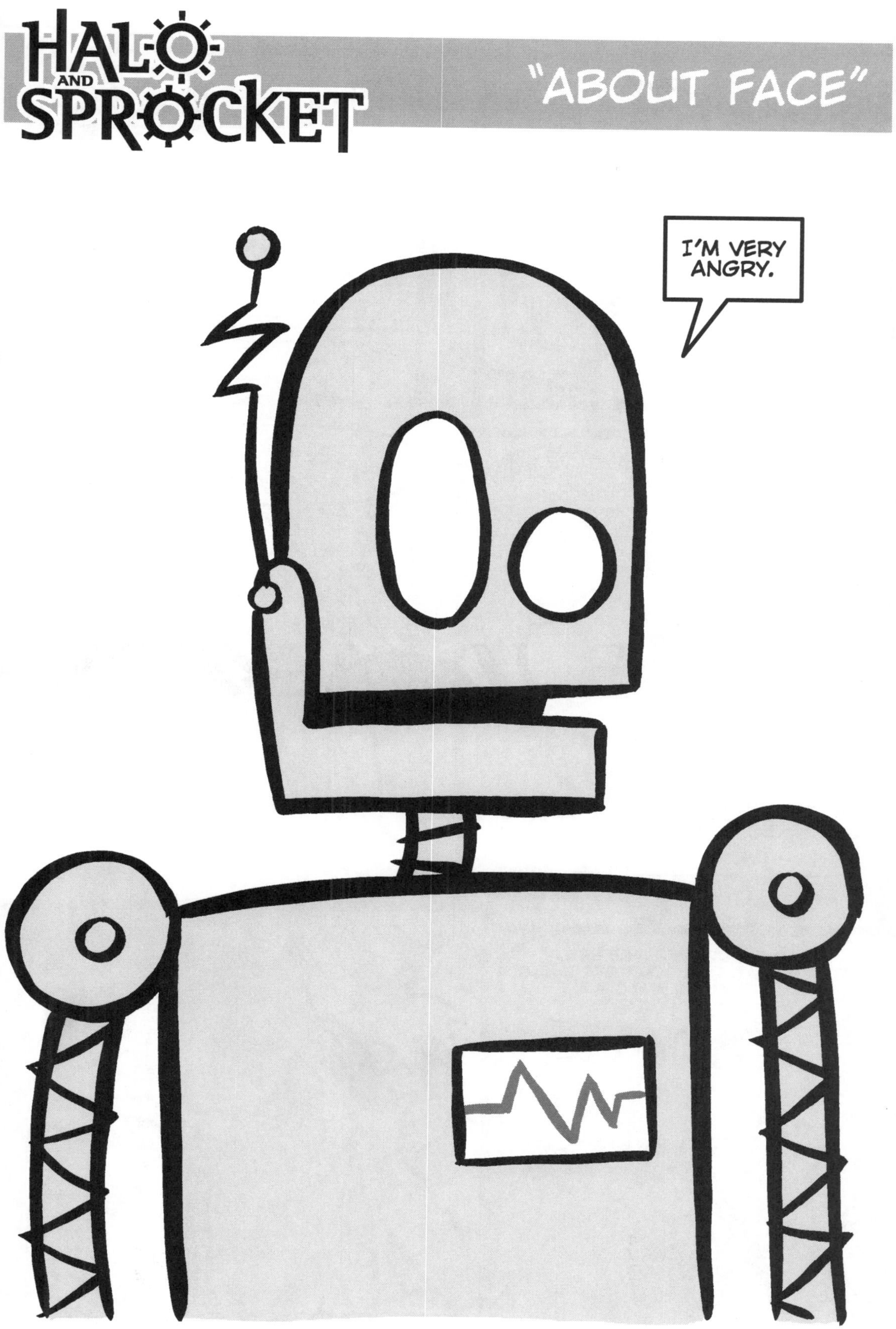
I'M VERY ANGRY.

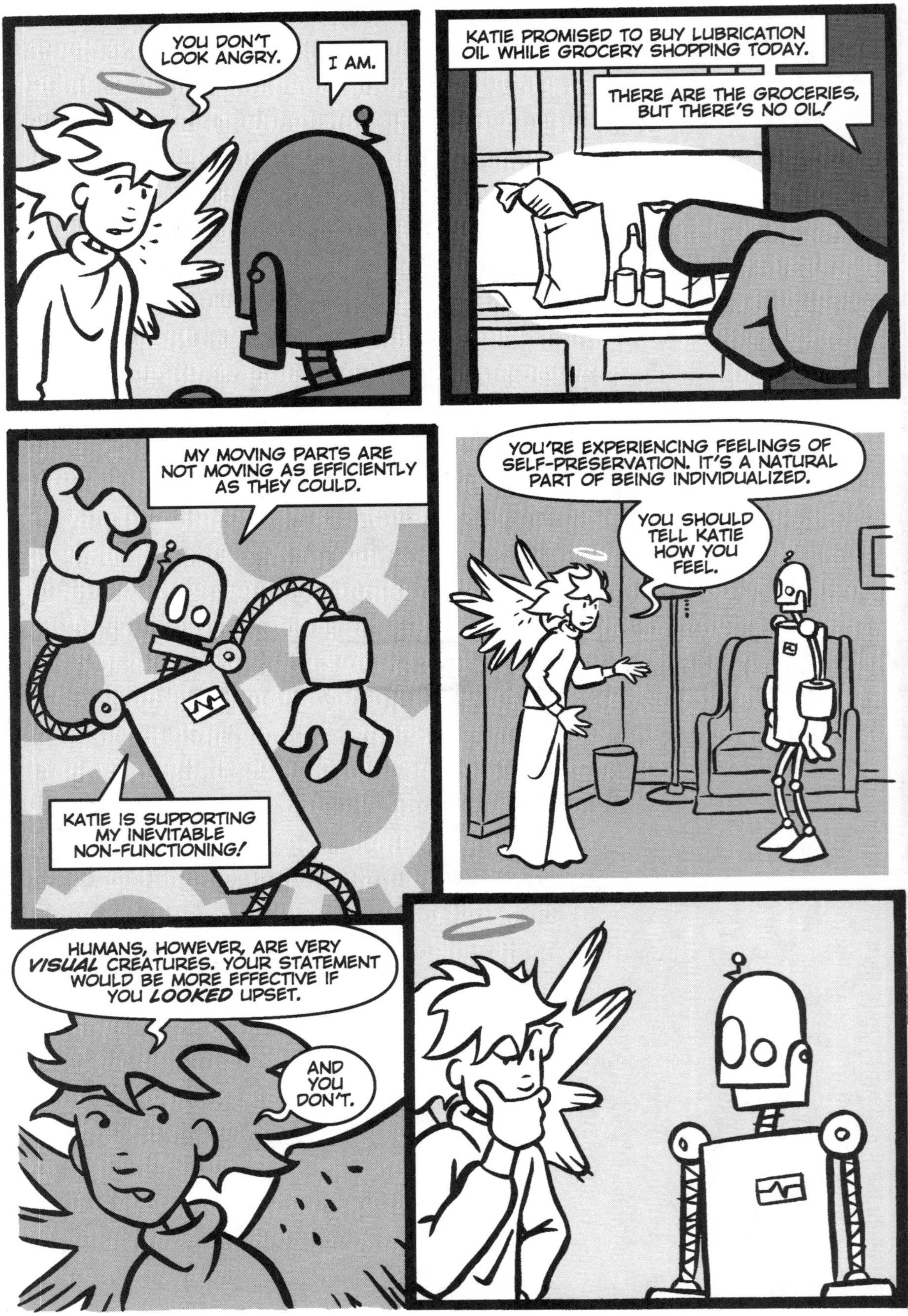
YOU DON'T LOOK ANGRY.
I AM.
KATIE PROMISED TO BUY LUBRICATION OIL WHILE GROCERY SHOPPING TODAY.
THERE ARE THE GROCERIES, BUT THERE'S NO OIL!
MY MOVING PARTS ARE NOT MOVING AS EFFICIENTLY AS THEY COULD.
KATIE IS SUPPORTING MY INEVITABLE NON-FUNCTIONING!
YOU'RE EXPERIENCING FEELINGS OF SELF-PRESERVATION. IT'S A NATURAL PART OF BEING INDIVIDUALIZED.
YOU SHOULD TELL KATIE HOW YOU FEEL.
HUMANS, HOWEVER, ARE VERY *VISUAL* CREATURES. YOUR STATEMENT WOULD BE MORE EFFECTIVE IF YOU *LOOKED* UPSET.
AND YOU DON'T.

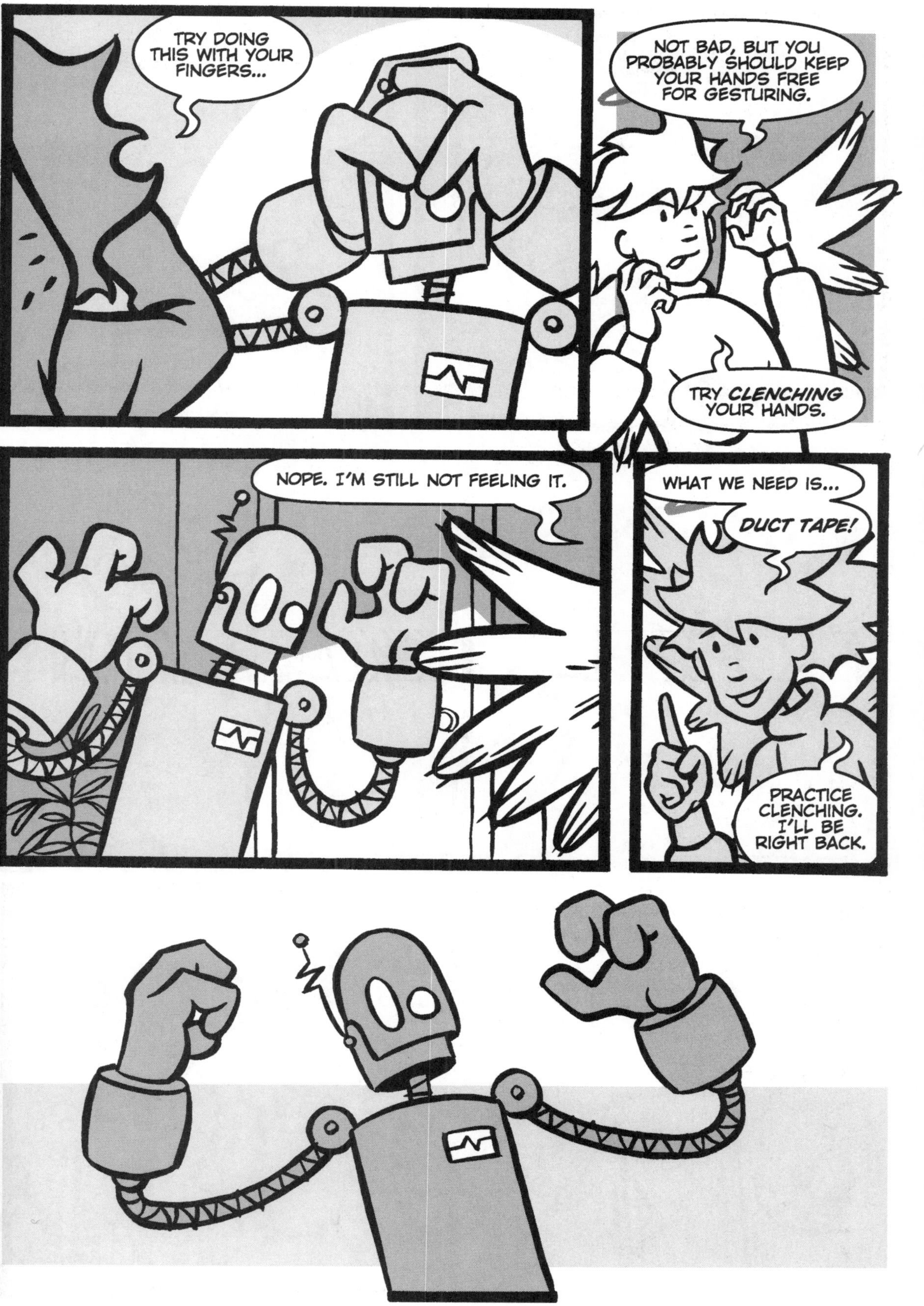
TRY DOING THIS WITH YOUR FINGERS...
NOT BAD, BUT YOU PROBABLY SHOULD KEEP YOUR HANDS FREE FOR GESTURING.
TRY *CLENCHING* YOUR HANDS.
NOPE. I'M STILL NOT FEELING IT.
WHAT WE NEED IS...
DUCT TAPE!
PRACTICE CLENCHING. I'LL BE RIGHT BACK.

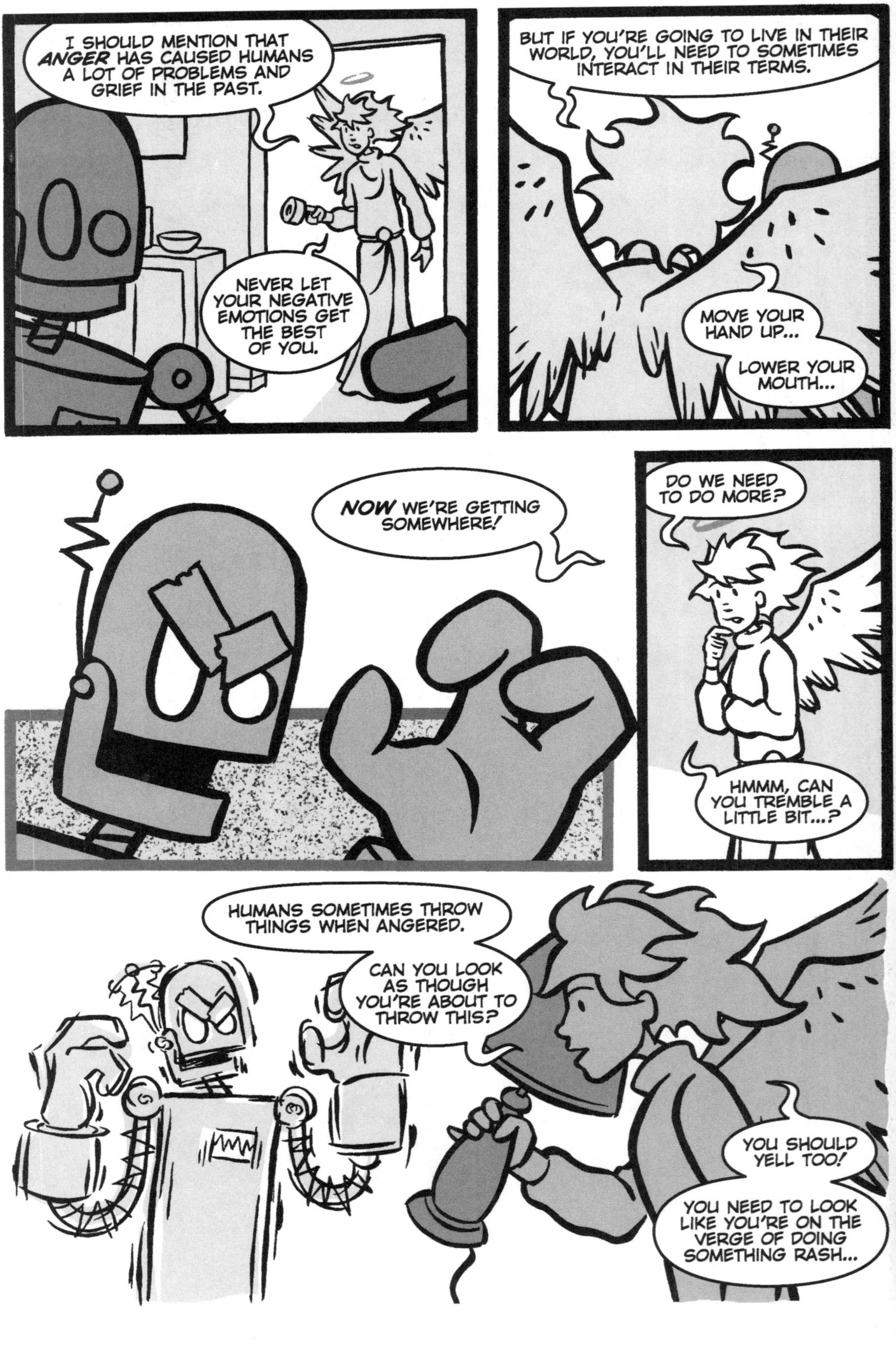
I SHOULD MENTION THAT ANGER HAS CAUSED HUMANS A LOT OF PROBLEMS AND GRIEF IN THE PAST.
NEVER LET YOUR NEGATIVE EMOTIONS GET THE BEST OF YOU.
BUT IF YOU'RE GOING TO LIVE IN THEIR WORLD, YOU'LL NEED TO SOMETIMES INTERACT IN THEIR TERMS.
MOVE YOUR HAND UP...
LOWER YOUR MOUTH...
NOW WE'RE GETTING SOMEWHERE!
DO WE NEED TO DO MORE?
HMMM, CAN YOU TREMBLE A LITTLE BIT...?
HUMANS SOMETIMES THROW THINGS WHEN ANGERED.
CAN YOU LOOK AS THOUGH YOU'RE ABOUT TO THROW THIS?
YOU SHOULD YELL TOO!
YOU NEED TO LOOK LIKE YOU'RE ON THE VERGE OF DOING SOMETHING RASH...

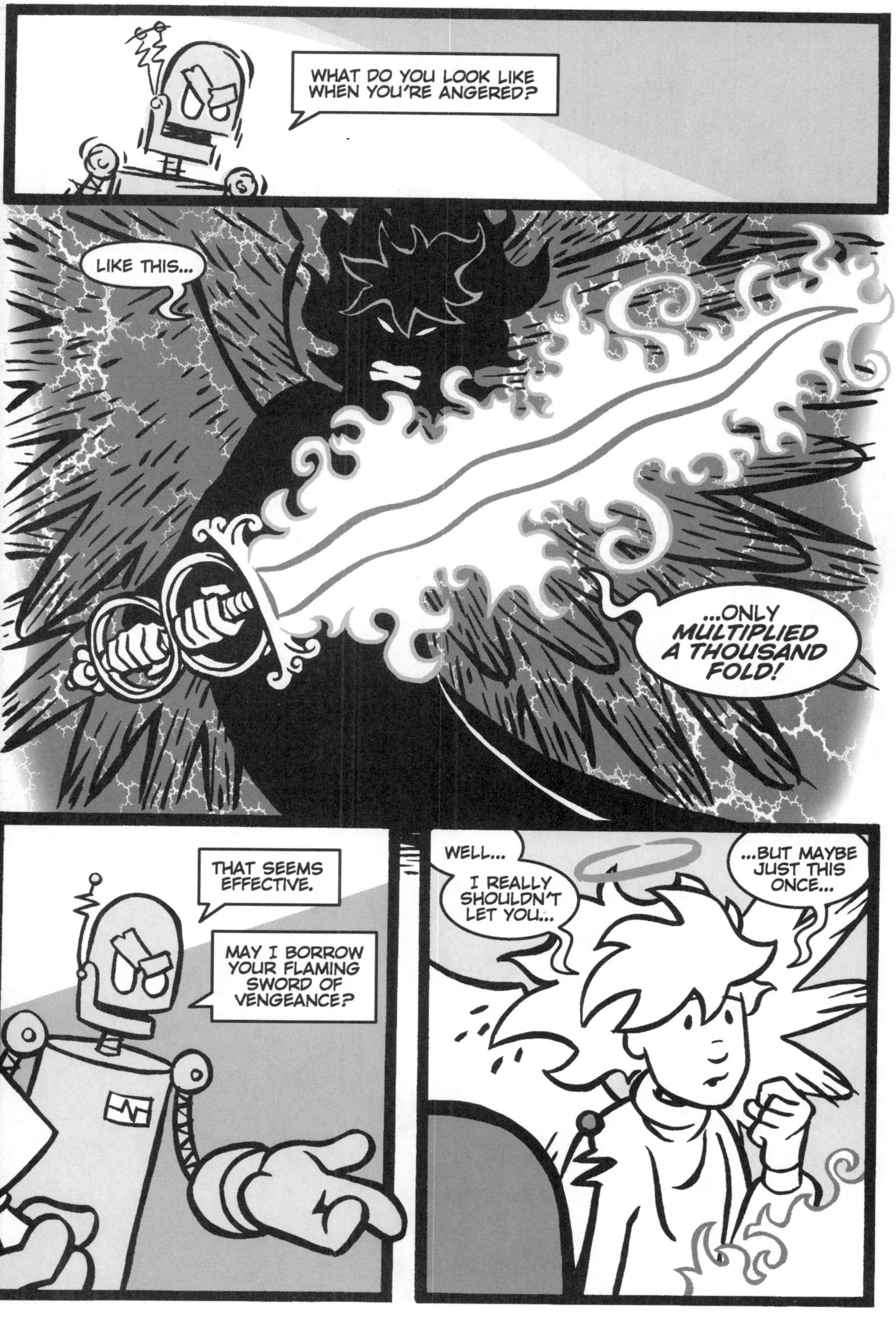
WHAT DO YOU LOOK LIKE WHEN YOU'RE ANGERED?
LIKE THIS...
...ONLY MULTIPLIED A THOUSAND FOLD!
THAT SEEMS EFFECTIVE.
MAY I BORROW YOUR FLAMING SWORD OF VENGEANCE?
WELL...
I REALLY SHOULDN'T LET YOU...
...BUT MAYBE JUST THIS ONCE...

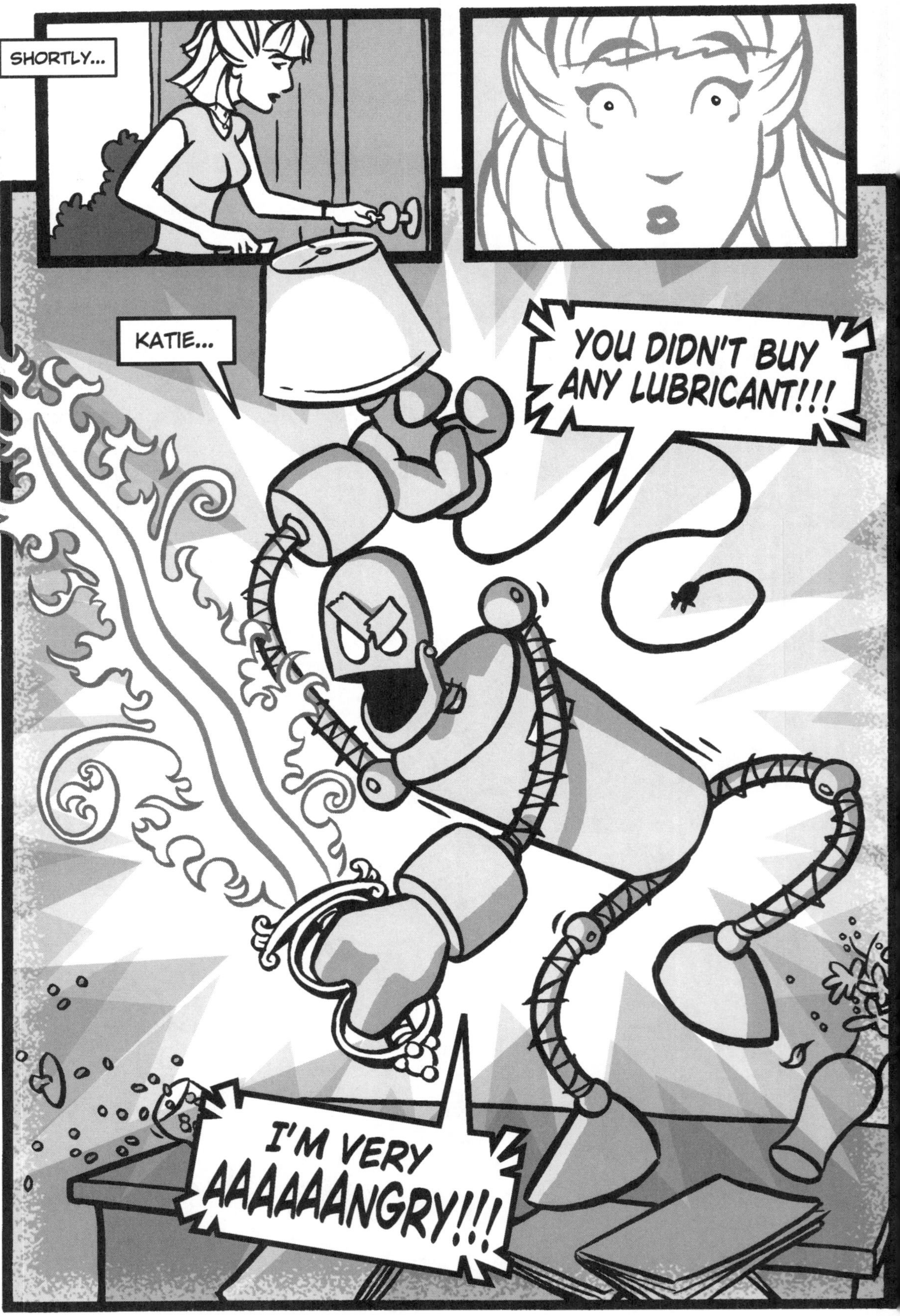
SHORTLY...
KATIE...
YOU DIDN'T BUY ANY LUBRICANT!!!
I'M VERY AAAAAANGRY!!!

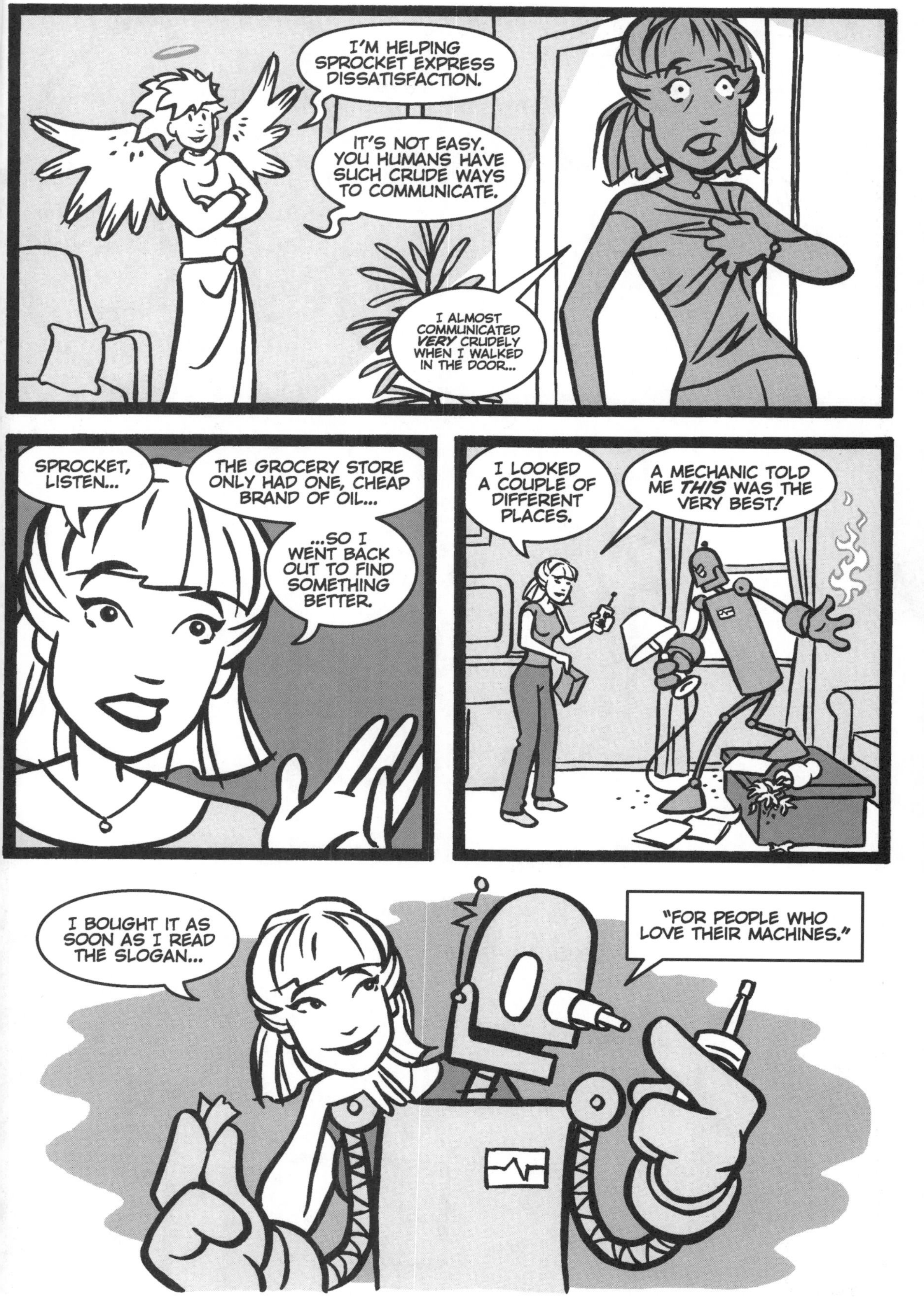
I'M HELPING SPROCKET EXPRESS DISSATISFACTION.
IT'S NOT EASY. YOU HUMANS HAVE SUCH CRUDE WAYS TO COMMUNICATE.
I ALMOST COMMUNICATED *VERY* CRUDELY WHEN I WALKED IN THE DOOR...
SPROCKET, LISTEN...
THE GROCERY STORE ONLY HAD ONE, CHEAP BRAND OF OIL...
...SO I WENT BACK OUT TO FIND SOMETHING BETTER.
I LOOKED A COUPLE OF DIFFERENT PLACES.
A MECHANIC TOLD ME *THIS* WAS THE VERY BEST!
I BOUGHT IT AS SOON AS I READ THE SLOGAN...
"FOR PEOPLE WHO LOVE THEIR MACHINES."

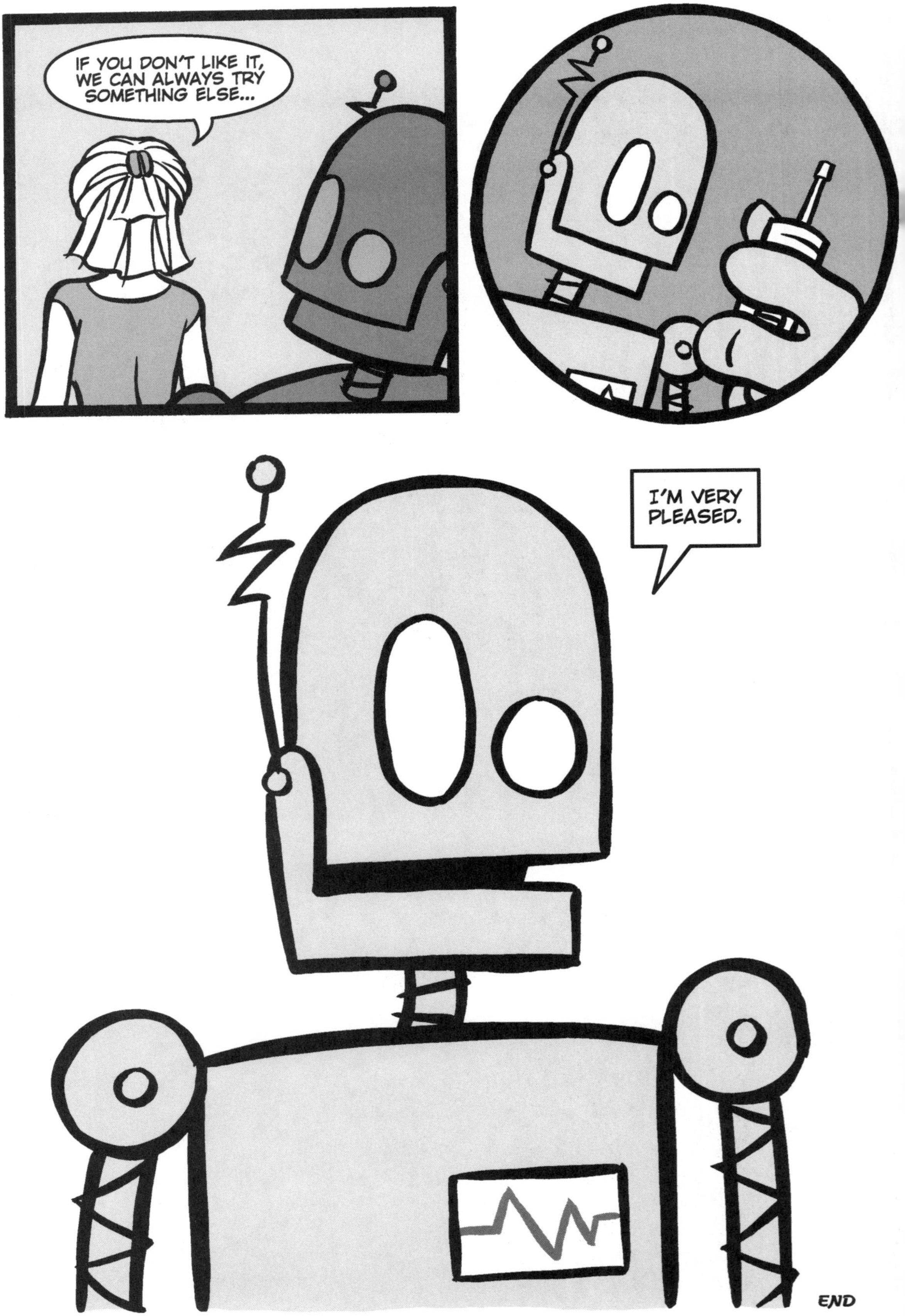
IF YOU DON'T LIKE IT, WE CAN ALWAYS TRY SOMETHING ELSE...
I'M VERY PLEASED.
END

HALO AND SPROCKET

"THE LITTLE THINGS"

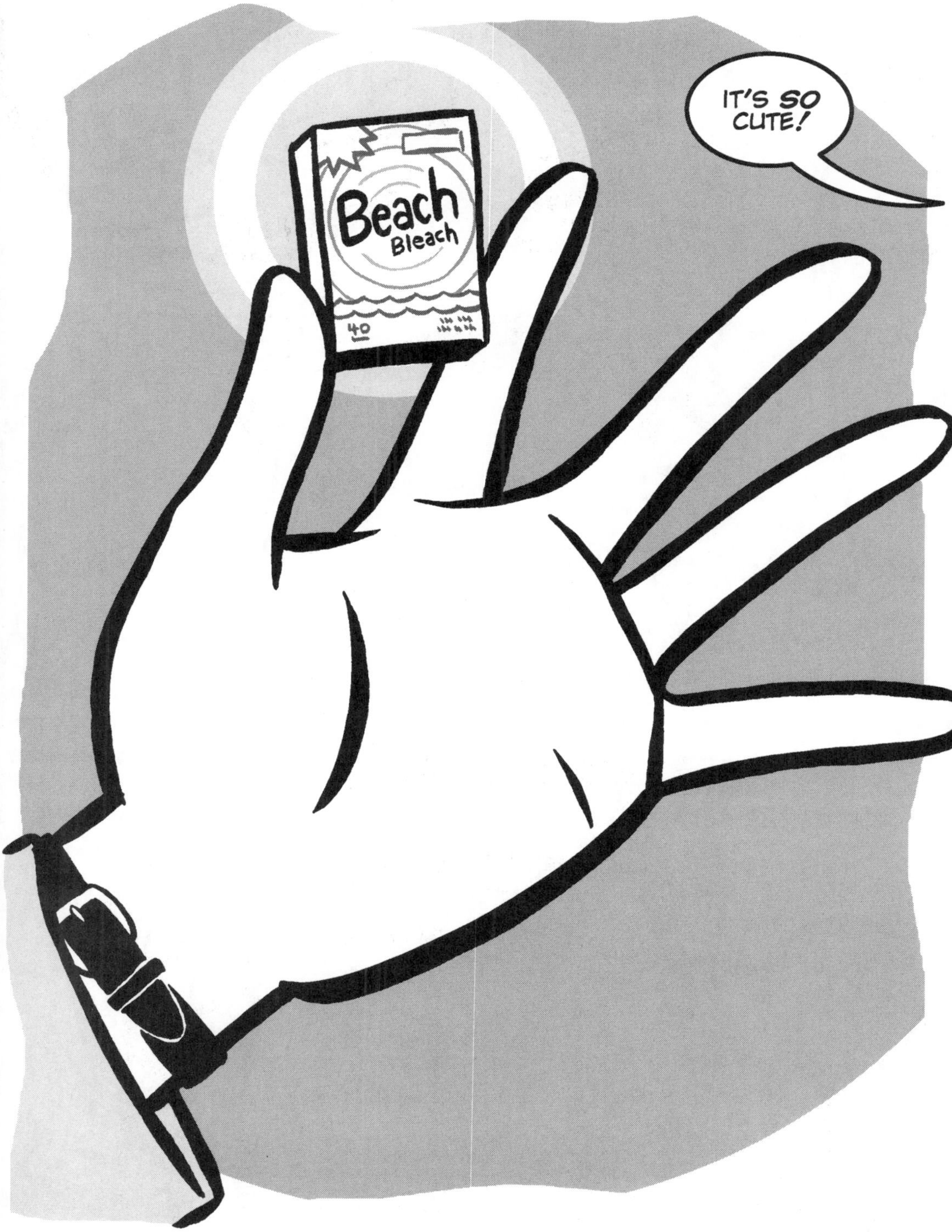
IT'S SO CUTE!
Beach
Bleach
40

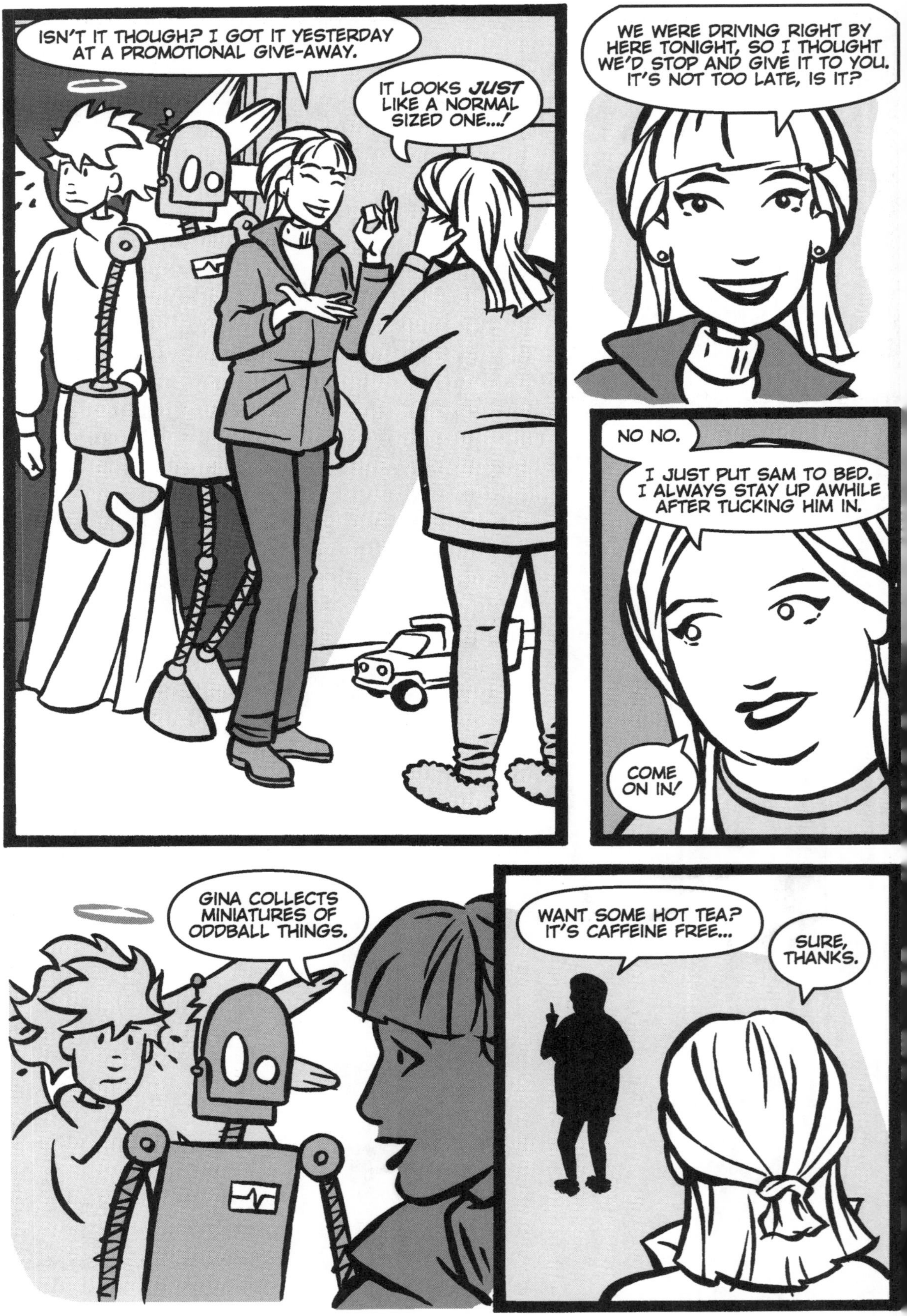
ISN'T IT THOUGH? I GOT IT YESTERDAY AT A PROMOTIONAL GIVE-AWAY.
IT LOOKS *JUST* LIKE A NORMAL SIZED ONE...!
WE WERE DRIVING RIGHT BY HERE TONIGHT, SO I THOUGHT WE'D STOP AND GIVE IT TO YOU. IT'S NOT TOO LATE, IS IT?
NO NO.
I JUST PUT SAM TO BED. I ALWAYS STAY UP AWHILE AFTER TUCKING HIM IN.
COME ON IN!
GINA COLLECTS MINIATURES OF ODDBALL THINGS.
WANT SOME HOT TEA? IT'S CAFFEINE FREE...
SURE, THANKS.

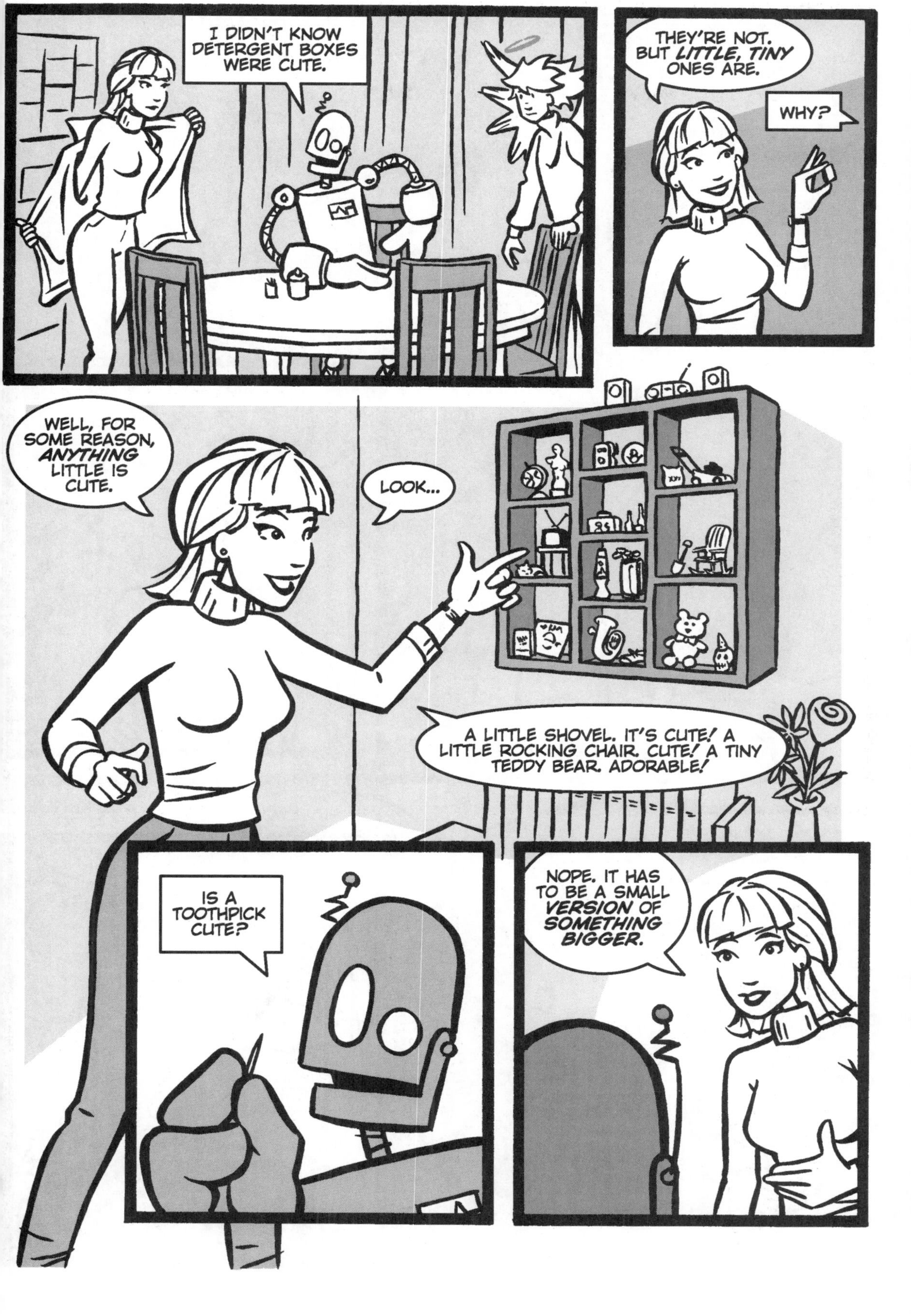
I DIDN'T KNOW DETERGENT BOXES WERE CUTE.
THEY'RE NOT. BUT *LITTLE, TINY* ONES ARE.
WHY?
WELL, FOR SOME REASON, ***ANYTHING*** LITTLE IS CUTE.
LOOK...
A LITTLE SHOVEL. IT'S CUTE! A LITTLE ROCKING CHAIR. CUTE! A TINY TEDDY BEAR. ADORABLE!
IS A TOOTHPICK CUTE?
NOPE. IT HAS TO BE A SMALL ***VERSION*** OF ***SOMETHING BIGGER.***

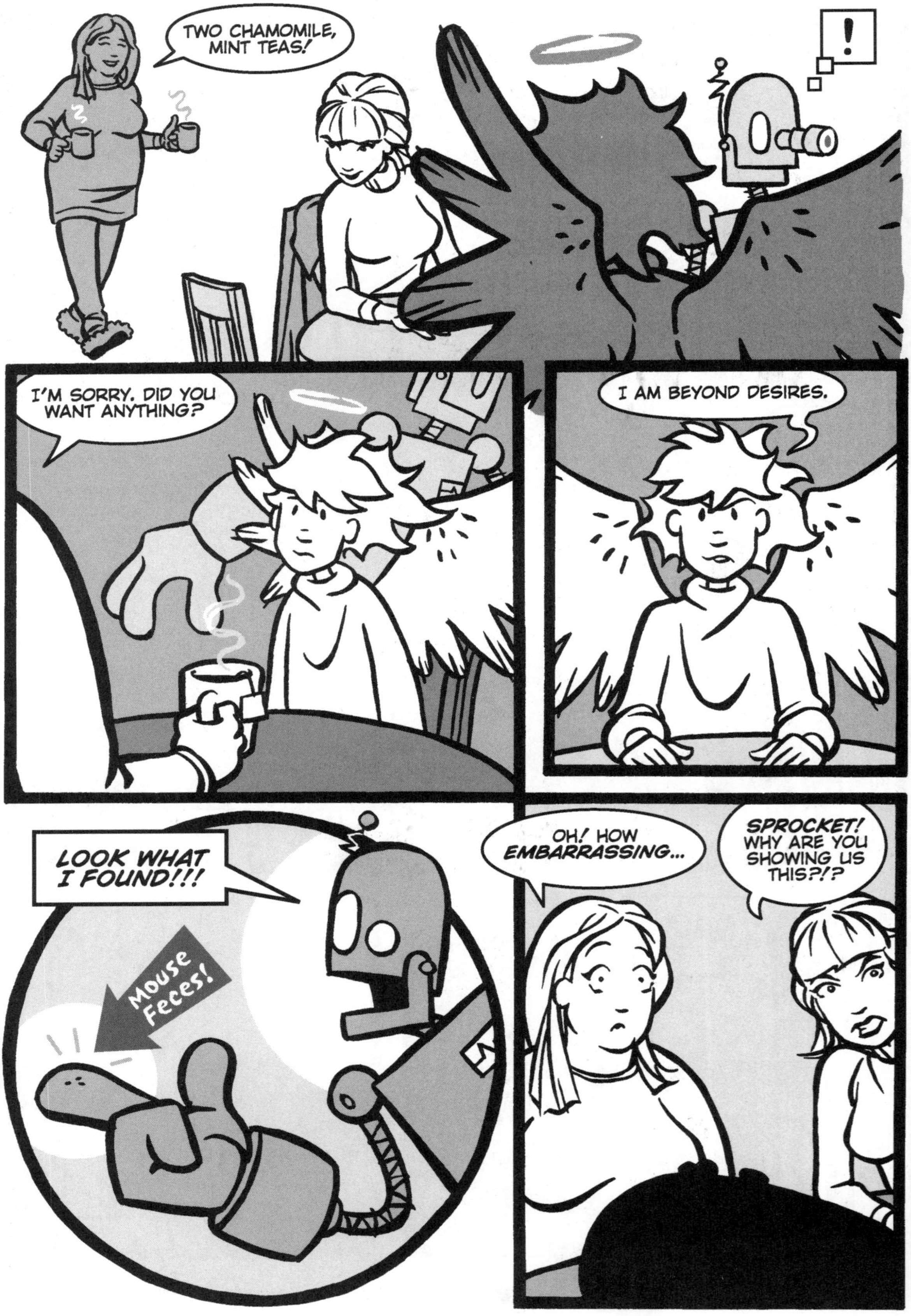
TWO CHAMOMILE, MINT TEAS!
!
I'M SORRY. DID YOU WANT ANYTHING?
I AM BEYOND DESIRES.
LOOK WHAT I FOUND!!!
Mouse Feces!
OH! HOW EMBARRASSING...
SPROCKET! WHY ARE YOU SHOWING US THIS?!?

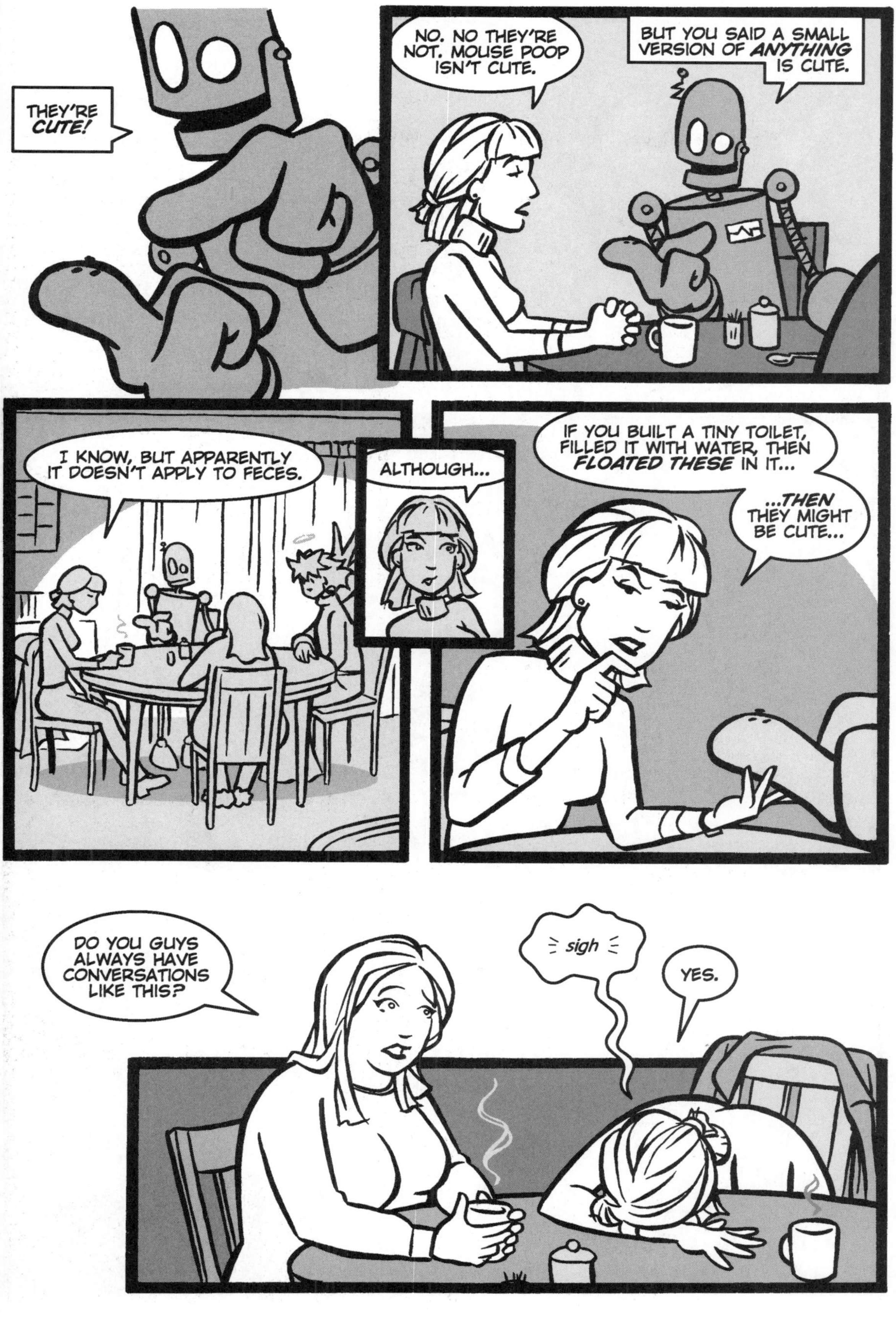
THEY'RE *CUTE!*
NO. NO THEY'RE NOT. MOUSE POOP ISN'T CUTE.
BUT YOU SAID A SMALL VERSION OF *ANYTHING* IS CUTE.
I KNOW, BUT APPARENTLY IT DOESN'T APPLY TO FECES.
ALTHOUGH...
IF YOU BUILT A TINY TOILET, FILLED IT WITH WATER, THEN *FLOATED THESE* IN IT...
...THEN THEY MIGHT BE CUTE...
DO YOU GUYS ALWAYS HAVE CONVERSATIONS LIKE THIS?
sigh
YES.

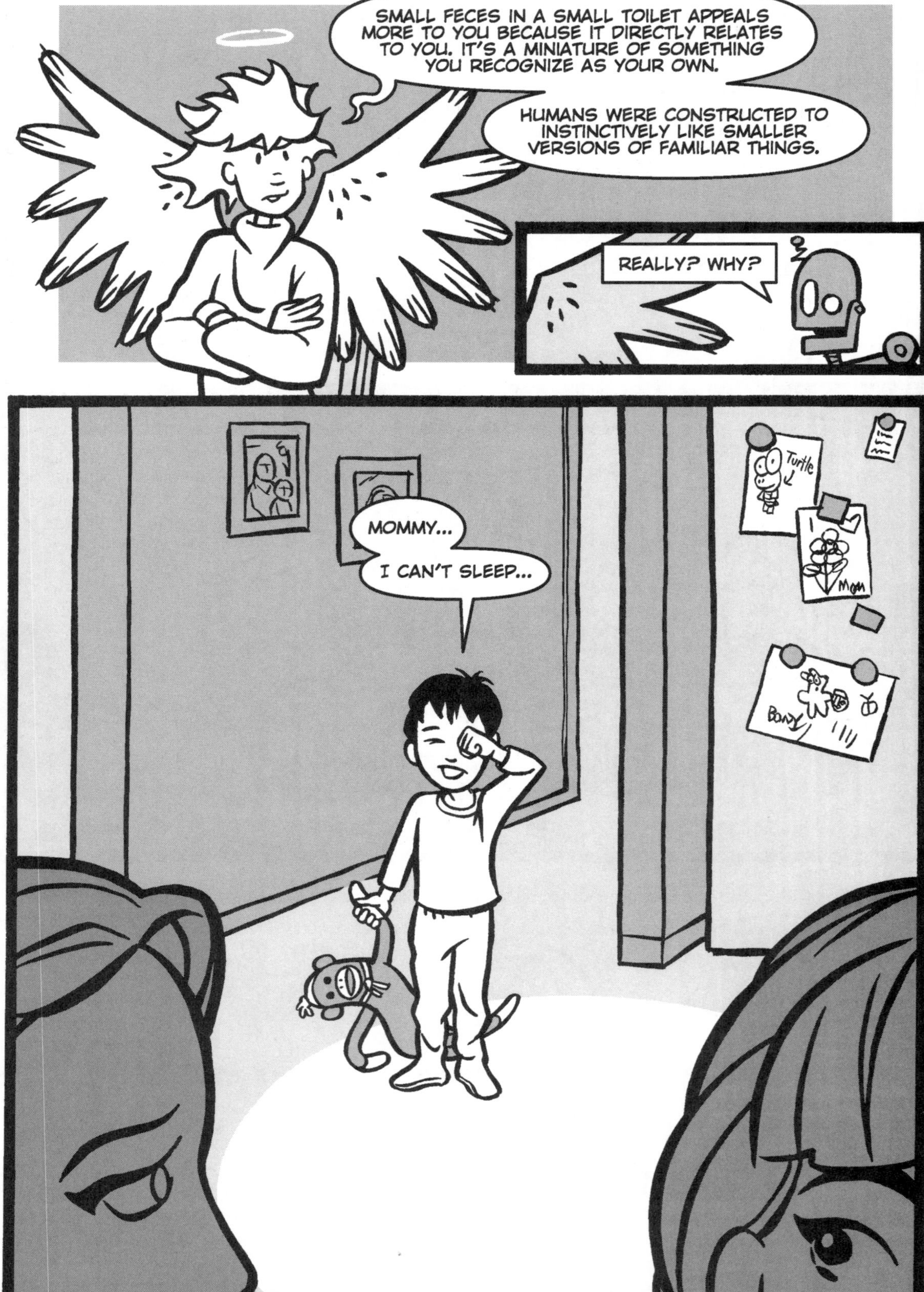
SMALL FECES IN A SMALL TOILET APPEALS MORE TO YOU BECAUSE IT DIRECTLY RELATES TO YOU. IT'S A MINIATURE OF SOMETHING YOU RECOGNIZE AS YOUR OWN.
HUMANS WERE CONSTRUCTED TO INSTINCTIVELY LIKE SMALLER VERSIONS OF FAMILIAR THINGS.
REALLY? WHY?
MOMMY...
I CAN'T SLEEP...
Turtle
MOM

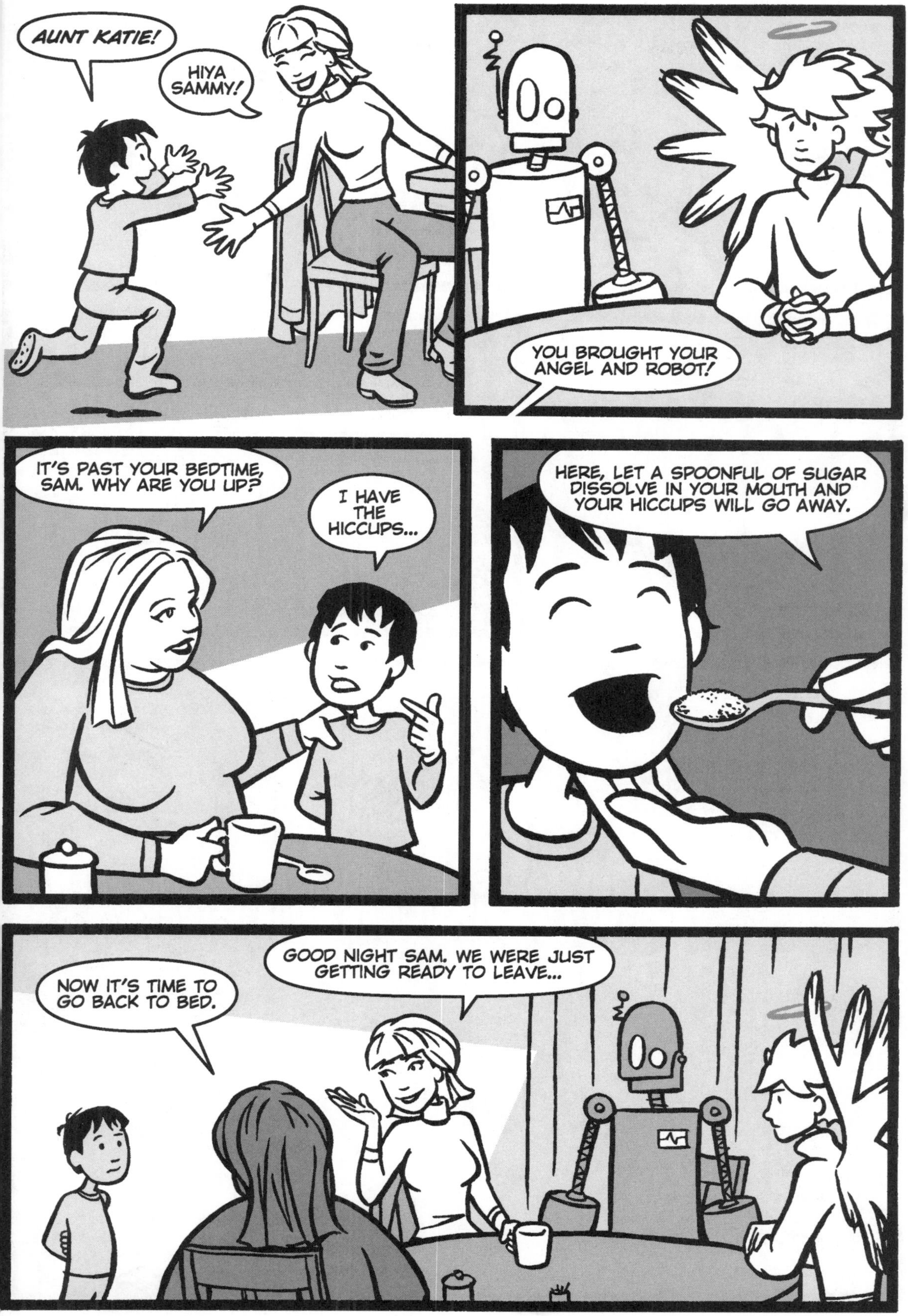
AUNT KATIE!
HIYA SAMMY!
YOU BROUGHT YOUR ANGEL AND ROBOT!
IT'S PAST YOUR BEDTIME, SAM. WHY ARE YOU UP?
I HAVE THE HICCUPS...
HERE, LET A SPOONFUL OF SUGAR DISSOLVE IN YOUR MOUTH AND YOUR HICCUPS WILL GO AWAY.
NOW IT'S TIME TO GO BACK TO BED.
GOOD NIGHT SAM. WE WERE JUST GETTING READY TO LEAVE...

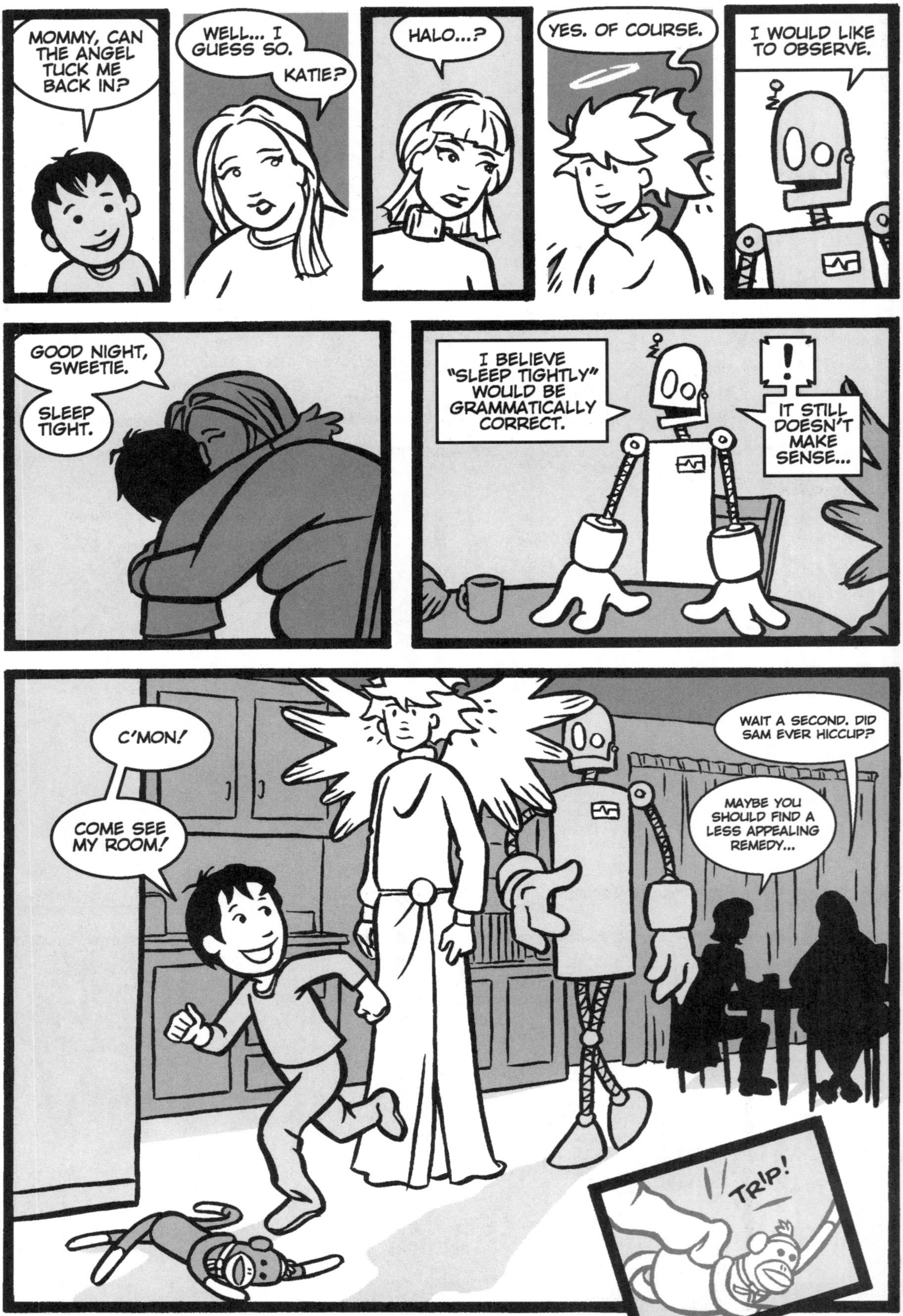
MOMMY, CAN THE ANGEL TUCK ME BACK IN?
WELL... I GUESS SO.
KATIE?
HALO...?
YES. OF COURSE.
I WOULD LIKE TO OBSERVE.
GOOD NIGHT, SWEETIE.
SLEEP TIGHT.
I BELIEVE "SLEEP TIGHTLY" WOULD BE GRAMMATICALLY CORRECT.
!
IT STILL DOESN'T MAKE SENSE...
C'MON!
COME SEE MY ROOM!
WAIT A SECOND. DID SAM EVER HICCUP?
MAYBE YOU SHOULD FIND A LESS APPEALING REMEDY...
TRIP!

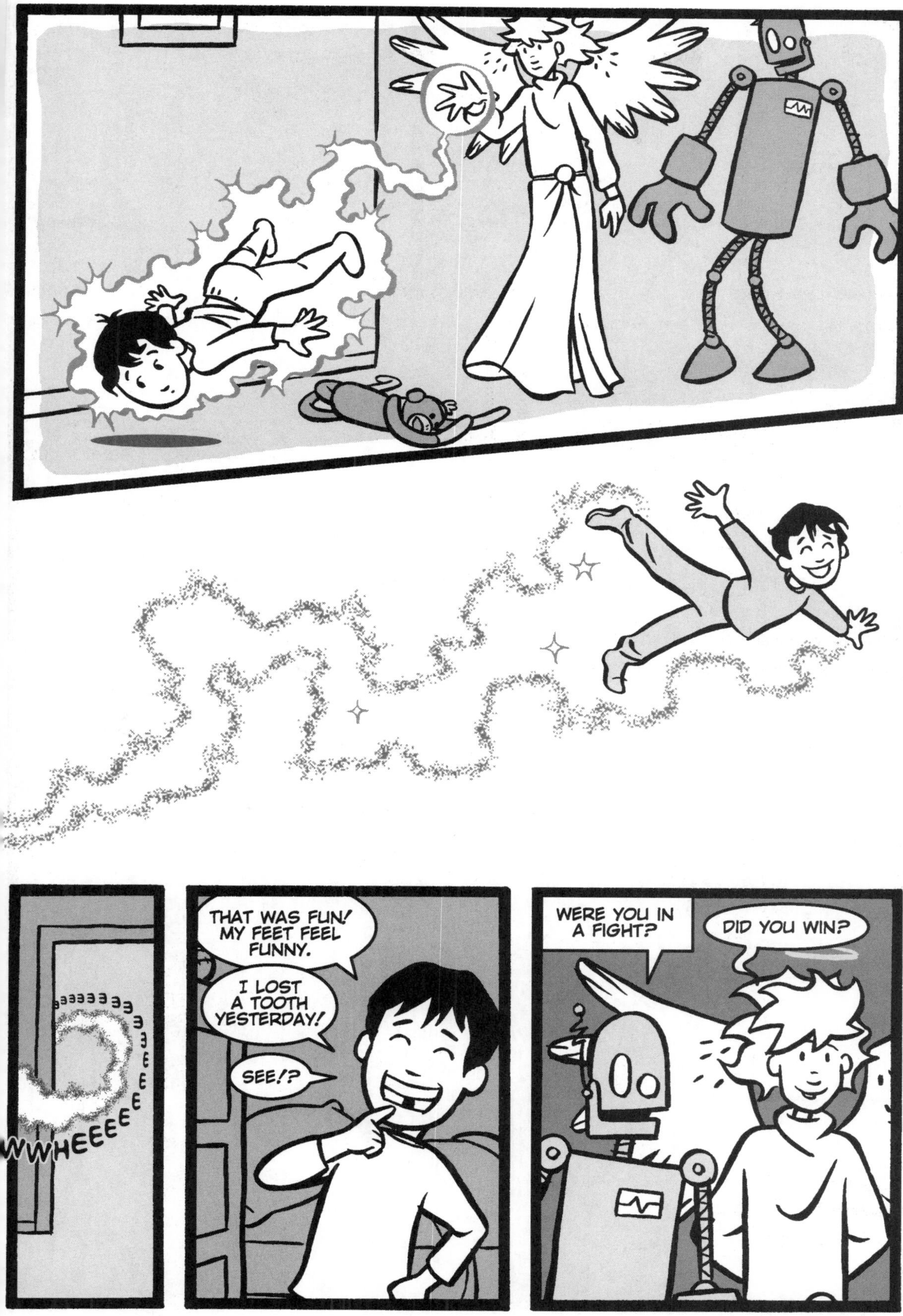
WWHEEEEEEEEEEEEEEEE
THAT WAS FUN! MY FEET FEEL FUNNY.
I LOST A TOOTH YESTERDAY!
SEE!?
WERE YOU IN A FIGHT?
DID YOU WIN?

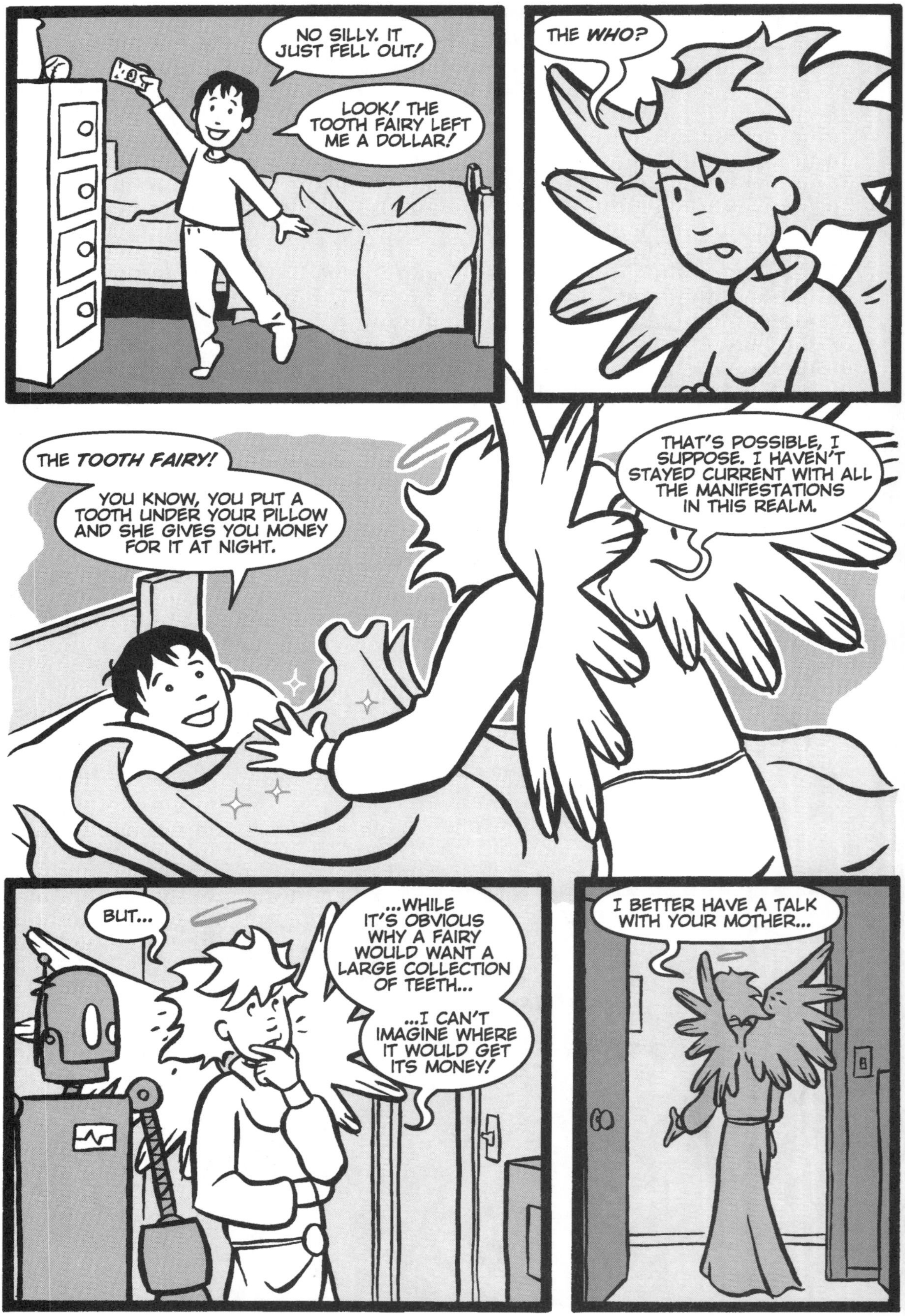
NO SILLY. IT JUST FELL OUT!
LOOK! THE TOOTH FAIRY LEFT ME A DOLLAR!
THE *WHO?*
THE *TOOTH FAIRY!*
YOU KNOW, YOU PUT A TOOTH UNDER YOUR PILLOW AND SHE GIVES YOU MONEY FOR IT AT NIGHT.
THAT'S POSSIBLE, I SUPPOSE. I HAVEN'T STAYED CURRENT WITH ALL THE MANIFESTATIONS IN THIS REALM.
BUT...
...WHILE IT'S OBVIOUS WHY A FAIRY WOULD WANT A LARGE COLLECTION OF TEETH...
...I CAN'T IMAGINE WHERE IT WOULD GET ITS MONEY!
I BETTER HAVE A TALK WITH YOUR MOTHER...

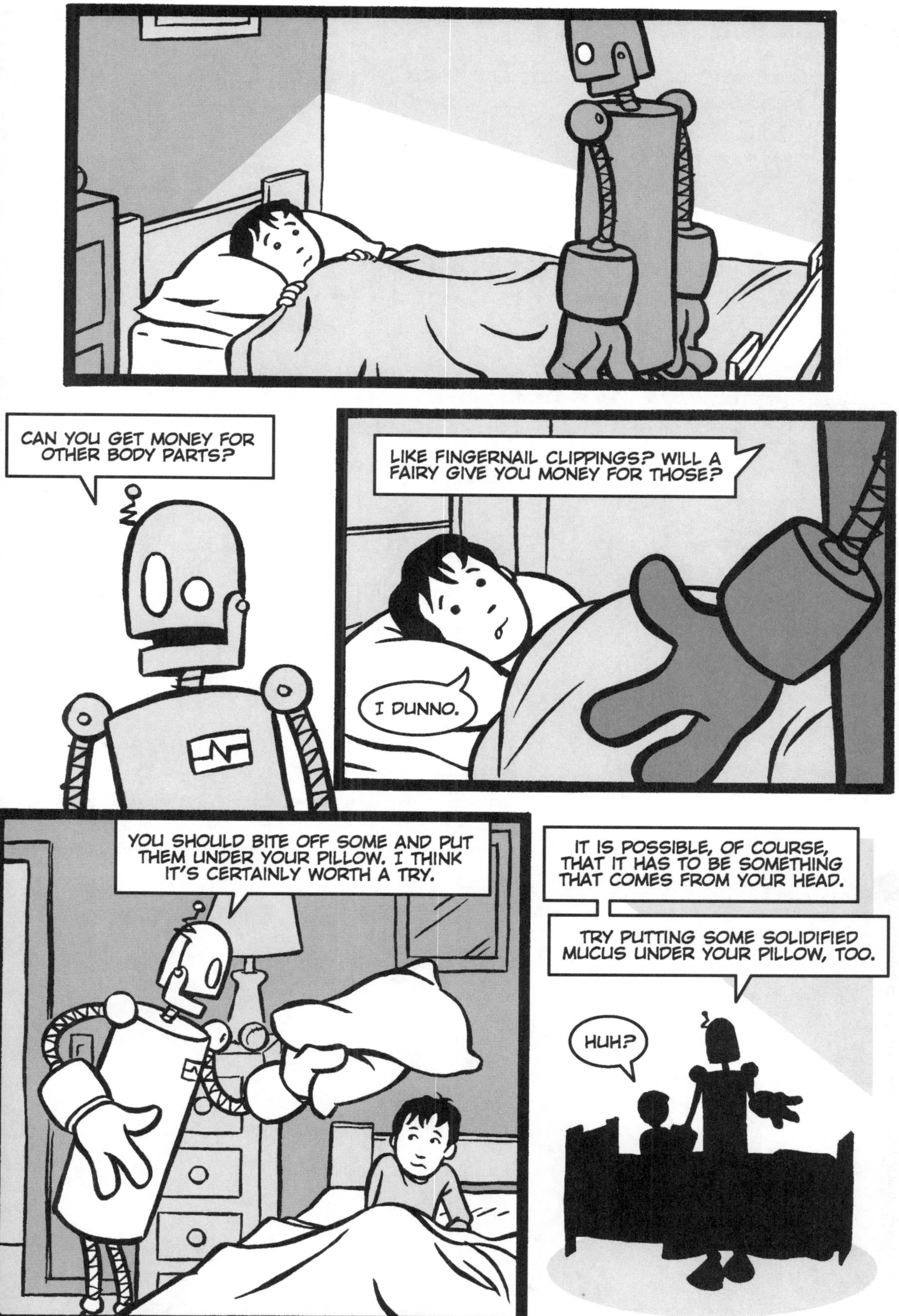
CAN YOU GET MONEY FOR OTHER BODY PARTS?
LIKE FINGERNAIL CLIPPINGS? WILL A FAIRY GIVE YOU MONEY FOR THOSE?
I DUNNO.
YOU SHOULD BITE OFF SOME AND PUT THEM UNDER YOUR PILLOW. I THINK IT'S CERTAINLY WORTH A TRY.
IT IS POSSIBLE, OF COURSE, THAT IT HAS TO BE SOMETHING THAT COMES FROM YOUR HEAD.
TRY PUTTING SOME SOLIDIFIED MUCUS UNDER YOUR PILLOW, TOO.
HUH?

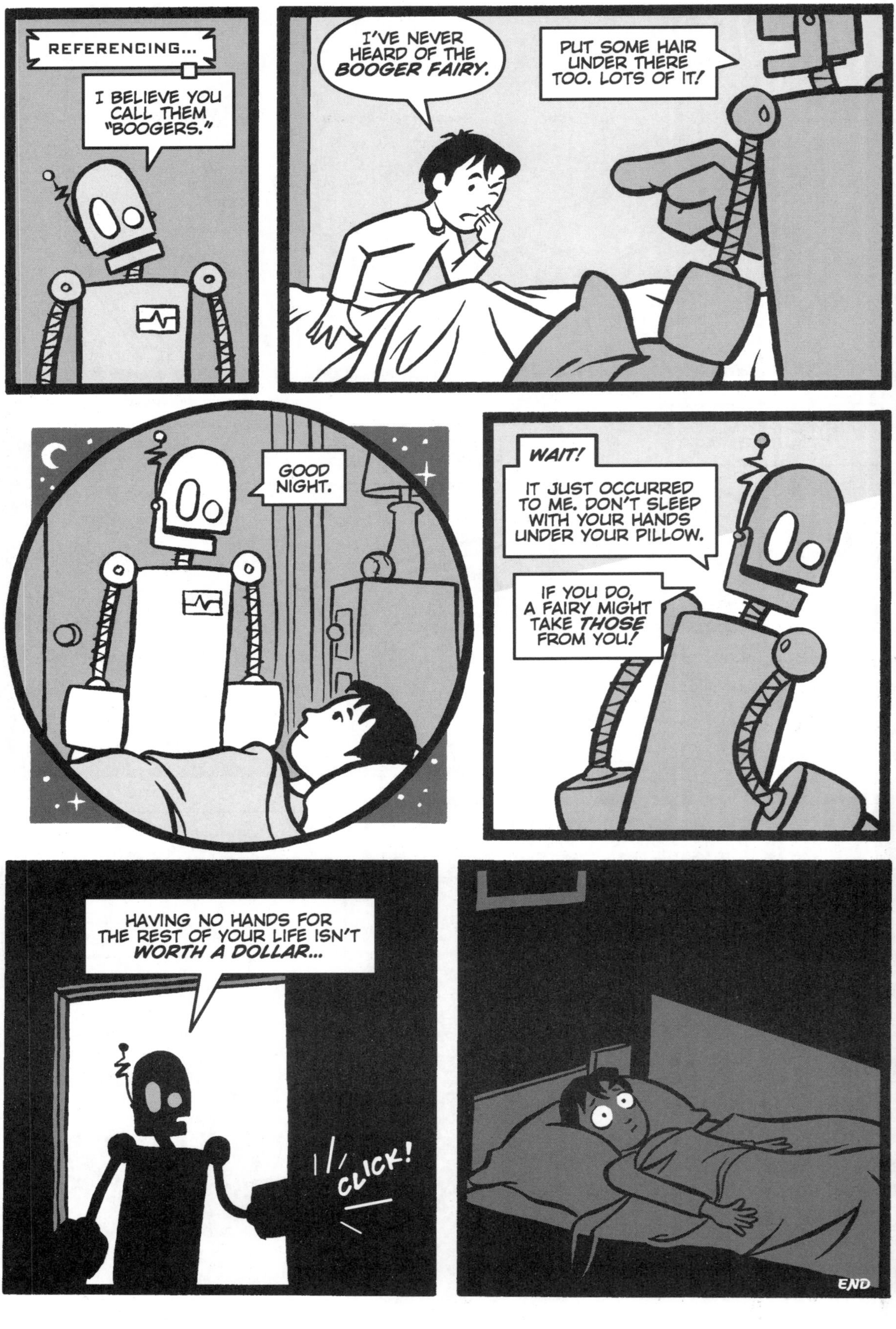
REFERENCING...
I BELIEVE YOU CALL THEM "BOOGERS."
I'VE NEVER HEARD OF THE BOOGER FAIRY.
PUT SOME HAIR UNDER THERE TOO. LOTS OF IT!
GOOD NIGHT.
WAIT!
IT JUST OCCURRED TO ME. DON'T SLEEP WITH YOUR HANDS UNDER YOUR PILLOW.
IF YOU DO, A FAIRY MIGHT TAKE THOSE FROM YOU!
HAVING NO HANDS FOR THE REST OF YOUR LIFE ISN'T WORTH A DOLLAR...
CLICK!
END

People Stories

"THE TELEMARKETER"

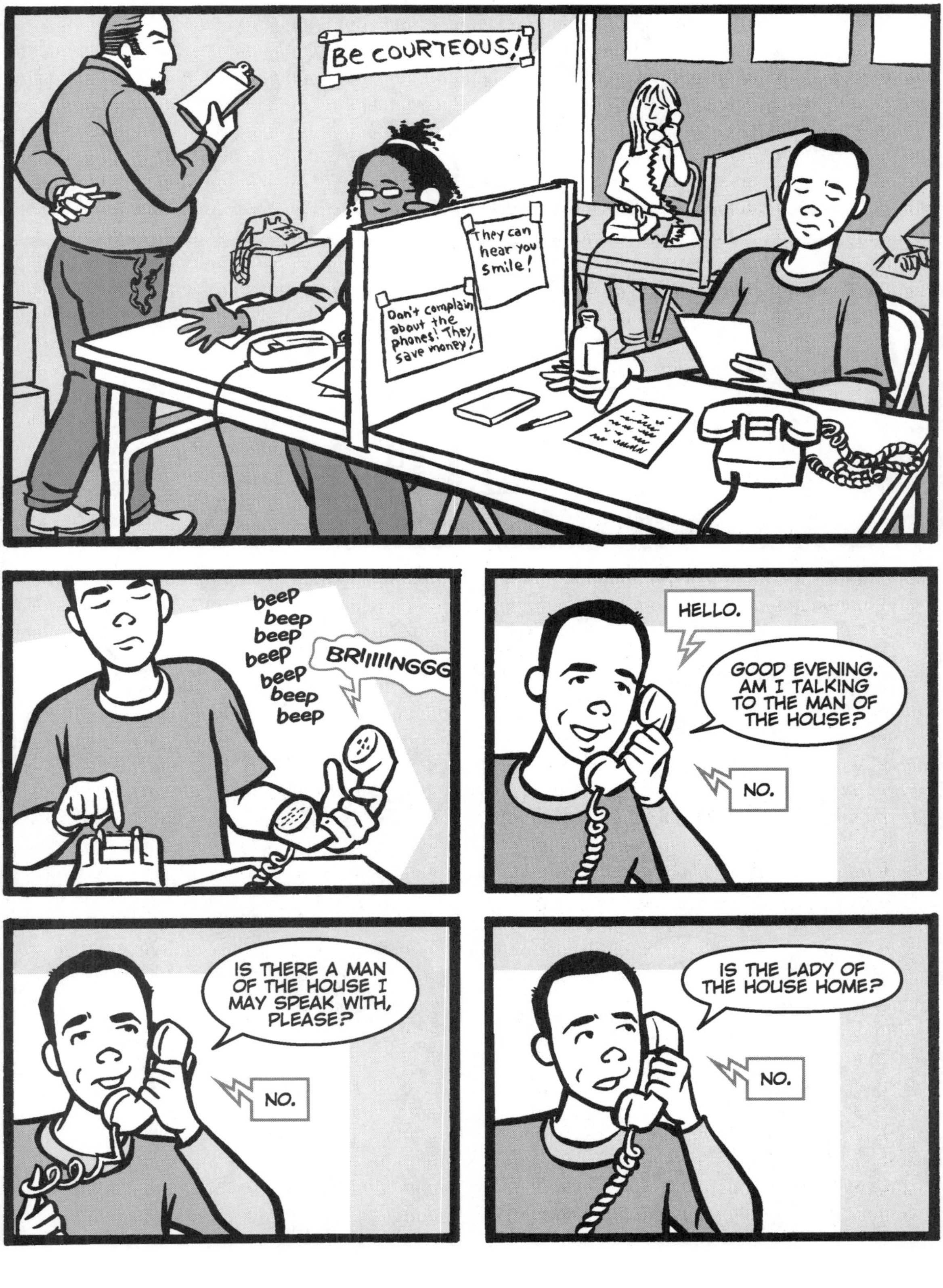
Be COURTEOUS!
They can hear you smile!
Don't complain about the phones! They save money!
beep
beep
beep
beep
beep
beep
beep
BRIIIIINGGG
HELLO.
GOOD EVENING. AM I TALKING TO THE MAN OF THE HOUSE?
NO.
IS THERE A MAN OF THE HOUSE I MAY SPEAK WITH, PLEASE?
NO.
IS THE LADY OF THE HOUSE HOME?
NO.

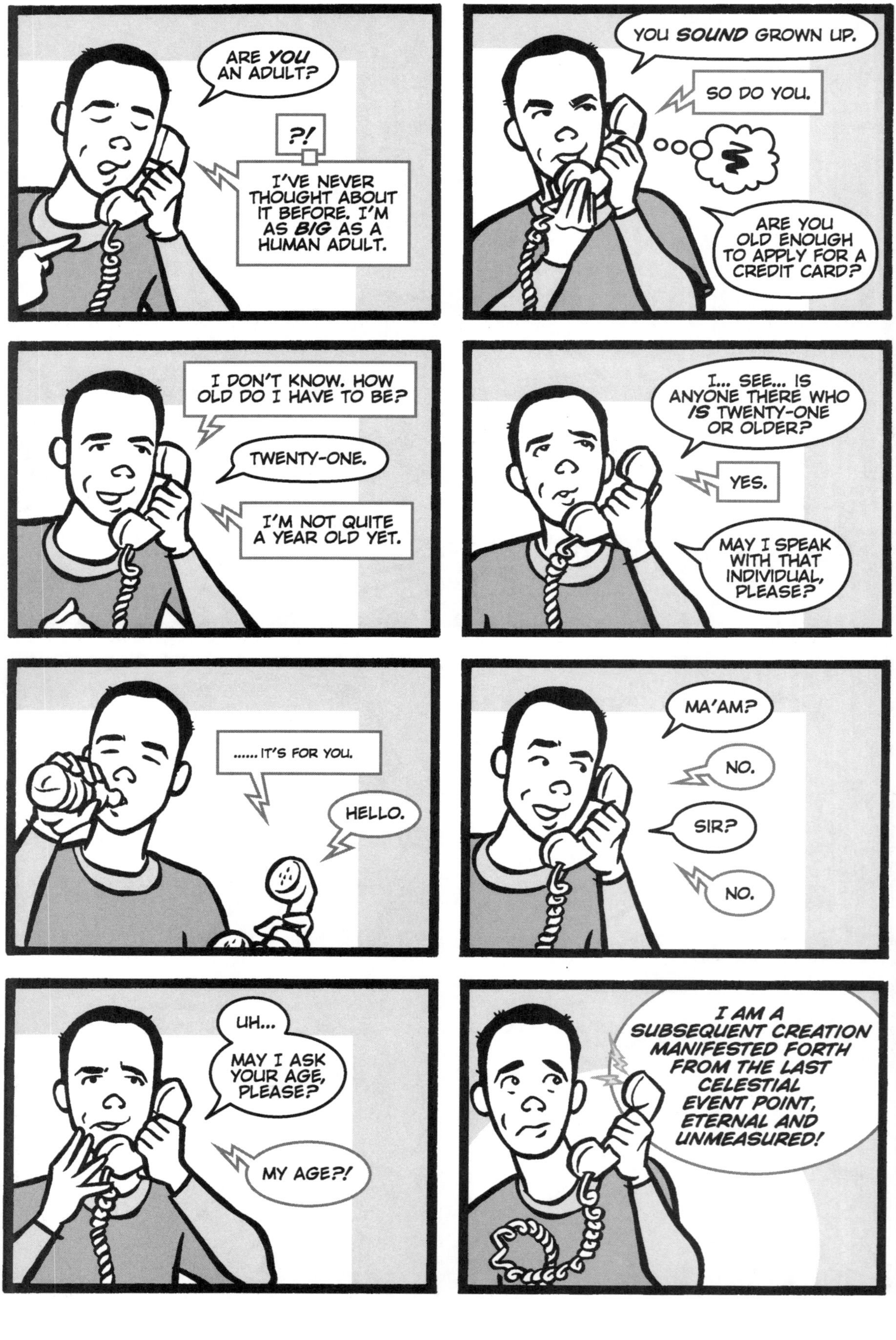
ARE YOU AN ADULT?
?!
I'VE NEVER THOUGHT ABOUT IT BEFORE. I'M AS BIG AS A HUMAN ADULT.
YOU SOUND GROWN UP.
SO DO YOU.
ARE YOU OLD ENOUGH TO APPLY FOR A CREDIT CARD?
I DON'T KNOW. HOW OLD DO I HAVE TO BE?
TWENTY-ONE.
I'M NOT QUITE A YEAR OLD YET.
I... SEE... IS ANYONE THERE WHO IS TWENTY-ONE OR OLDER?
YES.
MAY I SPEAK WITH THAT INDIVIDUAL, PLEASE?
......IT'S FOR YOU.
HELLO.
MA'AM?
NO.
SIR?
NO.
UH...
MAY I ASK YOUR AGE, PLEASE?
MY AGE?!
I AM A SUBSEQUENT CREATION MANIFESTED FORTH FROM THE LAST CELESTIAL EVENT POINT, ETERNAL AND UNMEASURED!

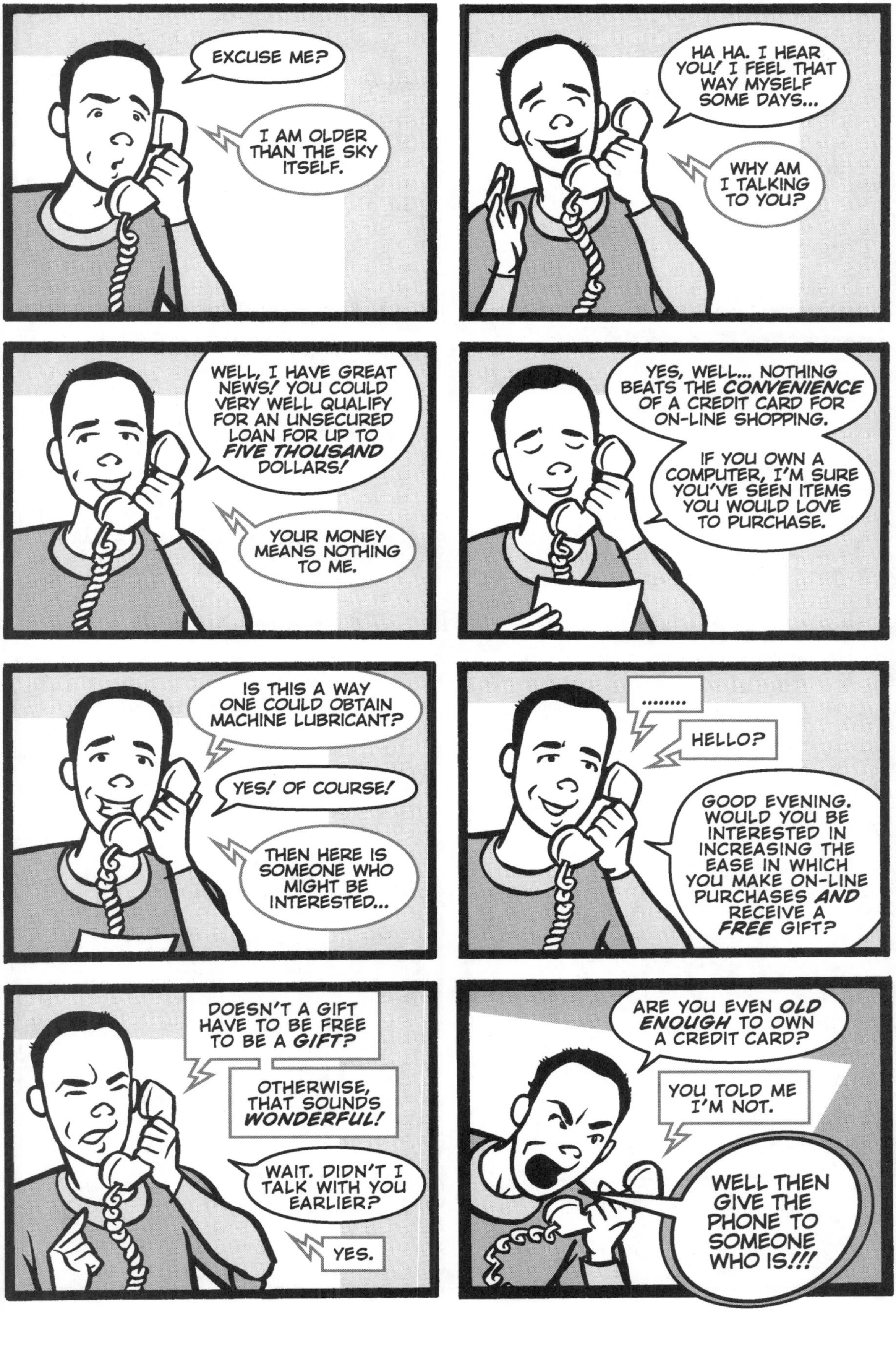
EXCUSE ME?
I AM OLDER THAN THE SKY ITSELF.
HA HA. I HEAR YOU! I FEEL THAT WAY MYSELF SOME DAYS...
WHY AM I TALKING TO YOU?
WELL, I HAVE GREAT NEWS! YOU COULD VERY WELL QUALIFY FOR AN UNSECURED LOAN FOR UP TO FIVE THOUSAND DOLLARS!
YOUR MONEY MEANS NOTHING TO ME.
YES, WELL... NOTHING BEATS THE CONVENIENCE OF A CREDIT CARD FOR ON-LINE SHOPPING.
IF YOU OWN A COMPUTER, I'M SURE YOU'VE SEEN ITEMS YOU WOULD LOVE TO PURCHASE.
IS THIS A WAY ONE COULD OBTAIN MACHINE LUBRICANT?
YES! OF COURSE!
THEN HERE IS SOMEONE WHO MIGHT BE INTERESTED...
....
HELLO?
GOOD EVENING. WOULD YOU BE INTERESTED IN INCREASING THE EASE IN WHICH YOU MAKE ON-LINE PURCHASES AND RECEIVE A FREE GIFT?
DOESN'T A GIFT HAVE TO BE FREE TO BE A GIFT?
OTHERWISE, THAT SOUNDS WONDERFUL!
WAIT. DIDN'T I TALK WITH YOU EARLIER?
YES.
ARE YOU EVEN OLD ENOUGH TO OWN A CREDIT CARD?
YOU TOLD ME I'M NOT.
WELL THEN GIVE THE PHONE TO SOMEONE WHO IS!!!

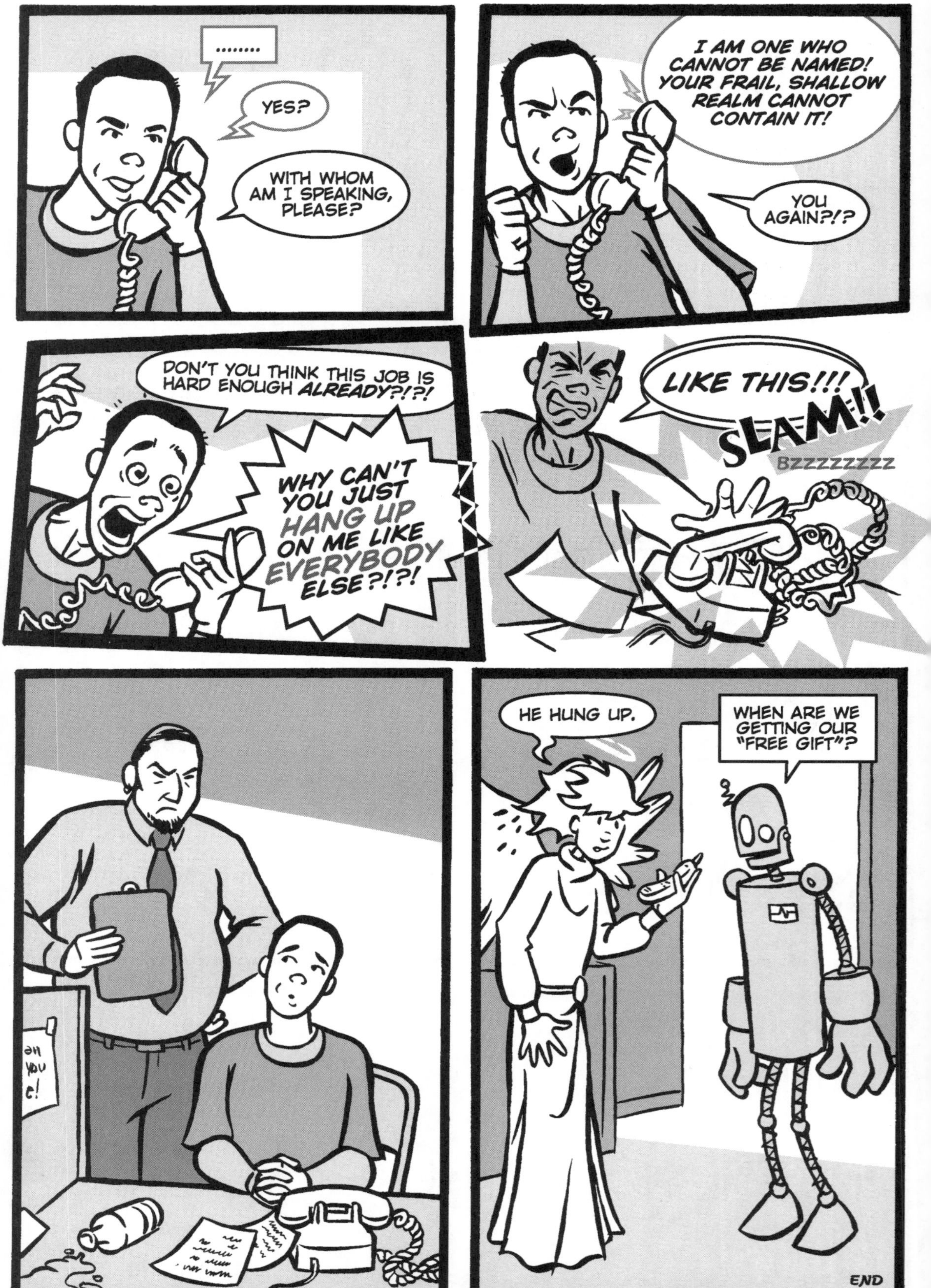
....
YES?
WITH WHOM AM I SPEAKING, PLEASE?
I AM ONE WHO CANNOT BE NAMED! YOUR FRAIL, SHALLOW REALM CANNOT CONTAIN IT!
YOU AGAIN?!?
DON'T YOU THINK THIS JOB IS HARD ENOUGH ALREADY?!?!
WHY CAN'T YOU JUST HANG UP ON ME LIKE EVERYBODY ELSE?!?!
LIKE THIS!!!
SLAM!!
BZZZZZZZZ
HE HUNG UP.
WHEN ARE WE GETTING OUR "FREE GIFT"?
END

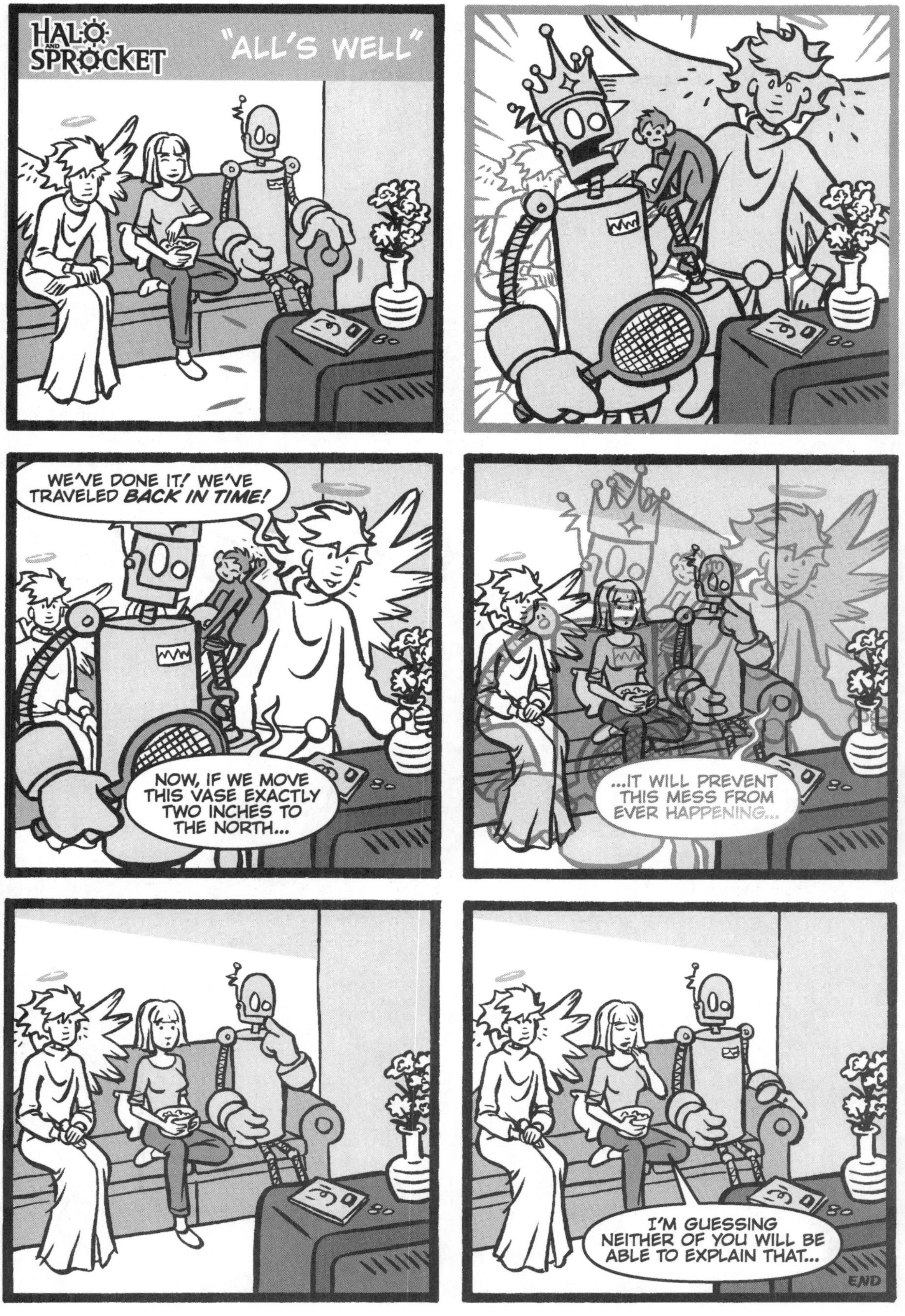
HALO AND SPROCKET
"ALL'S WELL"
WE'VE DONE IT! WE'VE TRAVELED BACK IN TIME!
NOW, IF WE MOVE THIS VASE EXACTLY TWO INCHES TO THE NORTH...
...IT WILL PREVENT THIS MESS FROM EVER HAPPENING...
I'M GUESSING NEITHER OF YOU WILL BE ABLE TO EXPLAIN THAT...
END

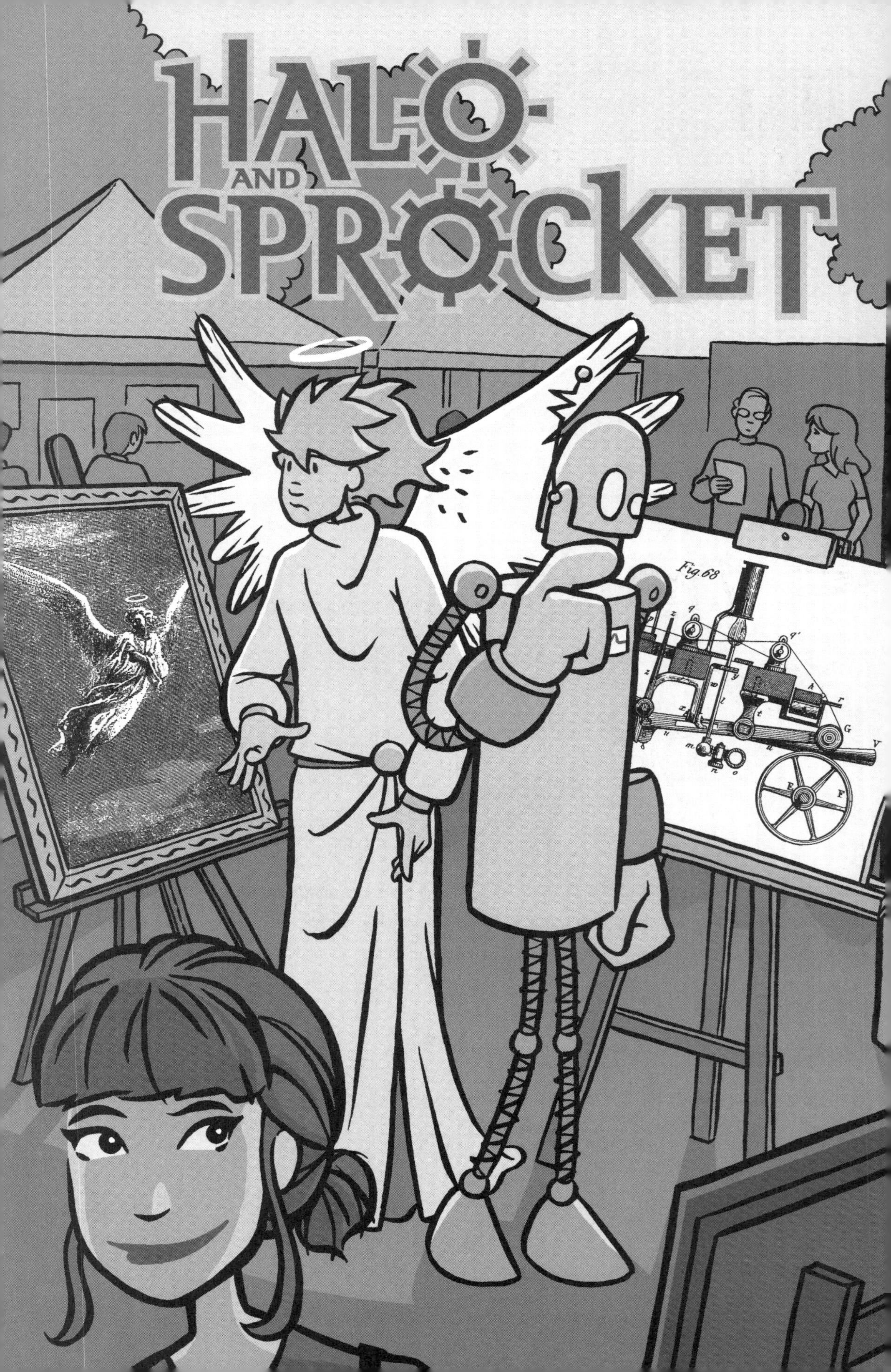
HALO AND SPROCKET
Fig. 68

HALO AND SPROCKET

"ONE TO NOTHING"

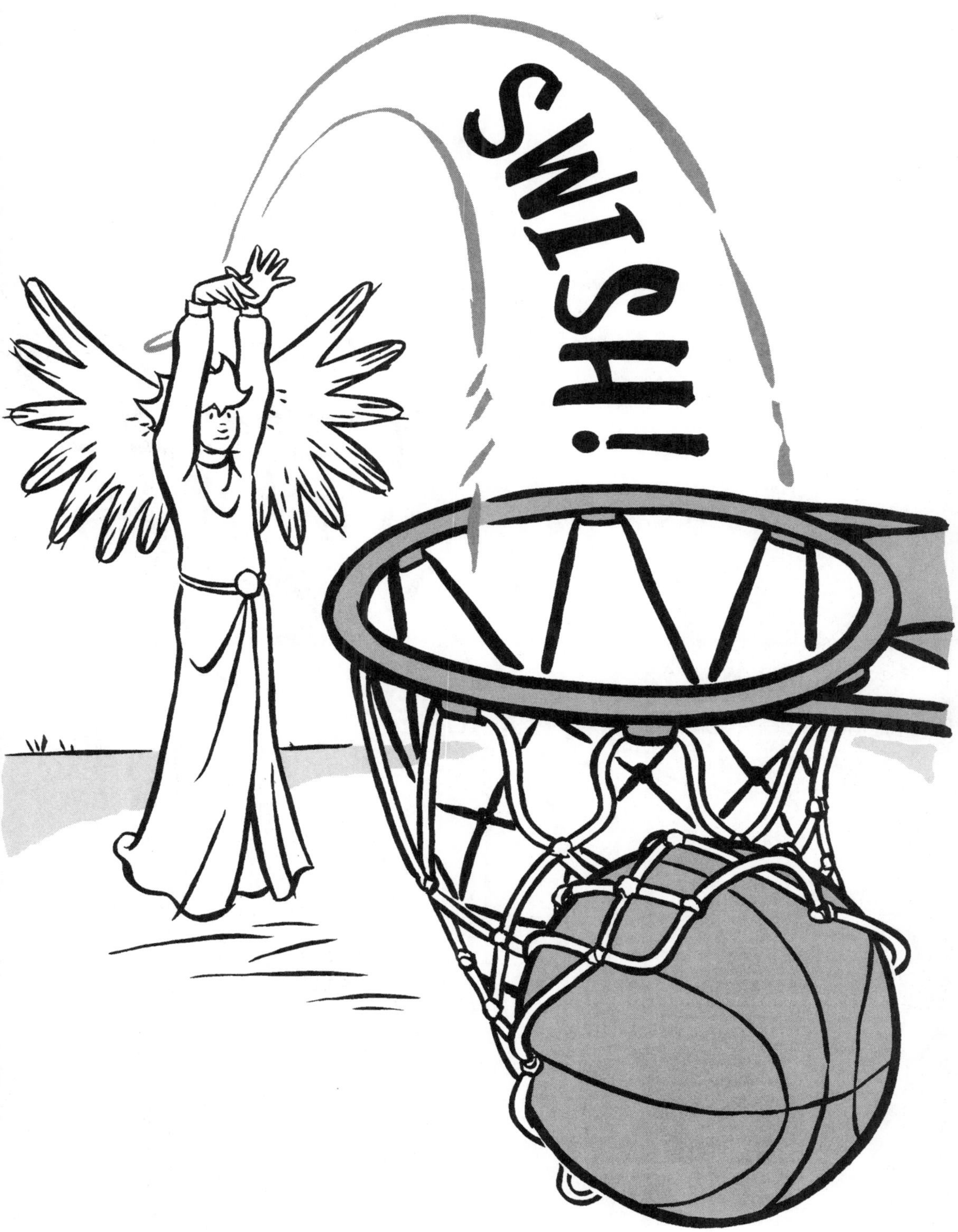
SWISH!

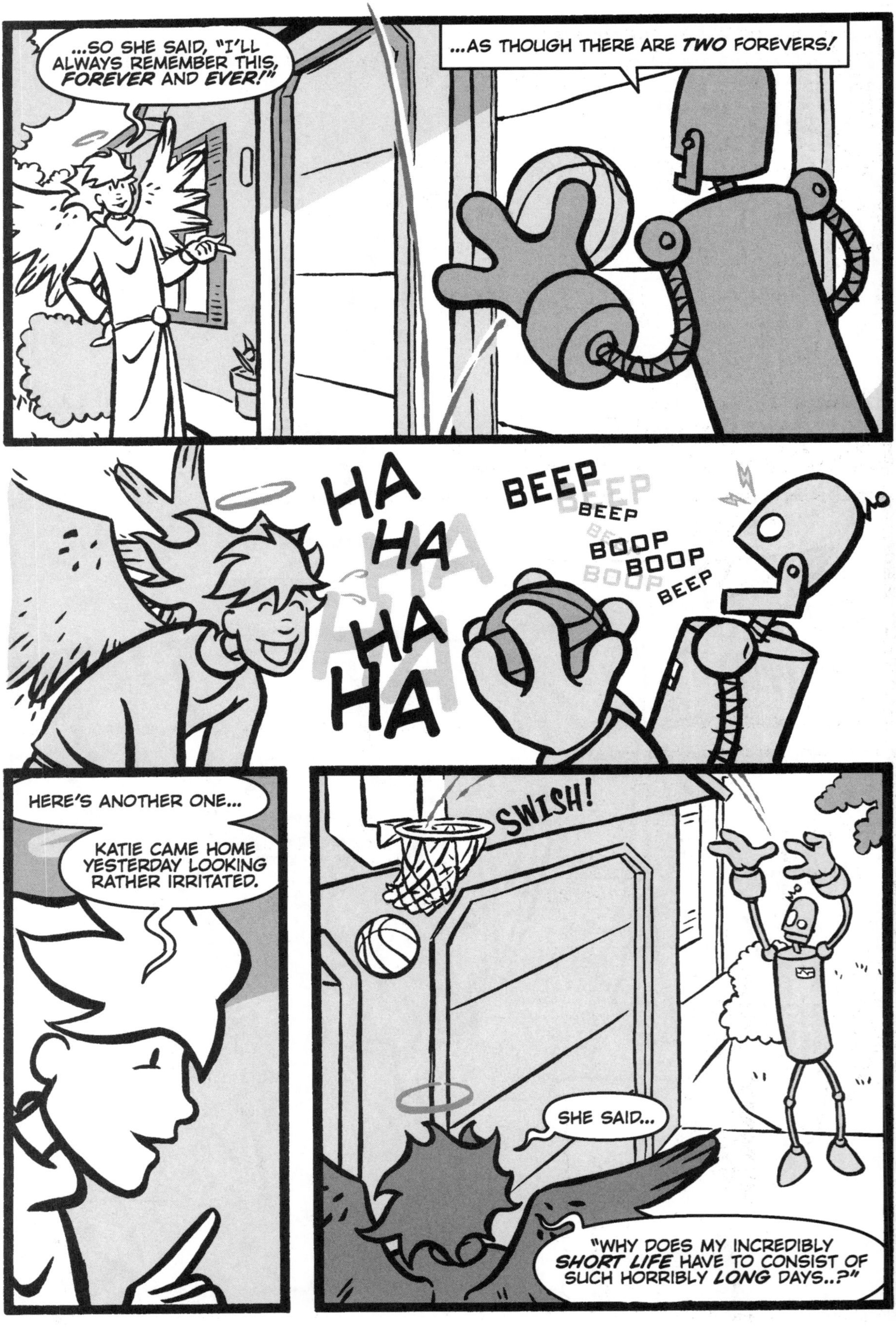
...SO SHE SAID, "I'LL ALWAYS REMEMBER THIS, FOREVER AND EVER!"
...AS THOUGH THERE ARE TWO FOREVERS!
HA HA HA HA
BEEP BEEP BOOP BOOP BEEP
HERE'S ANOTHER ONE...
KATIE CAME HOME YESTERDAY LOOKING RATHER IRRITATED.
SWISH!
SHE SAID...
"WHY DOES MY INCREDIBLY SHORT LIFE HAVE TO CONSIST OF SUCH HORRIBLY LONG DAYS..?"

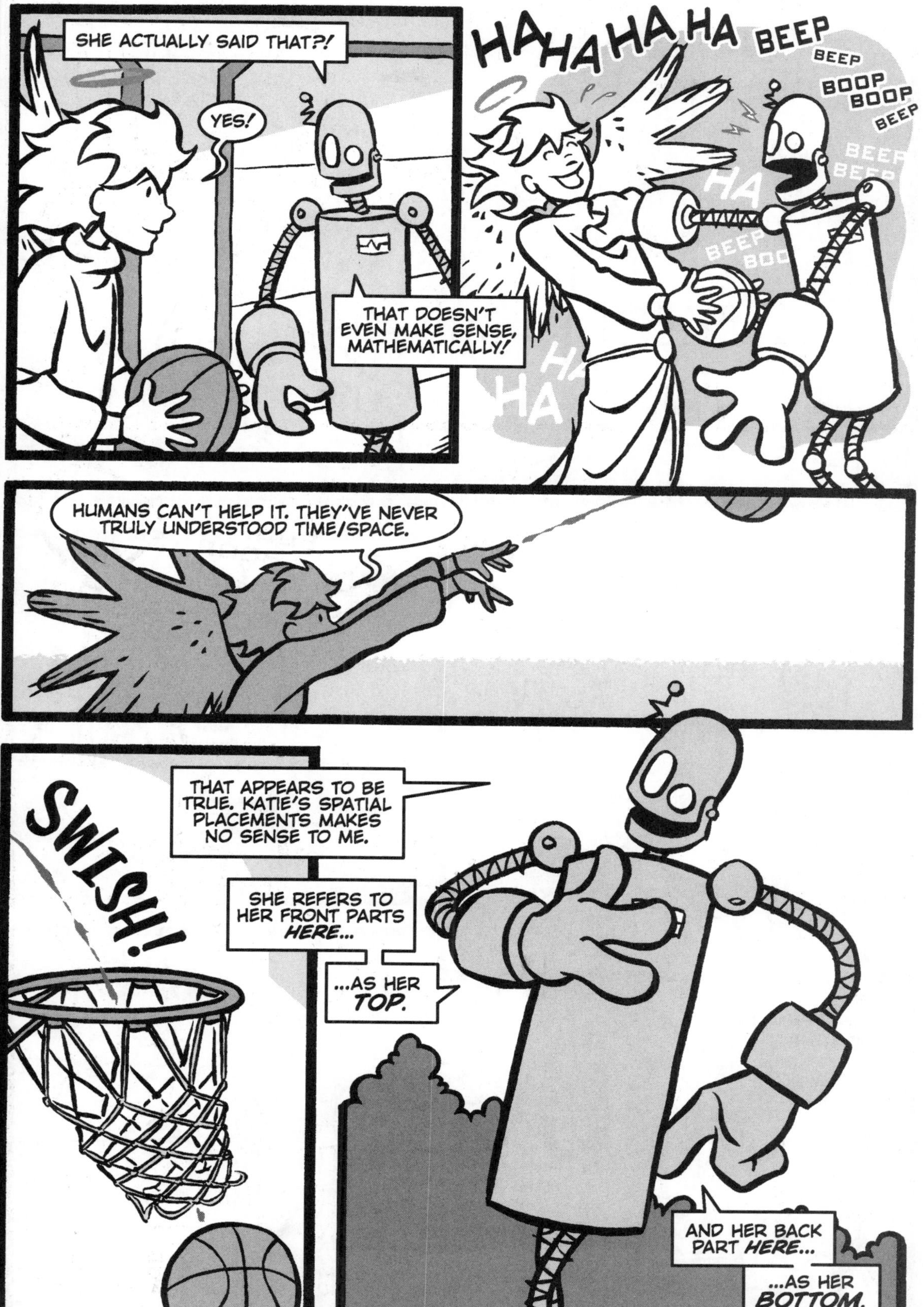
SHE ACTUALLY SAID THAT?!
YES!
THAT DOESN'T EVEN MAKE SENSE, MATHEMATICALLY!
HA HA HA HA HA BEEP
BEEP
BOOP BOOP
BEEP
HA
BEEP
BEEP
BOO
HA
HA
HUMANS CAN'T HELP IT. THEY'VE NEVER TRULY UNDERSTOOD TIME/SPACE.
SWISH!
THAT APPEARS TO BE TRUE. KATIE'S SPATIAL PLACEMENTS MAKES NO SENSE TO ME.
SHE REFERS TO HER FRONT PARTS *HERE*...
...AS HER *TOP*.
AND HER BACK PART *HERE*...
...AS HER *BOTTOM*.

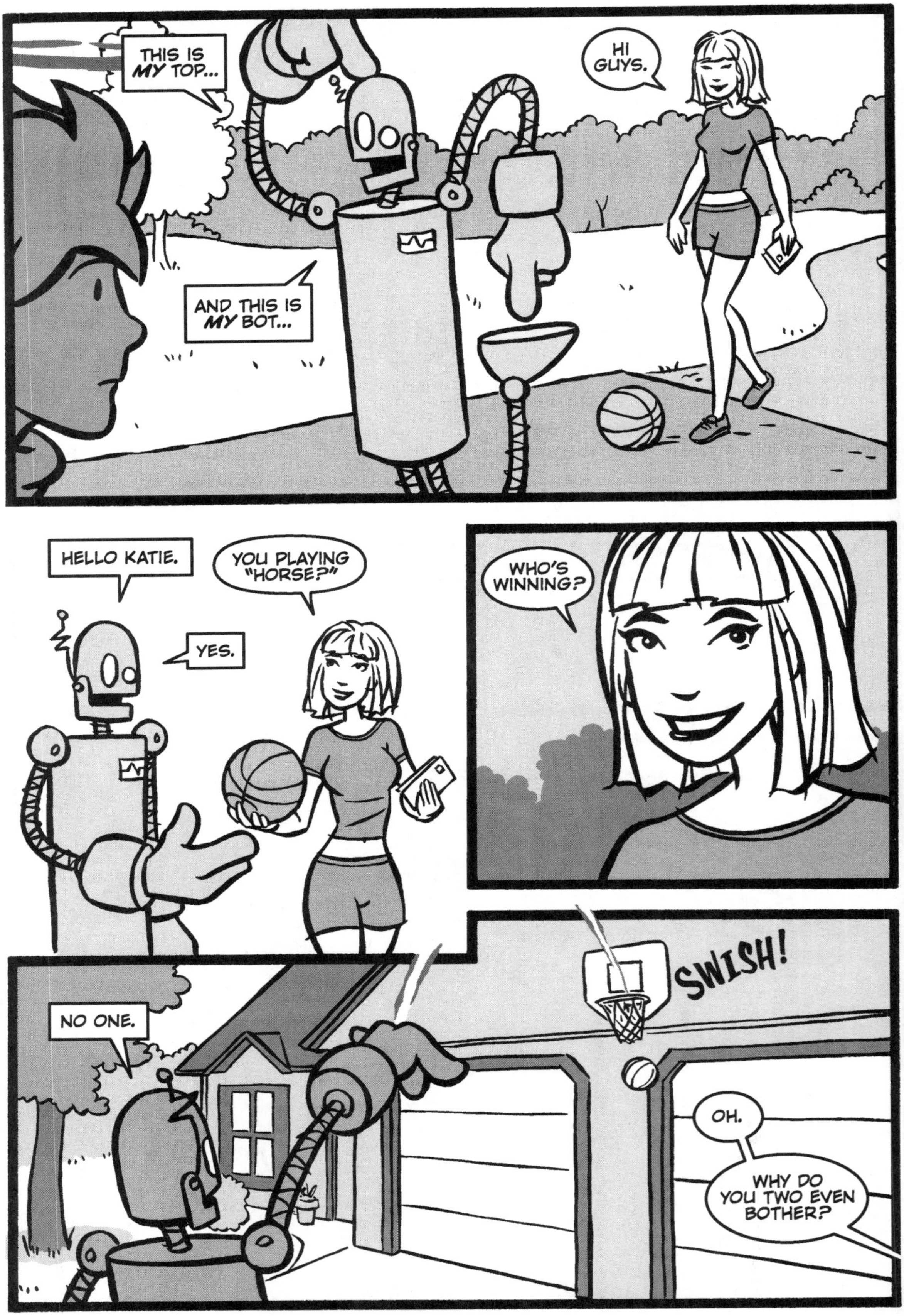
THIS IS MY TOP...
AND THIS IS MY BOT...
HI GUYS.
HELLO KATIE.
YOU PLAYING "HORSE?"
YES.
WHO'S WINNING?
NO ONE.
SWISH!
OH.
WHY DO YOU TWO EVEN BOTHER?

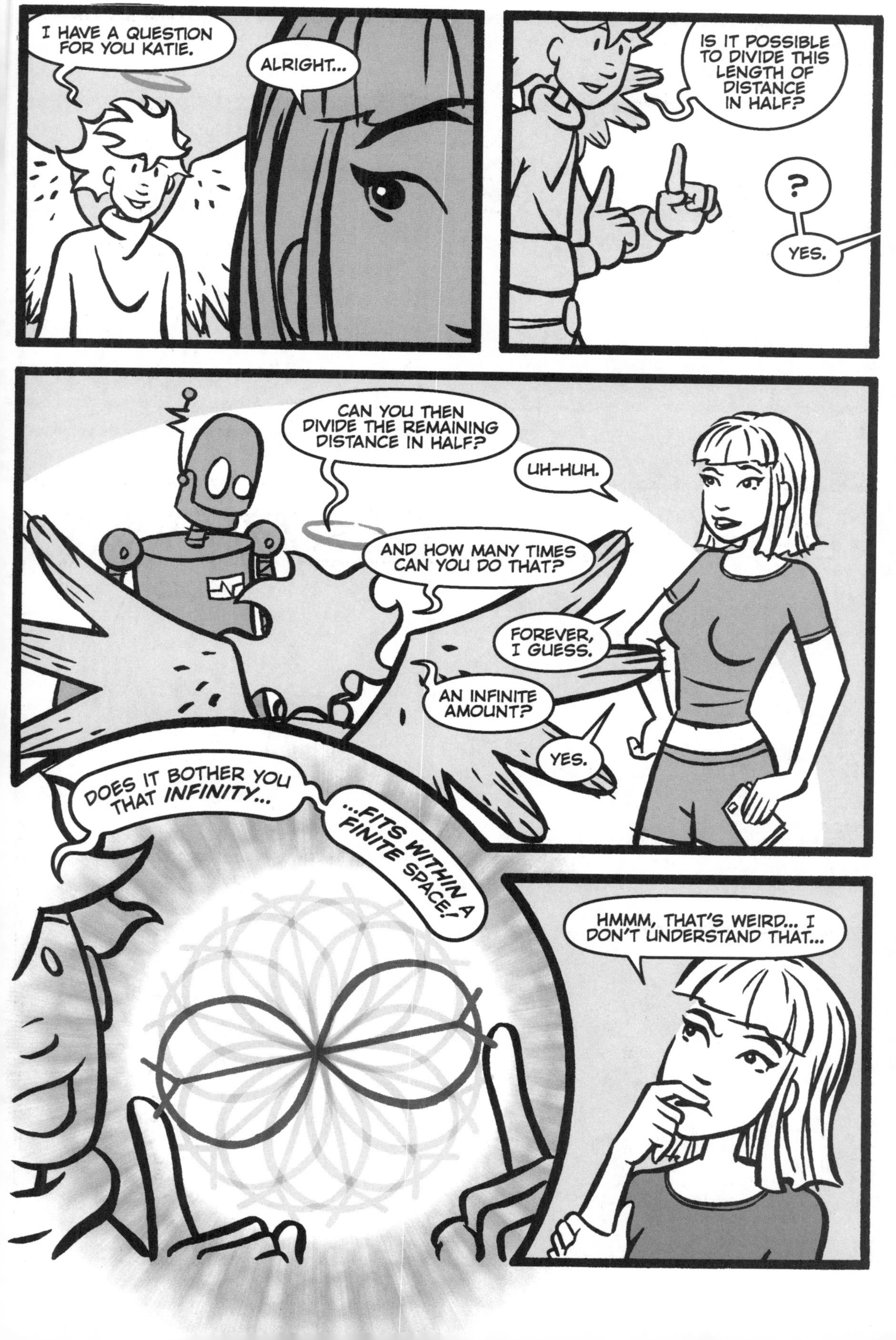
I HAVE A QUESTION FOR YOU KATIE.
ALRIGHT...
IS IT POSSIBLE TO DIVIDE THIS LENGTH OF DISTANCE IN HALF?
?
YES.
CAN YOU THEN DIVIDE THE REMAINING DISTANCE IN HALF?
UH-HUH.
AND HOW MANY TIMES CAN YOU DO THAT?
FOREVER, I GUESS.
AN INFINITE AMOUNT?
YES.
DOES IT BOTHER YOU THAT *INFINITY*...
...*FITS WITHIN A FINITE* SPACE?
HMMM, THAT'S WEIRD... I DON'T UNDERSTAND THAT...

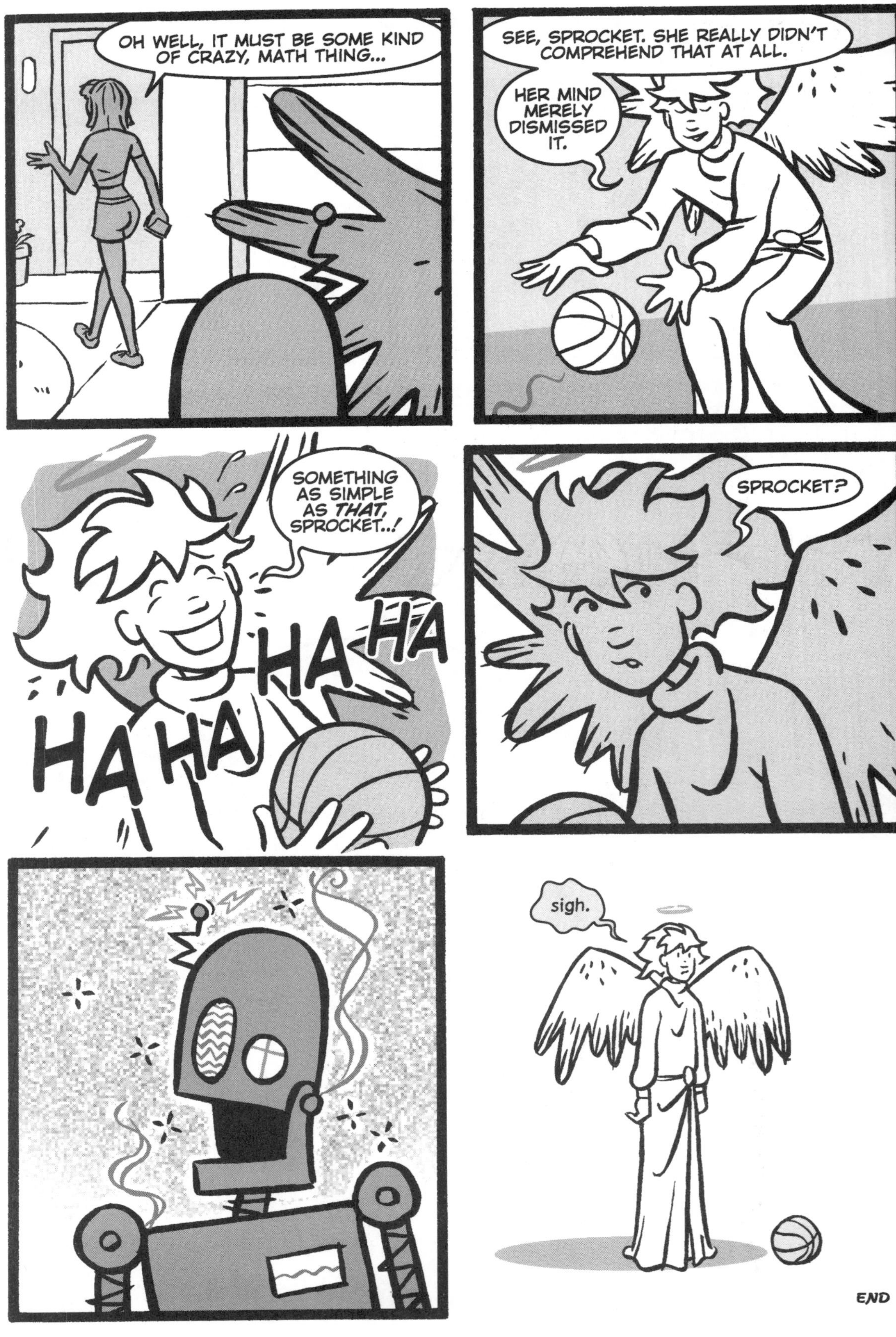

OH WELL, IT MUST BE SOME KIND OF CRAZY, MATH THING...
SEE, SPROCKET. SHE REALLY DIDN'T COMPREHEND THAT AT ALL.
HER MIND MERELY DISMISSED IT.
SOMETHING AS SIMPLE AS *THAT*, SPROCKET..!
HA HA HA HA HA
SPROCKET?
sigh.
END

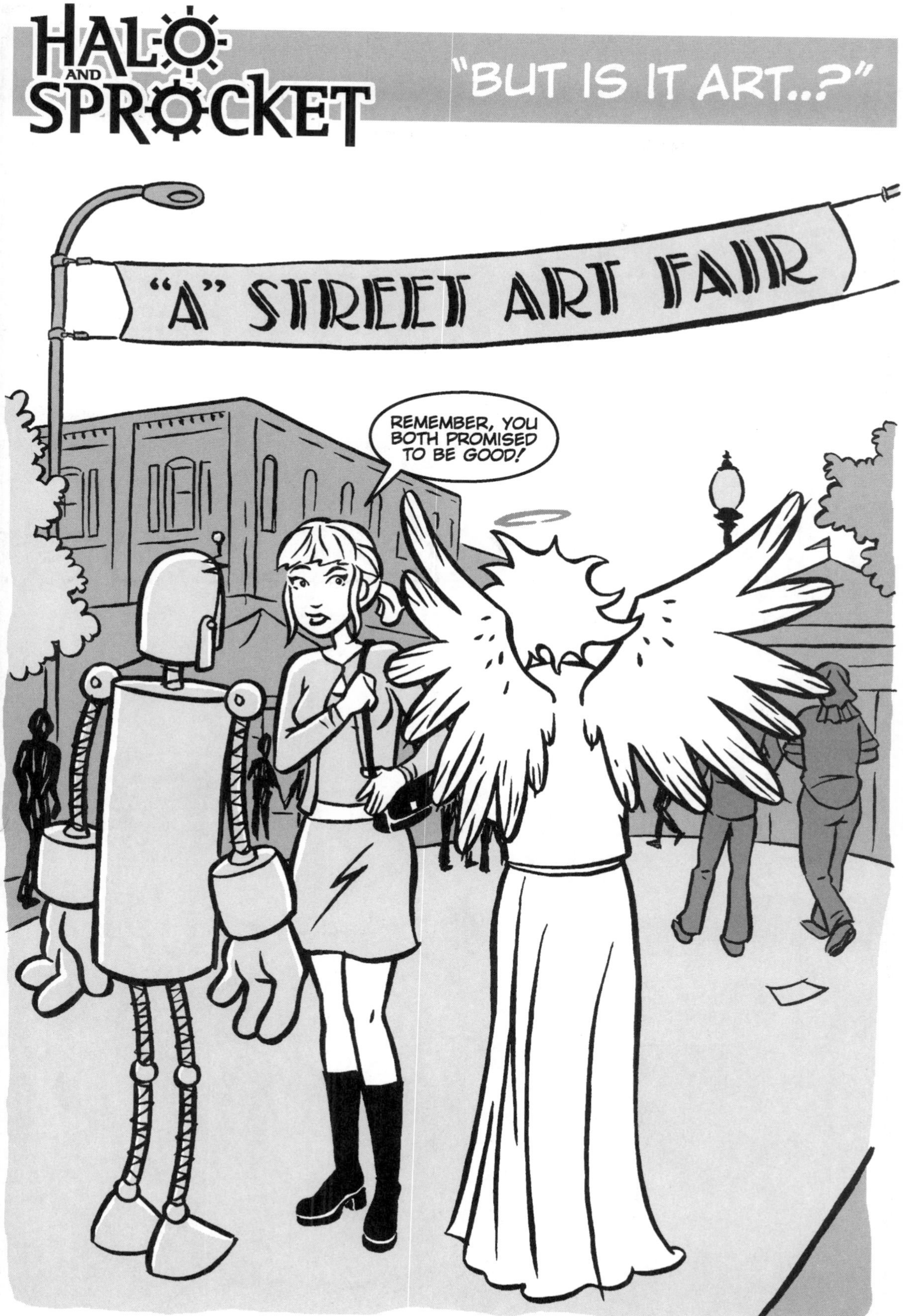
HALO AND SPROCKET
"BUT IS IT ART..?"
"A" STREET ART FAIR
REMEMBER, YOU BOTH PROMISED TO BE GOOD!

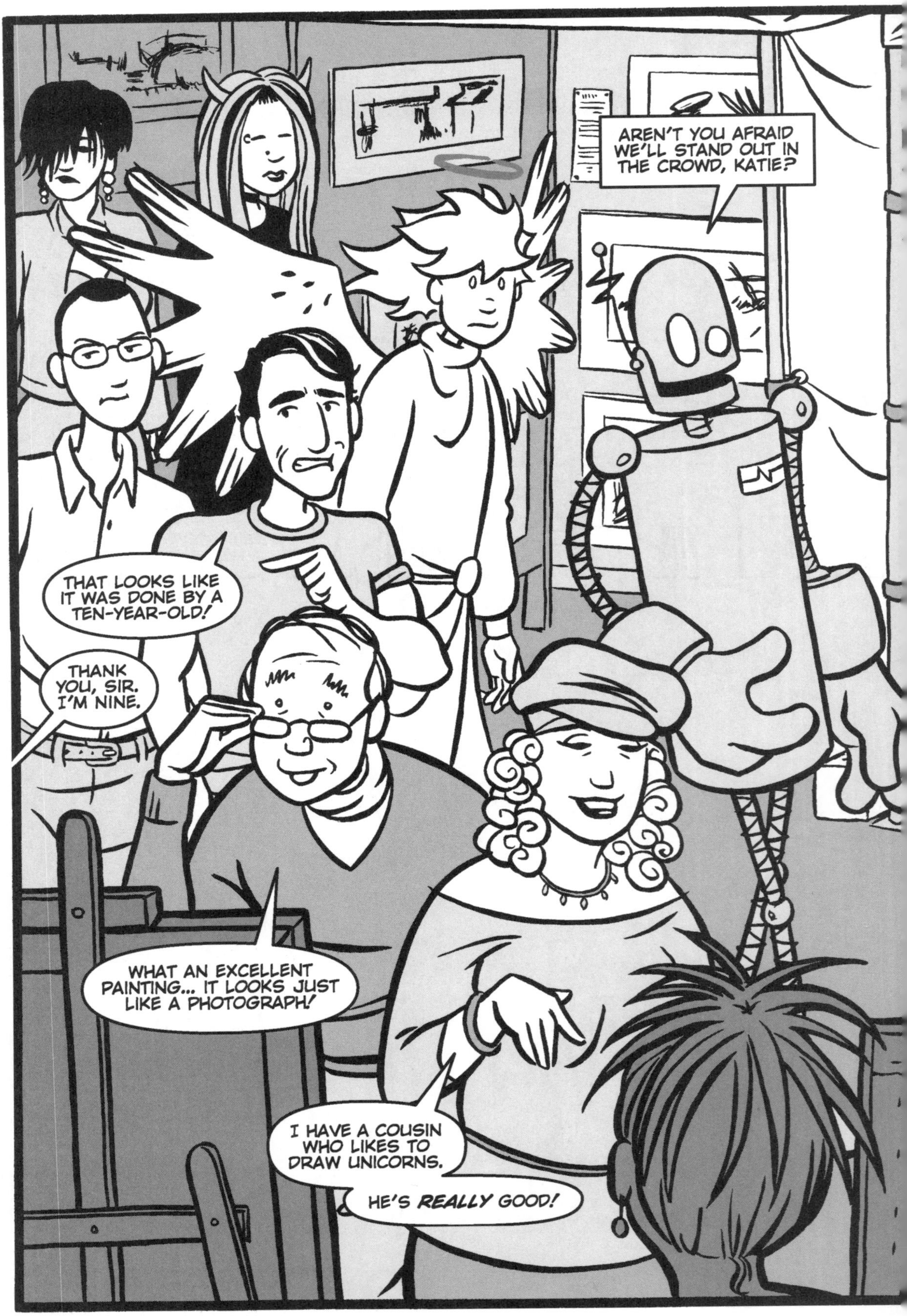
AREN'T YOU AFRAID WE'LL STAND OUT IN THE CROWD, KATIE?
THAT LOOKS LIKE IT WAS DONE BY A TEN-YEAR-OLD!
THANK YOU, SIR. I'M NINE.
WHAT AN EXCELLENT PAINTING... IT LOOKS JUST LIKE A PHOTOGRAPH!
I HAVE A COUSIN WHO LIKES TO DRAW UNICORNS.
HE'S REALLY GOOD!

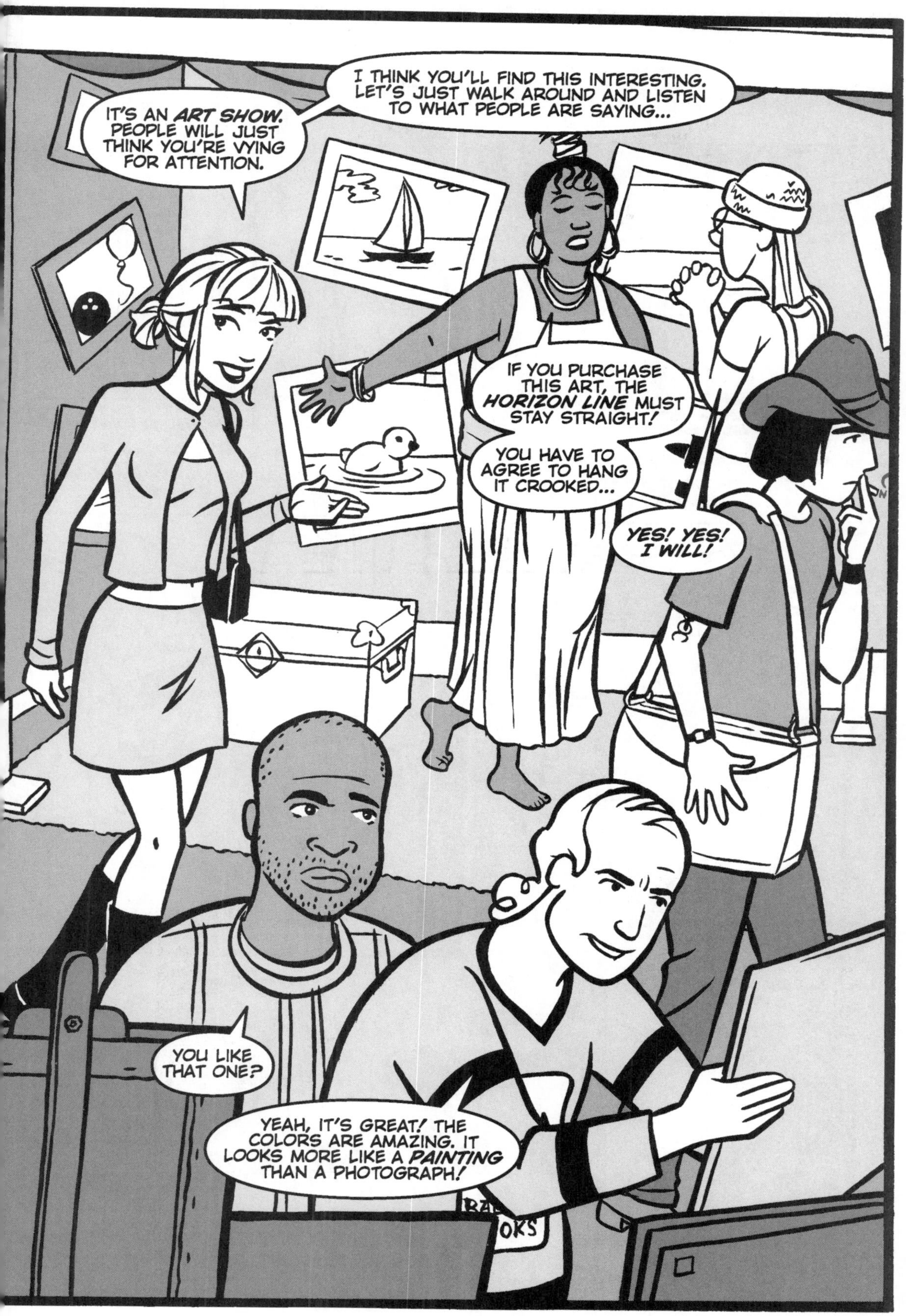
I THINK YOU'LL FIND THIS INTERESTING. LET'S JUST WALK AROUND AND LISTEN TO WHAT PEOPLE ARE SAYING...
IT'S AN ART SHOW. PEOPLE WILL JUST THINK YOU'RE VYING FOR ATTENTION.
IF YOU PURCHASE THIS ART, THE HORIZON LINE MUST STAY STRAIGHT!
YOU HAVE TO AGREE TO HANG IT CROOKED...
YES! YES! I WILL!
YOU LIKE THAT ONE?
YEAH, IT'S GREAT! THE COLORS ARE AMAZING. IT LOOKS MORE LIKE A PAINTING THAN A PHOTOGRAPH!

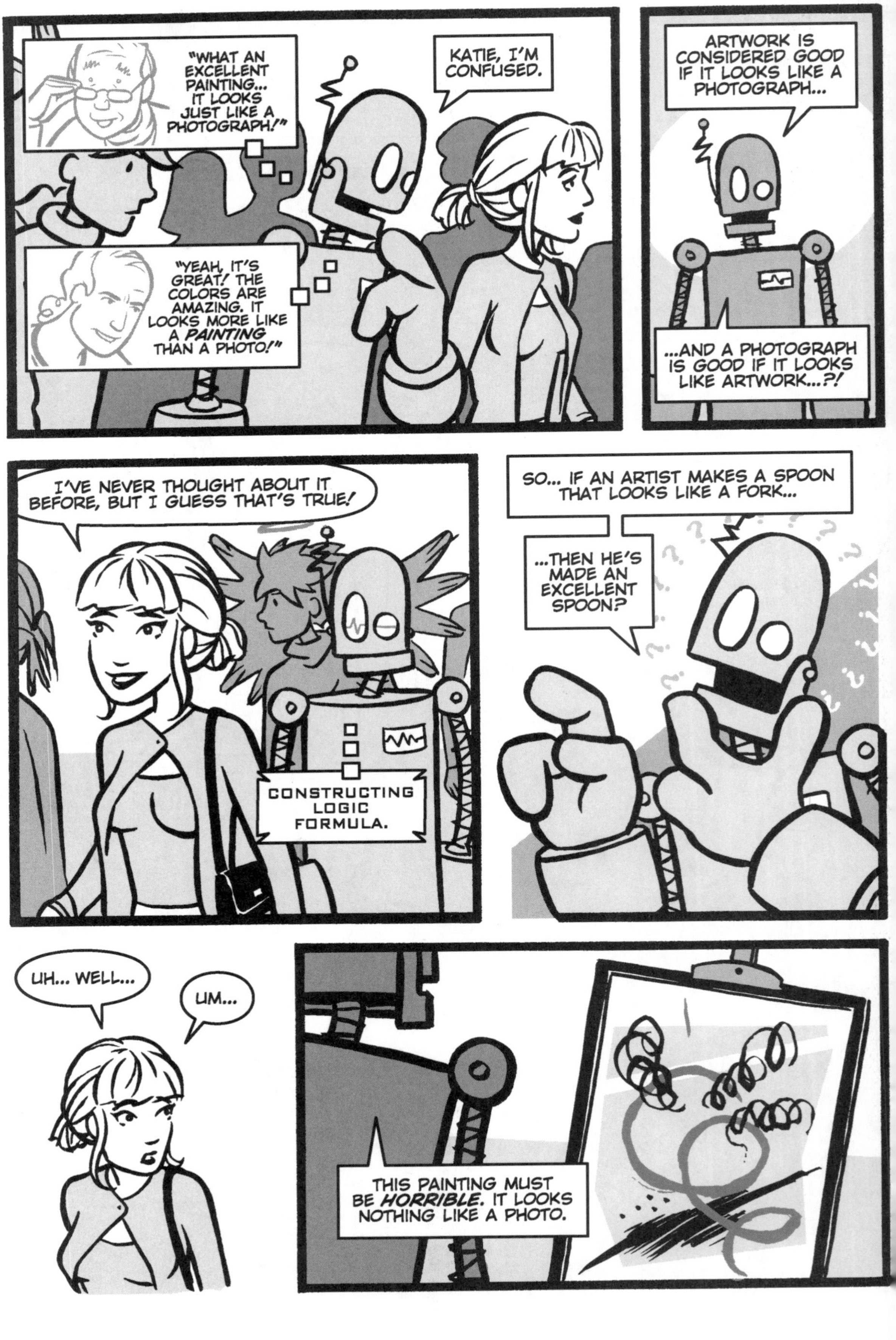
"WHAT AN EXCELLENT PAINTING... IT LOOKS JUST LIKE A PHOTOGRAPH!"
"YEAH, IT'S GREAT! THE COLORS ARE AMAZING. IT LOOKS MORE LIKE A PAINTING THAN A PHOTO!"
KATIE, I'M CONFUSED.
ARTWORK IS CONSIDERED GOOD IF IT LOOKS LIKE A PHOTOGRAPH...
...AND A PHOTOGRAPH IS GOOD IF IT LOOKS LIKE ARTWORK...?!
I'VE NEVER THOUGHT ABOUT IT BEFORE, BUT I GUESS THAT'S TRUE!
CONSTRUCTING LOGIC FORMULA.
SO... IF AN ARTIST MAKES A SPOON THAT LOOKS LIKE A FORK...
...THEN HE'S MADE AN EXCELLENT SPOON?
UH... WELL...
UM...
THIS PAINTING MUST BE HORRIBLE. IT LOOKS NOTHING LIKE A PHOTO.

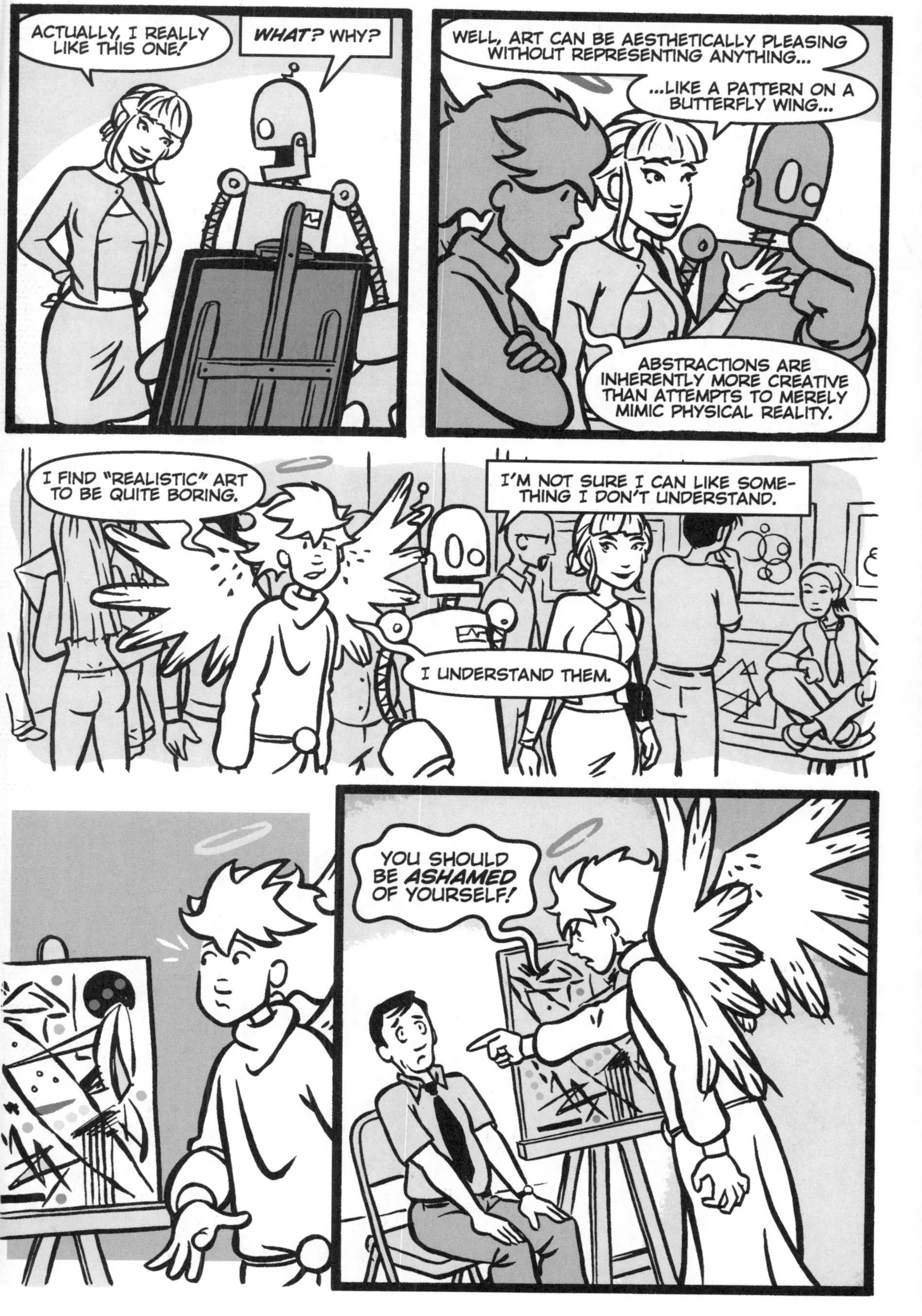
ACTUALLY, I REALLY LIKE THIS ONE!
WHAT? WHY?
WELL, ART CAN BE AESTHETICALLY PLEASING WITHOUT REPRESENTING ANYTHING...
...LIKE A PATTERN ON A BUTTERFLY WING...
ABSTRACTIONS ARE INHERENTLY MORE CREATIVE THAN ATTEMPTS TO MERELY MIMIC PHYSICAL REALITY.
I FIND "REALISTIC" ART TO BE QUITE BORING.
I'M NOT SURE I CAN LIKE SOMETHING I DON'T UNDERSTAND.
I UNDERSTAND THEM.
YOU SHOULD BE ASHAMED OF YOURSELF!

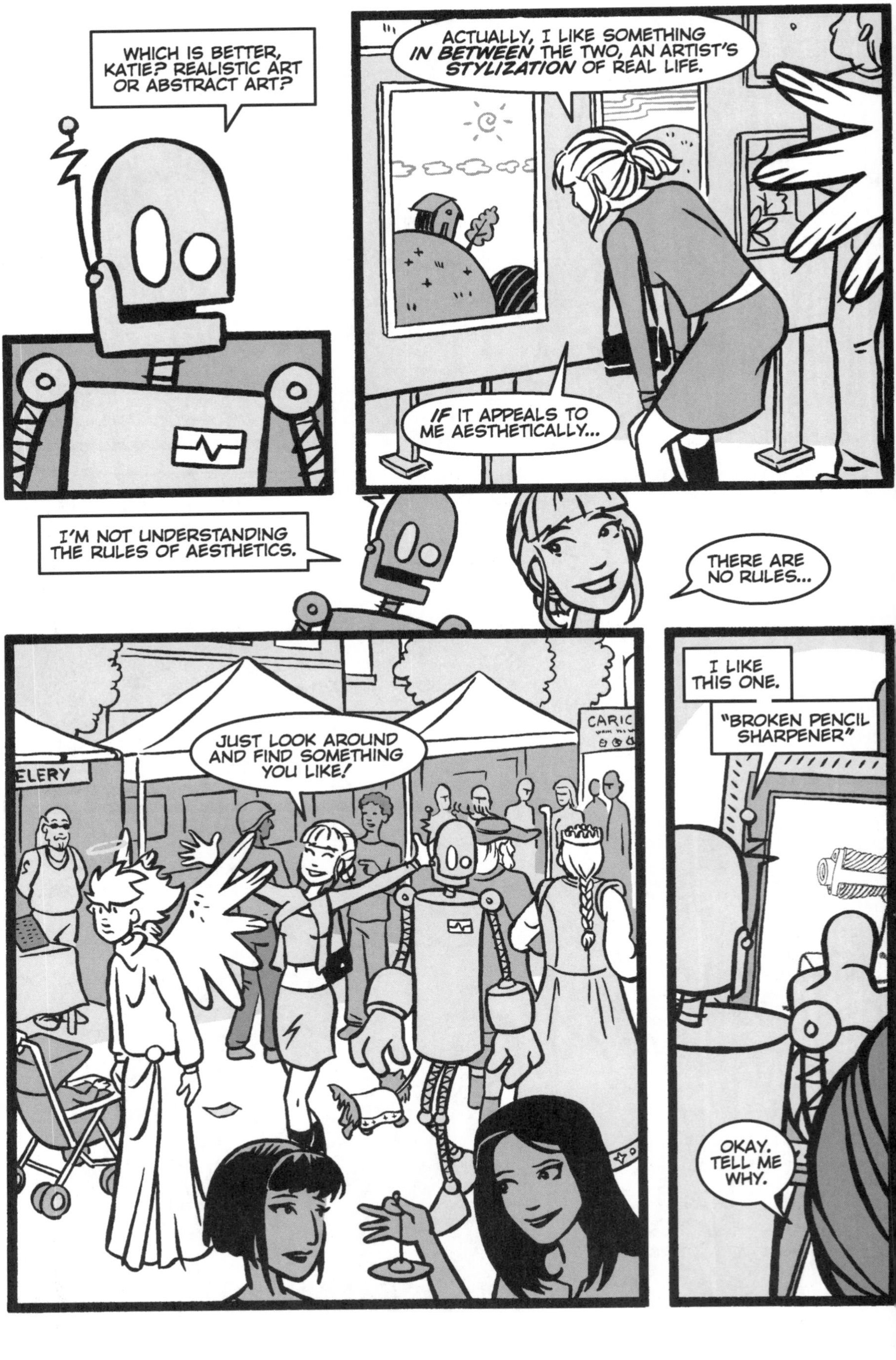
WHICH IS BETTER, KATIE? REALISTIC ART OR ABSTRACT ART?
ACTUALLY, I LIKE SOMETHING *IN BETWEEN* THE TWO, AN ARTIST'S *STYLIZATION* OF REAL LIFE.
IF IT APPEALS TO ME AESTHETICALLY...
I'M NOT UNDERSTANDING THE RULES OF AESTHETICS.
THERE ARE NO RULES...
JUST LOOK AROUND AND FIND SOMETHING YOU LIKE!
ELERY
CARIC
I LIKE THIS ONE.
"BROKEN PENCIL SHARPENER"
OKAY. TELL ME WHY.

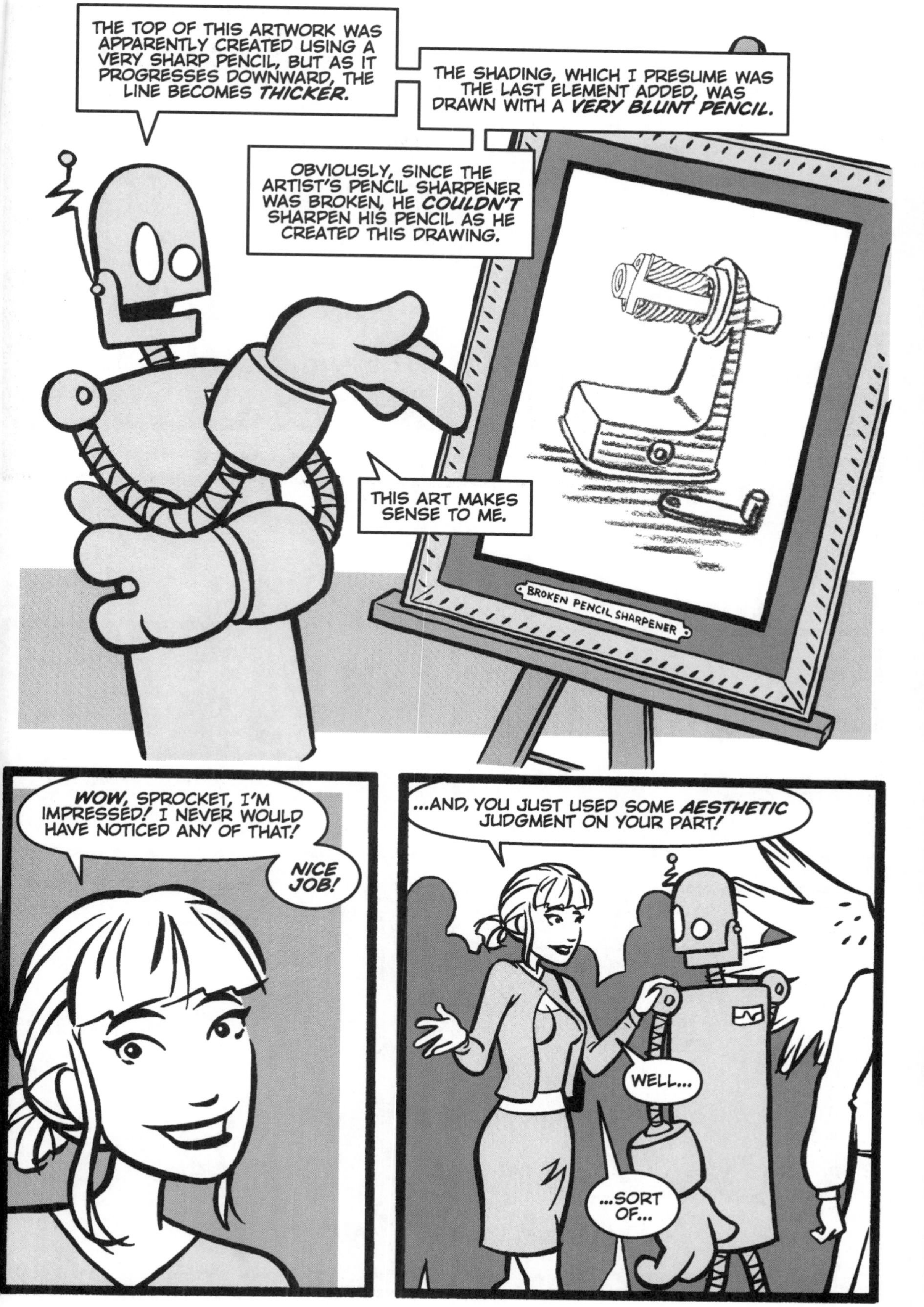
THE TOP OF THIS ARTWORK WAS APPARENTLY CREATED USING A VERY SHARP PENCIL, BUT AS IT PROGRESSES DOWNWARD, THE LINE BECOMES *THICKER.*
THE SHADING, WHICH I PRESUME WAS THE LAST ELEMENT ADDED, WAS DRAWN WITH A *VERY BLUNT PENCIL.*
OBVIOUSLY, SINCE THE ARTIST'S PENCIL SHARPENER WAS BROKEN, HE *COULDN'T* SHARPEN HIS PENCIL AS HE CREATED THIS DRAWING.
THIS ART MAKES SENSE TO ME.
BROKEN PENCIL SHARPENER
WOW, SPROCKET, I'M IMPRESSED! I NEVER WOULD HAVE NOTICED ANY OF THAT!
NICE JOB!
...AND, YOU JUST USED SOME *AESTHETIC* JUDGMENT ON YOUR PART!
WELL...
...SORT OF...

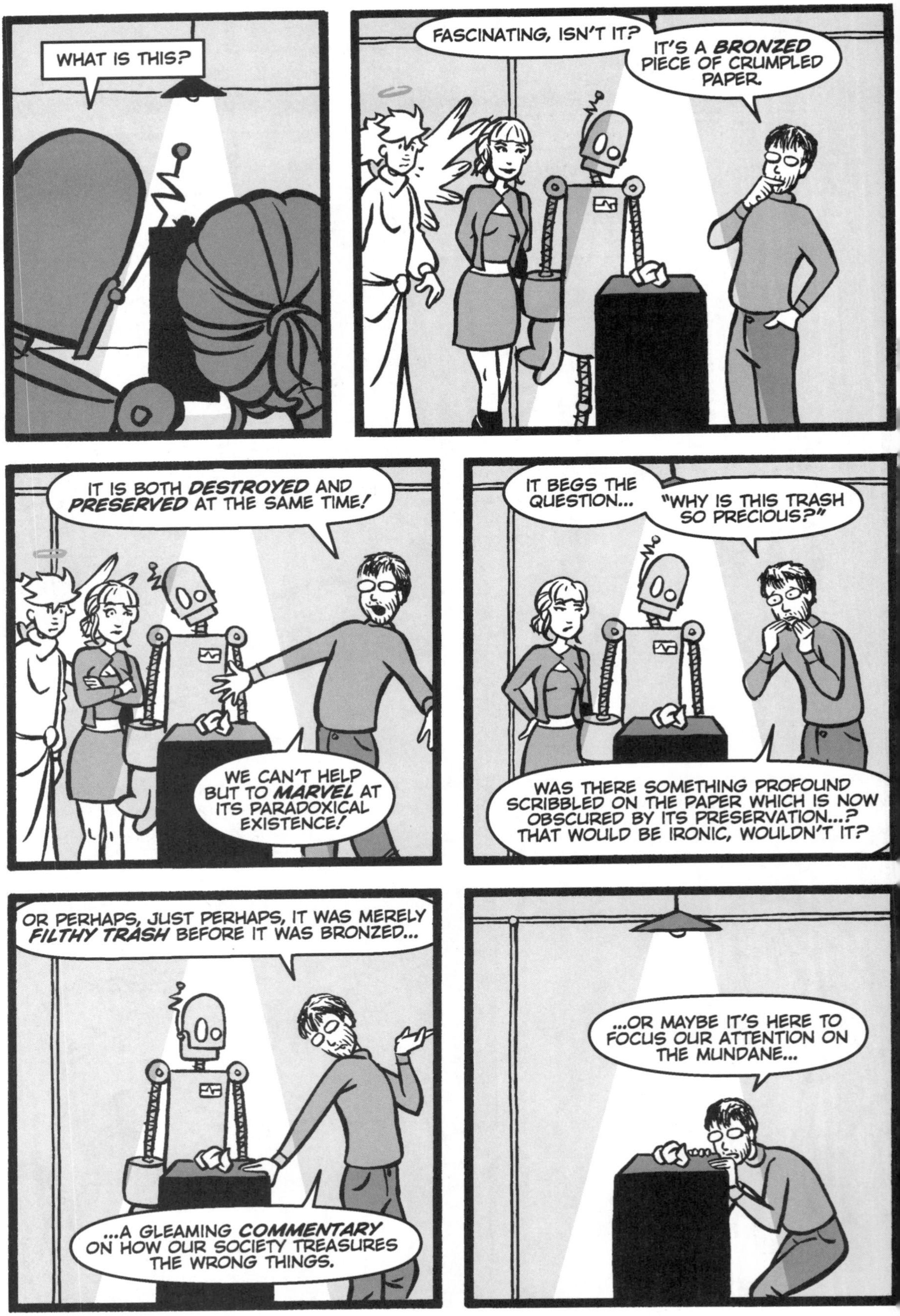
WHAT IS THIS?
FASCINATING, ISN'T IT?
IT'S A BRONZED PIECE OF CRUMPLED PAPER.
IT IS BOTH DESTROYED AND PRESERVED AT THE SAME TIME!
WE CAN'T HELP BUT TO MARVEL AT ITS PARADOXICAL EXISTENCE!
IT BEGS THE QUESTION...
"WHY IS THIS TRASH SO PRECIOUS?"
WAS THERE SOMETHING PROFOUND SCRIBBLED ON THE PAPER WHICH IS NOW OBSCURED BY ITS PRESERVATION...? THAT WOULD BE IRONIC, WOULDN'T IT?
OR PERHAPS, JUST PERHAPS, IT WAS MERELY FILTHY TRASH BEFORE IT WAS BRONZED...
...A GLEAMING COMMENTARY ON HOW OUR SOCIETY TREASURES THE WRONG THINGS.
...OR MAYBE IT'S HERE TO FOCUS OUR ATTENTION ON THE MUNDANE...

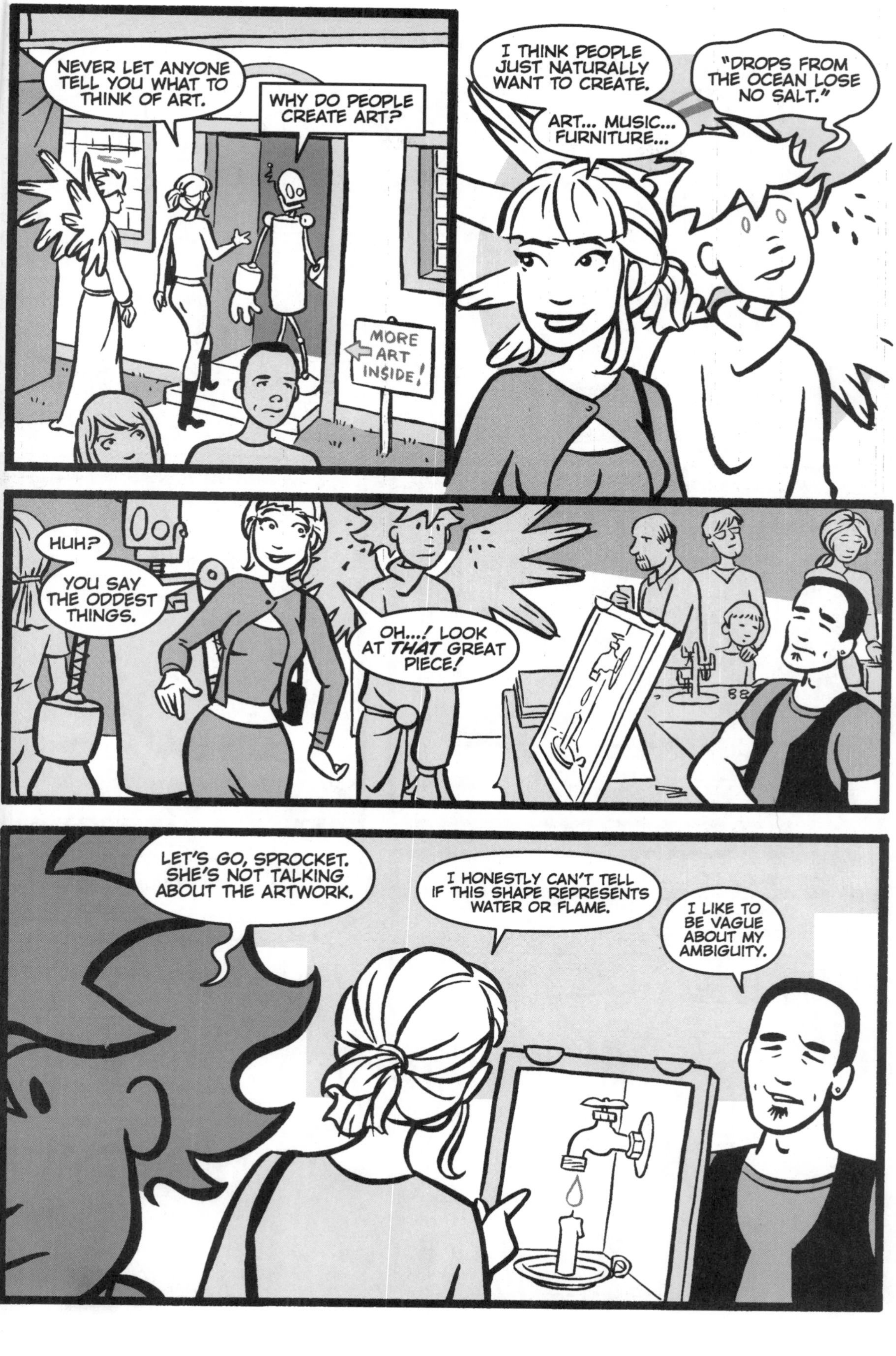
NEVER LET ANYONE TELL YOU WHAT TO THINK OF ART.
WHY DO PEOPLE CREATE ART?
MORE ART INSIDE!
I THINK PEOPLE JUST NATURALLY WANT TO CREATE.
ART... MUSIC... FURNITURE...
"DROPS FROM THE OCEAN LOSE NO SALT."
HUH?
YOU SAY THE ODDEST THINGS.
OH...! LOOK AT *THAT* GREAT PIECE!
LET'S GO, SPROCKET. SHE'S NOT TALKING ABOUT THE ARTWORK.
I HONESTLY CAN'T TELL IF THIS SHAPE REPRESENTS WATER OR FLAME.
I LIKE TO BE VAGUE ABOUT MY AMBIGUITY.

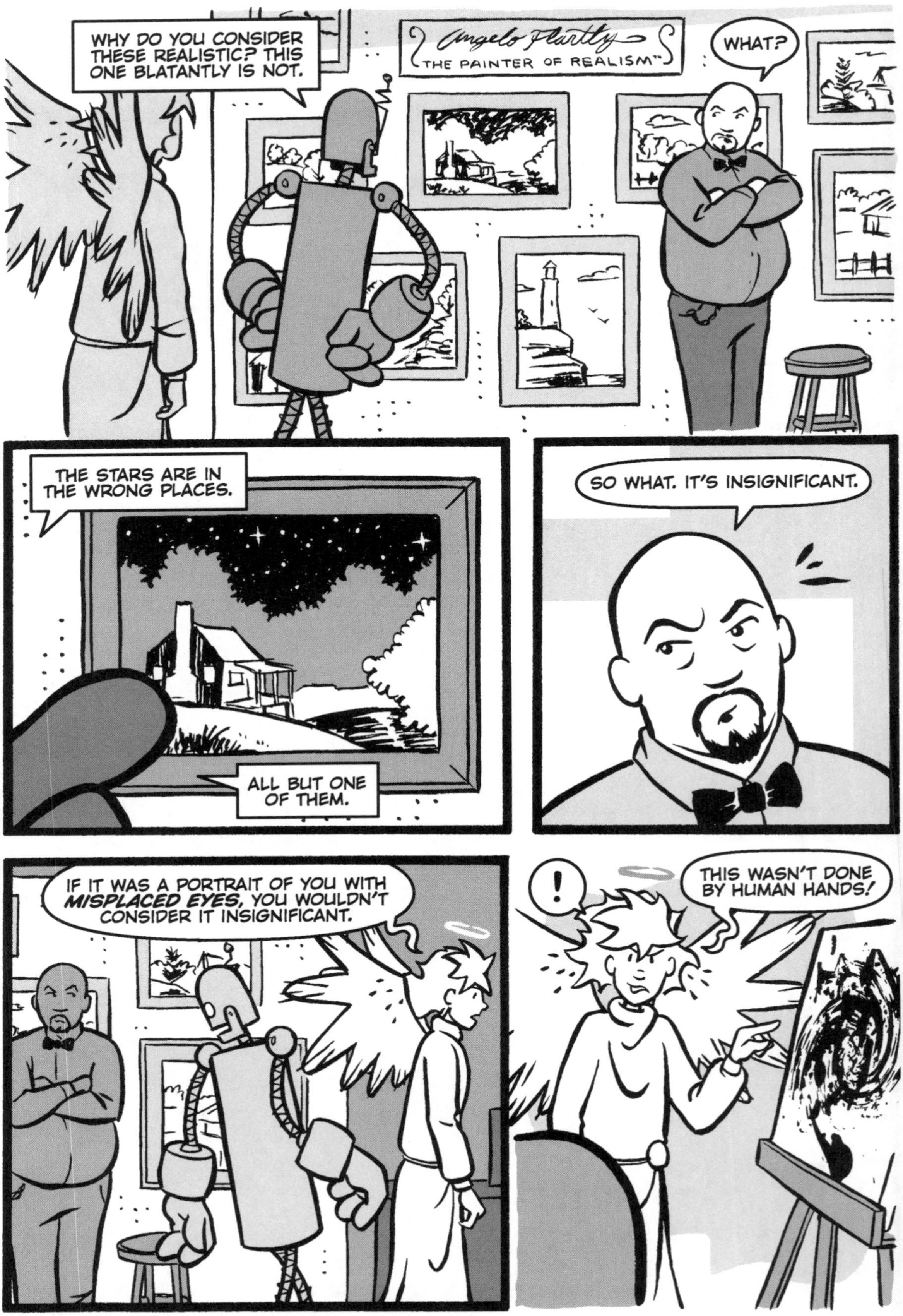
WHY DO YOU CONSIDER THESE REALISTIC? THIS ONE BLATANTLY IS NOT.
Angelo Flartty
THE PAINTER OF REALISM™
WHAT?
THE STARS ARE IN THE WRONG PLACES.
ALL BUT ONE OF THEM.
SO WHAT. IT'S INSIGNIFICANT.
IF IT WAS A PORTRAIT OF YOU WITH *MISPLACED EYES,* YOU WOULDN'T CONSIDER IT INSIGNIFICANT.
!
THIS WASN'T DONE BY HUMAN HANDS!

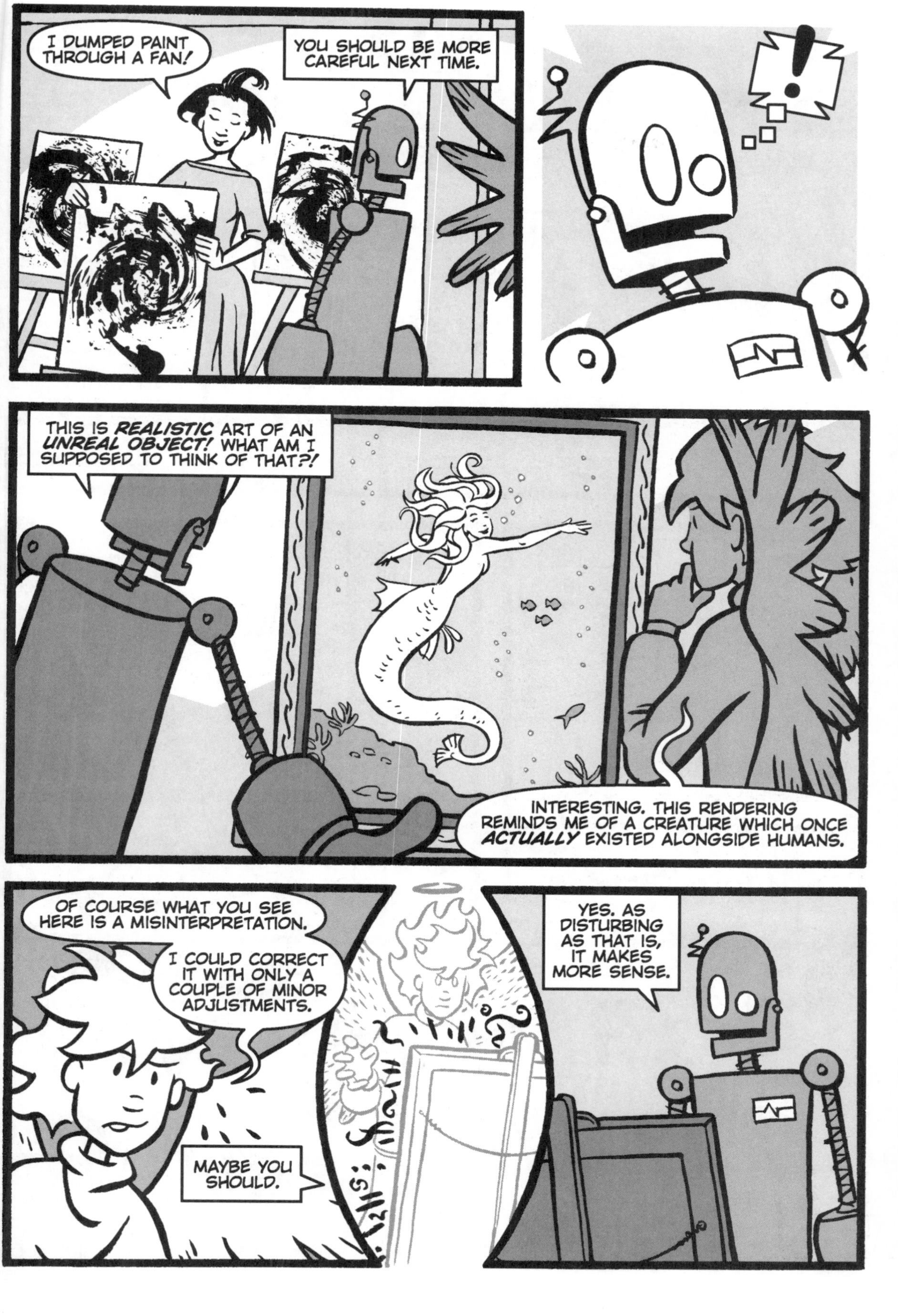
I DUMPED PAINT THROUGH A FAN!
YOU SHOULD BE MORE CAREFUL NEXT TIME.
!
THIS IS REALISTIC ART OF AN UNREAL OBJECT! WHAT AM I SUPPOSED TO THINK OF THAT?!
INTERESTING. THIS RENDERING REMINDS ME OF A CREATURE WHICH ONCE ACTUALLY EXISTED ALONGSIDE HUMANS.
OF COURSE WHAT YOU SEE HERE IS A MISINTERPRETATION.
I COULD CORRECT IT WITH ONLY A COUPLE OF MINOR ADJUSTMENTS.
MAYBE YOU SHOULD.
YES. AS DISTURBING AS THAT IS, IT MAKES MORE SENSE.

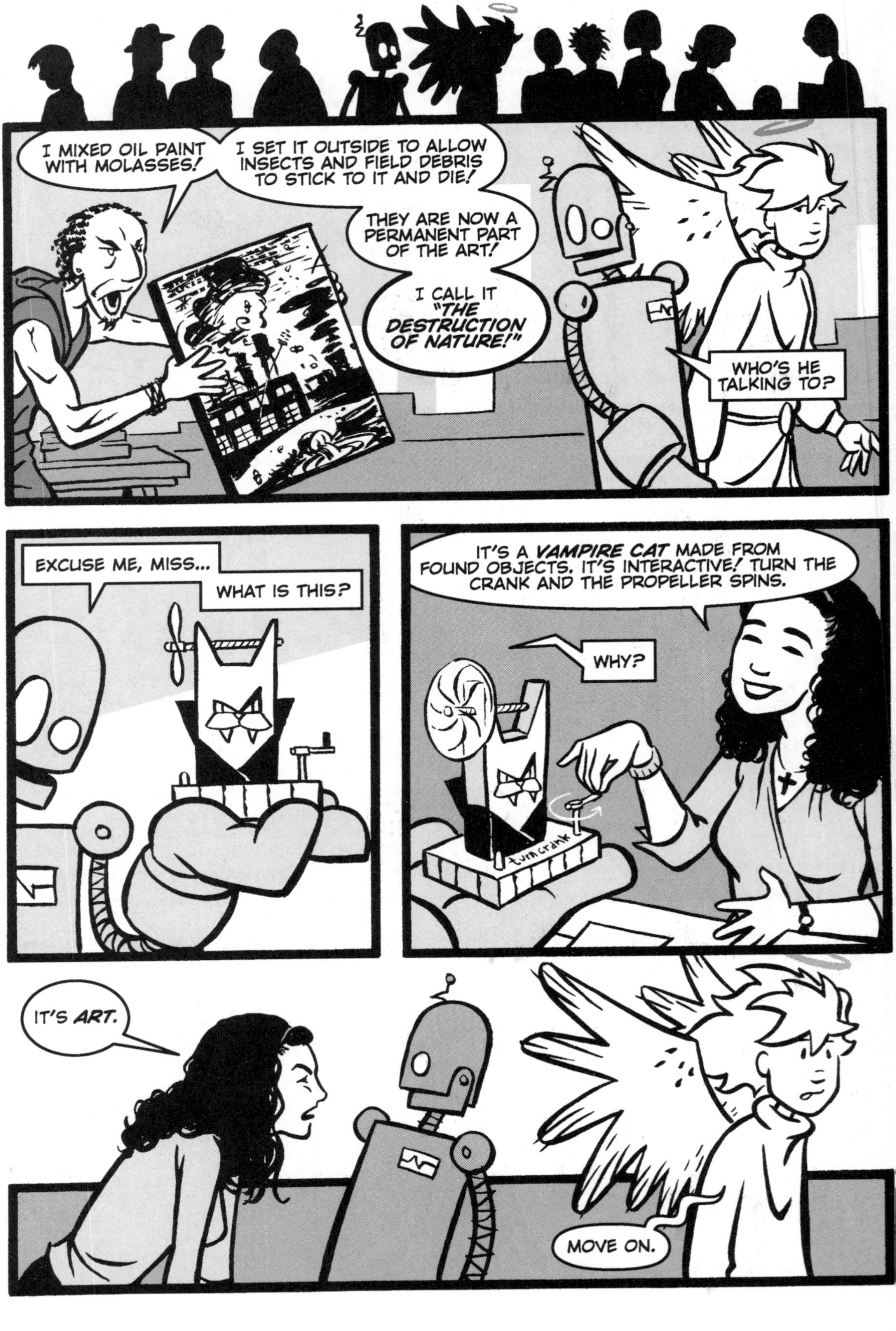
I MIXED OIL PAINT WITH MOLASSES!
I SET IT OUTSIDE TO ALLOW INSECTS AND FIELD DEBRIS TO STICK TO IT AND DIE!
THEY ARE NOW A PERMANENT PART OF THE ART!
I CALL IT "THE DESTRUCTION OF NATURE!"
WHO'S HE TALKING TO?
EXCUSE ME, MISS...
WHAT IS THIS?
IT'S A VAMPIRE CAT MADE FROM FOUND OBJECTS. IT'S INTERACTIVE! TURN THE CRANK AND THE PROPELLER SPINS.
WHY?
turn crank
IT'S ART.
MOVE ON.

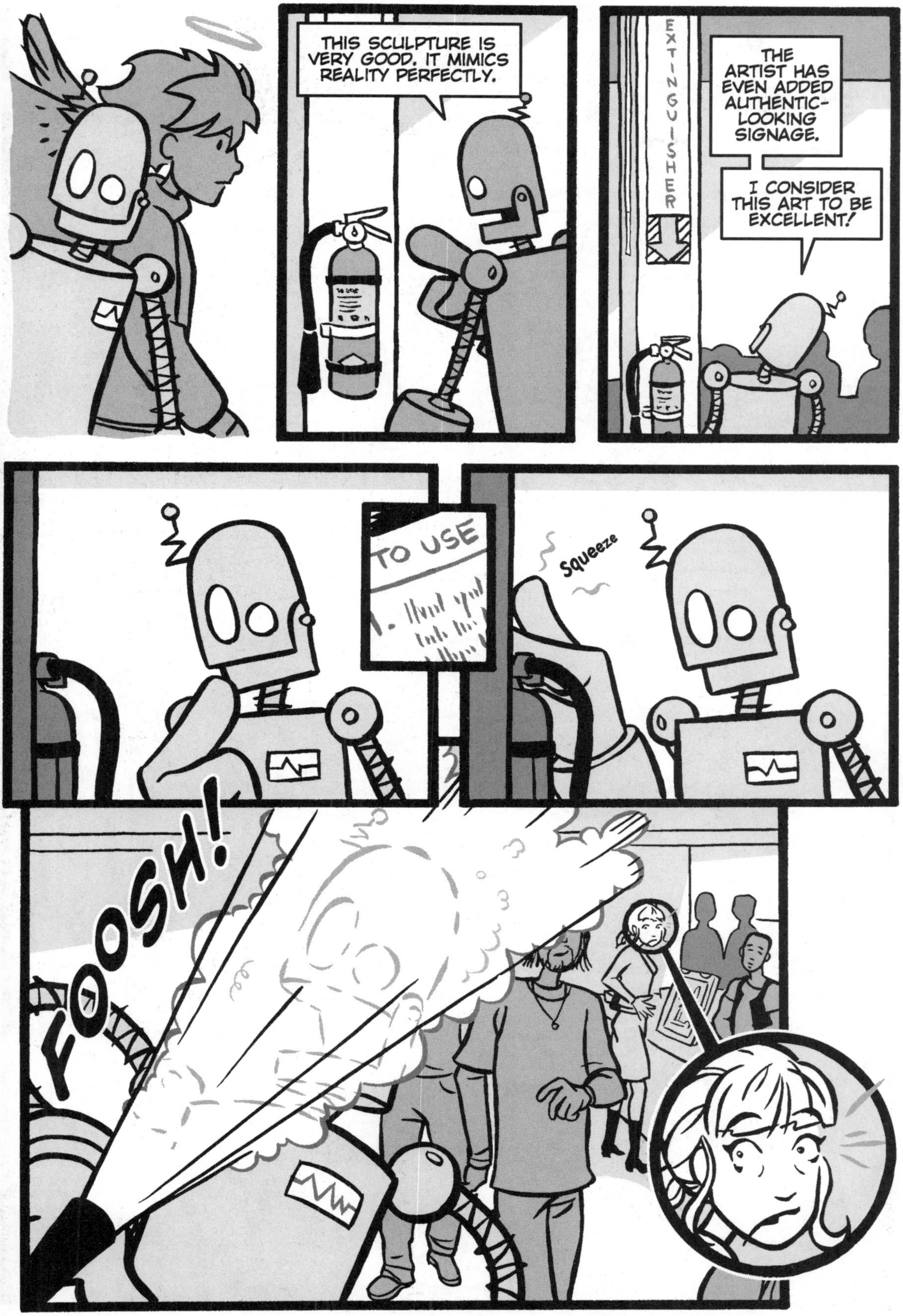
THIS SCULPTURE IS VERY GOOD. IT MIMICS REALITY PERFECTLY.
EXTINGUISHER
THE ARTIST HAS EVEN ADDED AUTHENTIC-LOOKING SIGNAGE.
I CONSIDER THIS ART TO BE EXCELLENT!
TO USE
Squeeze
FOOSH!

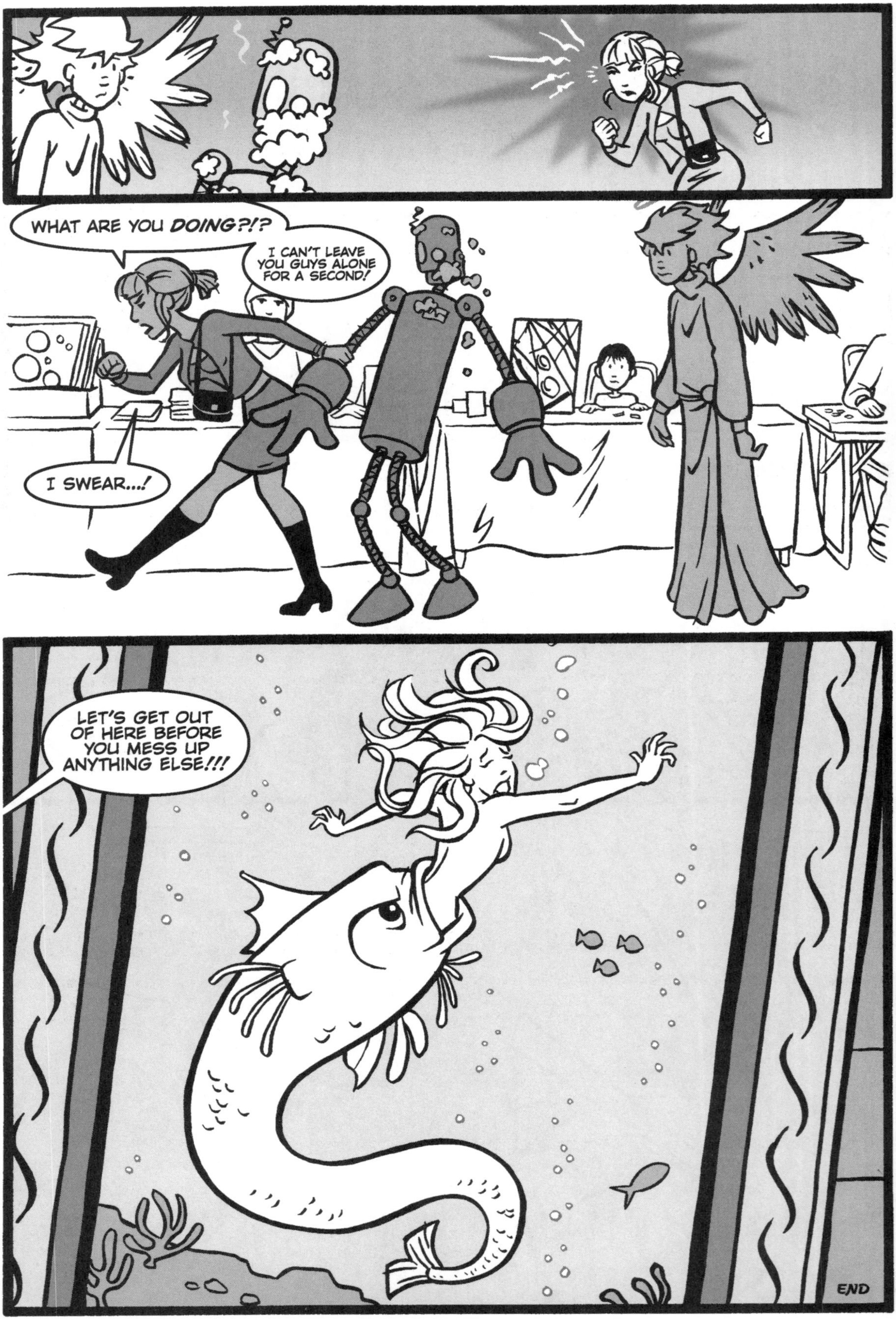
WHAT ARE YOU *DOING?!?*
I CAN'T LEAVE YOU GUYS ALONE FOR A SECOND!
I SWEAR...!
LET'S GET OUT OF HERE BEFORE YOU MESS UP ANYTHING ELSE!!!
END

THIS HAS NOTHING TO DO WITH HALO & SPROCKET,
BUT THIS QUESTION HAS BURNED INSIDE OF ME FOR YEARS...

ARE CATS HIGHLY INTELLIGENT (but aloof) OR JUST PLAIN STUPID?

IT SEEMS *EITHER* COULD BE TRUE...

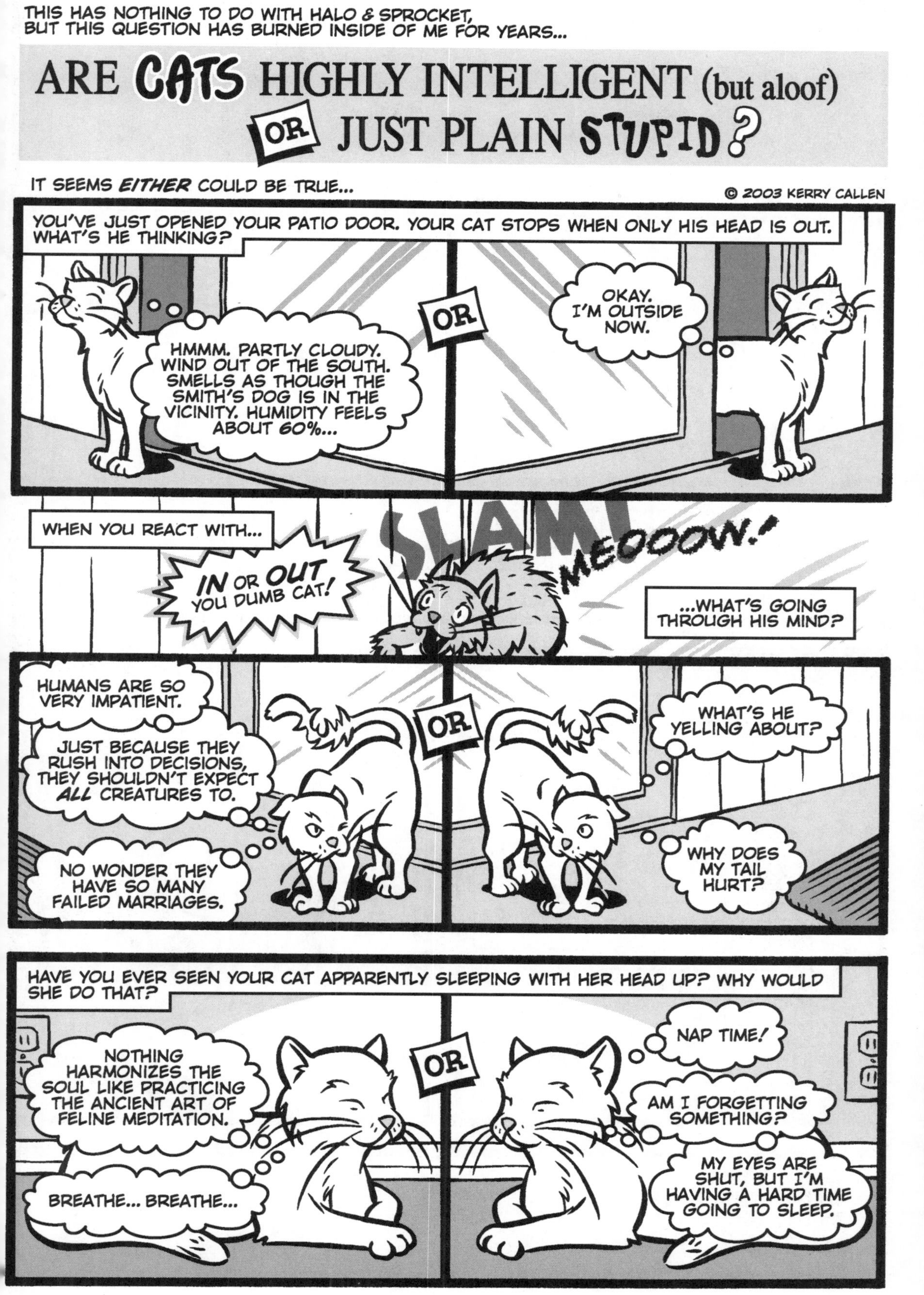

YOU'VE JUST OPENED YOUR PATIO DOOR. YOUR CAT STOPS WHEN ONLY HIS HEAD IS OUT. WHAT'S HE THINKING?
HMMM. PARTLY CLOUDY. WIND OUT OF THE SOUTH. SMELLS AS THOUGH THE SMITH'S DOG IS IN THE VICINITY. HUMIDITY FEELS ABOUT 60%...
OR
OKAY. I'M OUTSIDE NOW.
WHEN YOU REACT WITH...
IN OR OUT YOU DUMB CAT!
SLAM!
MEOOOW.!
...WHAT'S GOING THROUGH HIS MIND?
HUMANS ARE SO VERY IMPATIENT.
JUST BECAUSE THEY RUSH INTO DECISIONS, THEY SHOULDN'T EXPECT *ALL* CREATURES TO.
NO WONDER THEY HAVE SO MANY FAILED MARRIAGES.
OR
WHAT'S HE YELLING ABOUT?
WHY DOES MY TAIL HURT?
HAVE YOU EVER SEEN YOUR CAT APPARENTLY SLEEPING WITH HER HEAD UP? WHY WOULD SHE DO THAT?
NOTHING HARMONIZES THE SOUL LIKE PRACTICING THE ANCIENT ART OF FELINE MEDITATION.
BREATHE... BREATHE...
OR
NAP TIME!
AM I FORGETTING SOMETHING?
MY EYES ARE SHUT, BUT I'M HAVING A HARD TIME GOING TO SLEEP.

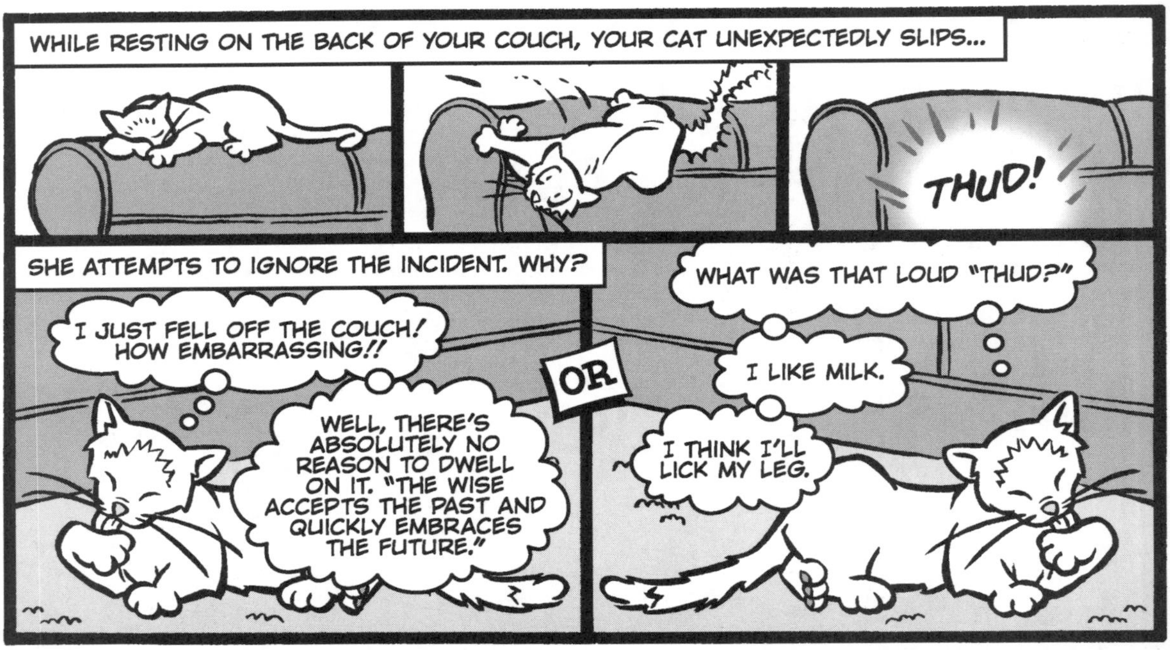
WHILE RESTING ON THE BACK OF YOUR COUCH, YOUR CAT UNEXPECTEDLY SLIPS...
THUD!
SHE ATTEMPTS TO IGNORE THE INCIDENT. WHY?
I JUST FELL OFF THE COUCH! HOW EMBARRASSING!!
WELL, THERE'S ABSOLUTELY NO REASON TO DWELL ON IT. "THE WISE ACCEPTS THE PAST AND QUICKLY EMBRACES THE FUTURE."
OR
WHAT WAS THAT LOUD "THUD?"
I LIKE MILK.
I THINK I'LL LICK MY LEG.

A CASE FOR INTELLIGENCE

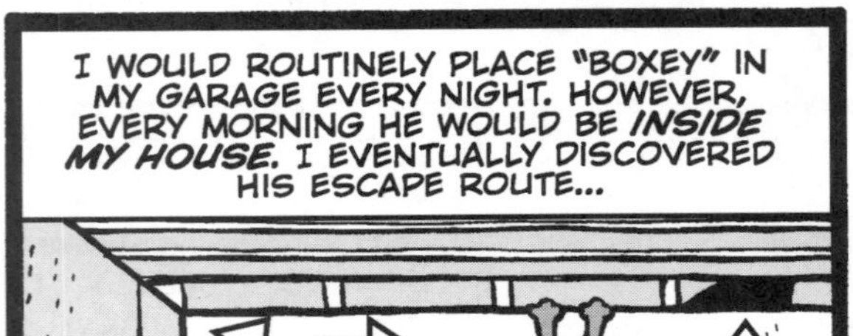
I WOULD ROUTINELY PLACE "BOXEY" IN MY GARAGE EVERY NIGHT. HOWEVER, EVERY MORNING HE WOULD BE *INSIDE MY HOUSE*. I EVENTUALLY DISCOVERED HIS ESCAPE ROUTE...
TOP EDGE OF WALL 1" THICK.
SIX FOOT EXPANSE ACCESSIBLE ONLY BY HANGING FROM FRONT PAWS.
TINY CAT-SIZED OPENING TO HOUSE.
SMALL 2"x 4" LEDGE HALFWAY UP WALL.
WHAT A GENIUS!

A CASE FOR STUPIDITY

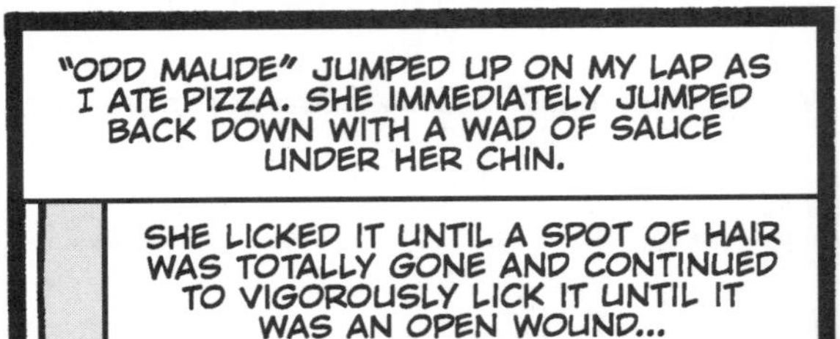
"ODD MAUDE" JUMPED UP ON MY LAP AS I ATE PIZZA. SHE IMMEDIATELY JUMPED BACK DOWN WITH A WAD OF SAUCE UNDER HER CHIN.
SHE LICKED IT UNTIL A SPOT OF HAIR WAS TOTALLY GONE AND CONTINUED TO VIGOROUSLY LICK IT UNTIL IT WAS AN OPEN WOUND...
YUM! MEAT!
STUPID CAT!

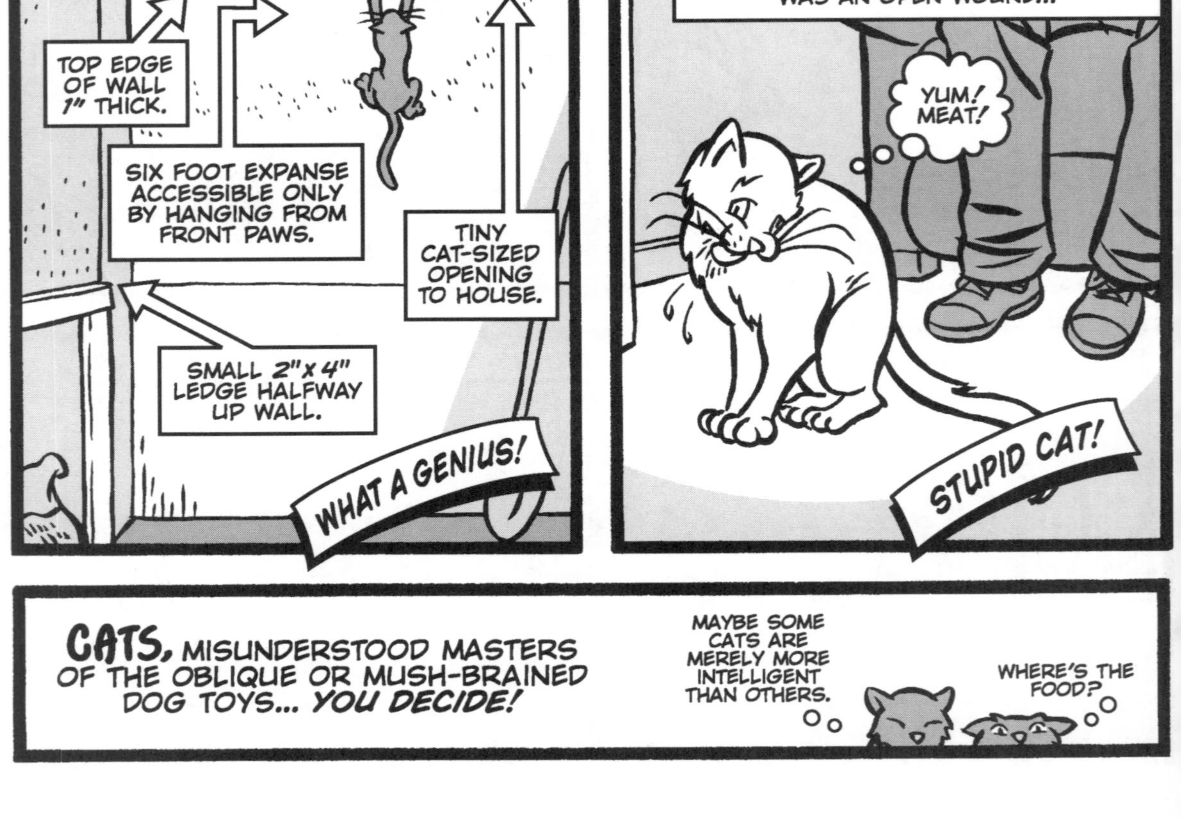
CATS, MISUNDERSTOOD MASTERS OF THE OBLIQUE OR MUSH-BRAINED DOG TOYS... *YOU DECIDE!*
MAYBE SOME CATS ARE MERELY MORE INTELLIGENT THAN OTHERS.
WHERE'S THE FOOD?

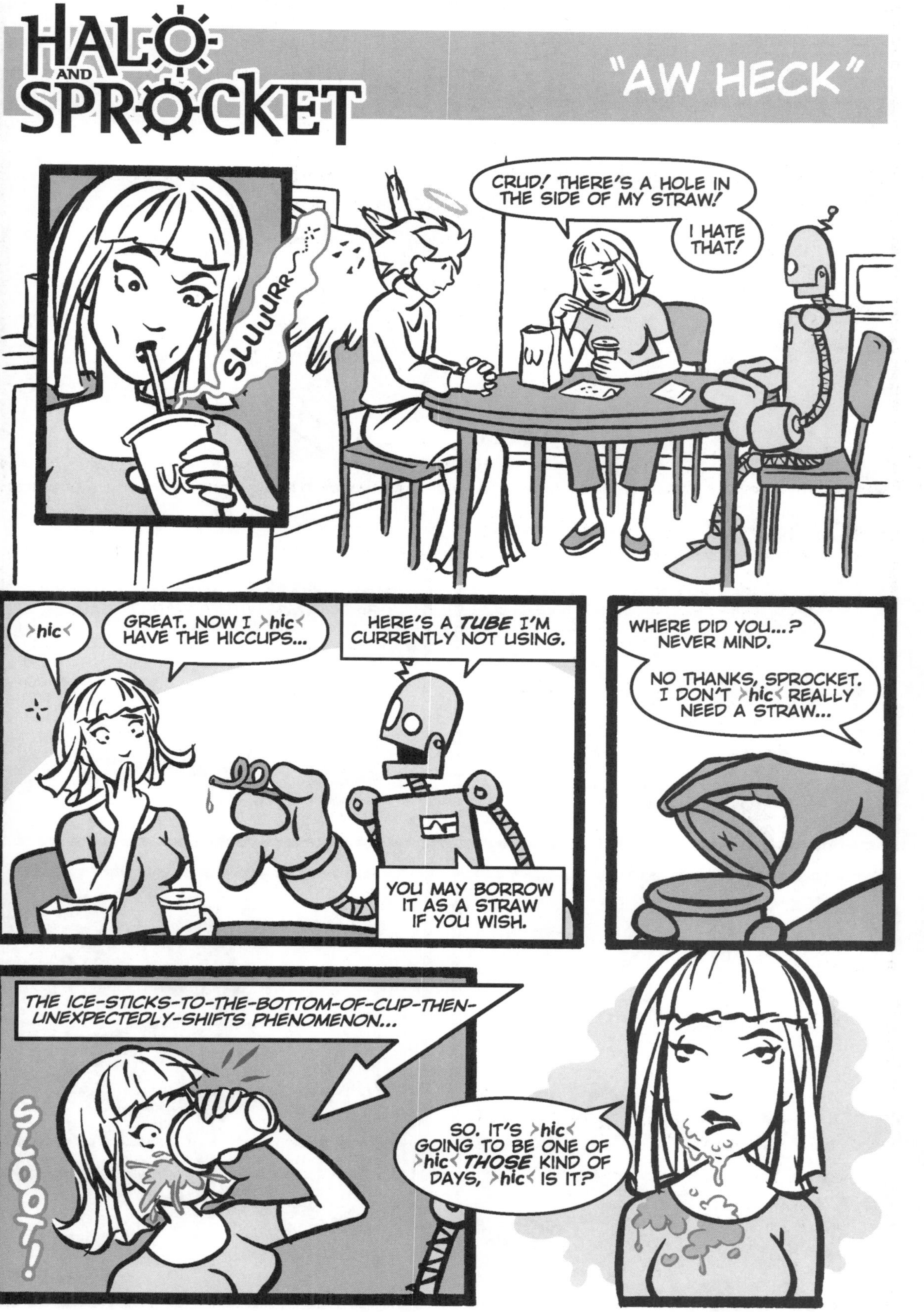
HALO AND SPROCKET
"AW HECK"
SLUUURR
CRUD! THERE'S A HOLE IN THE SIDE OF MY STRAW!
I HATE THAT!
>hic<
GREAT. NOW I >hic< HAVE THE HICCUPS...
HERE'S A TUBE I'M CURRENTLY NOT USING.
YOU MAY BORROW IT AS A STRAW IF YOU WISH.
WHERE DID YOU...? NEVER MIND.
NO THANKS, SPROCKET. I DON'T >hic< REALLY NEED A STRAW...
THE ICE-STICKS-TO-THE-BOTTOM-OF-CUP-THEN-UNEXPECTEDLY-SHIFTS PHENOMENON...
SLOOT!
SO. IT'S >hic< GOING TO BE ONE OF >hic< THOSE KIND OF DAYS, >hic< IS IT?

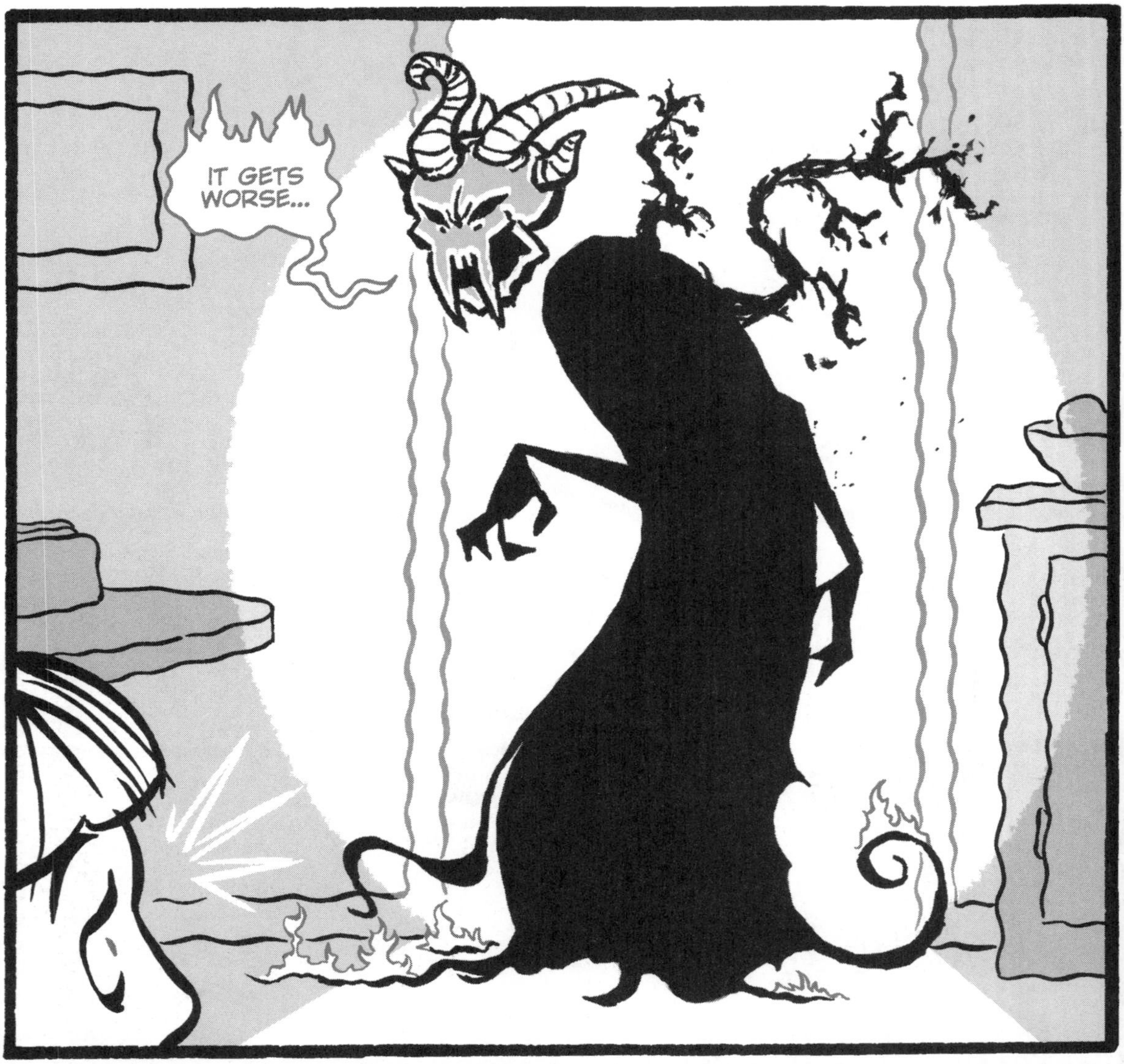
IT GETS WORSE...

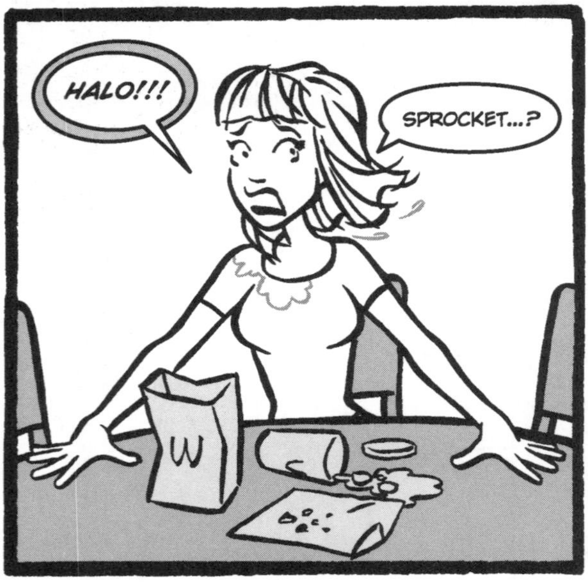
HALO!!!
SPROCKET...?

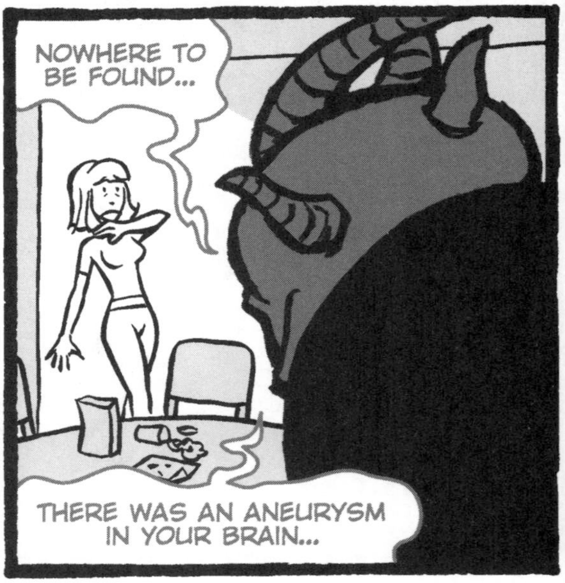
NOWHERE TO BE FOUND...
THERE WAS AN ANEURYSM IN YOUR BRAIN...

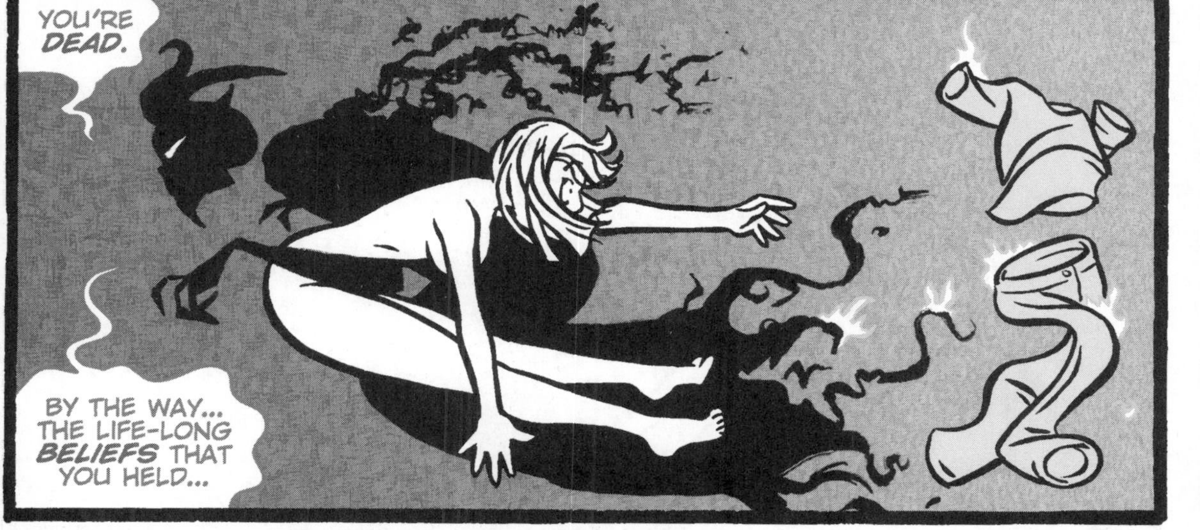
YOU'RE DEAD.
BY THE WAY... THE LIFE-LONG BELIEFS THAT YOU HELD...

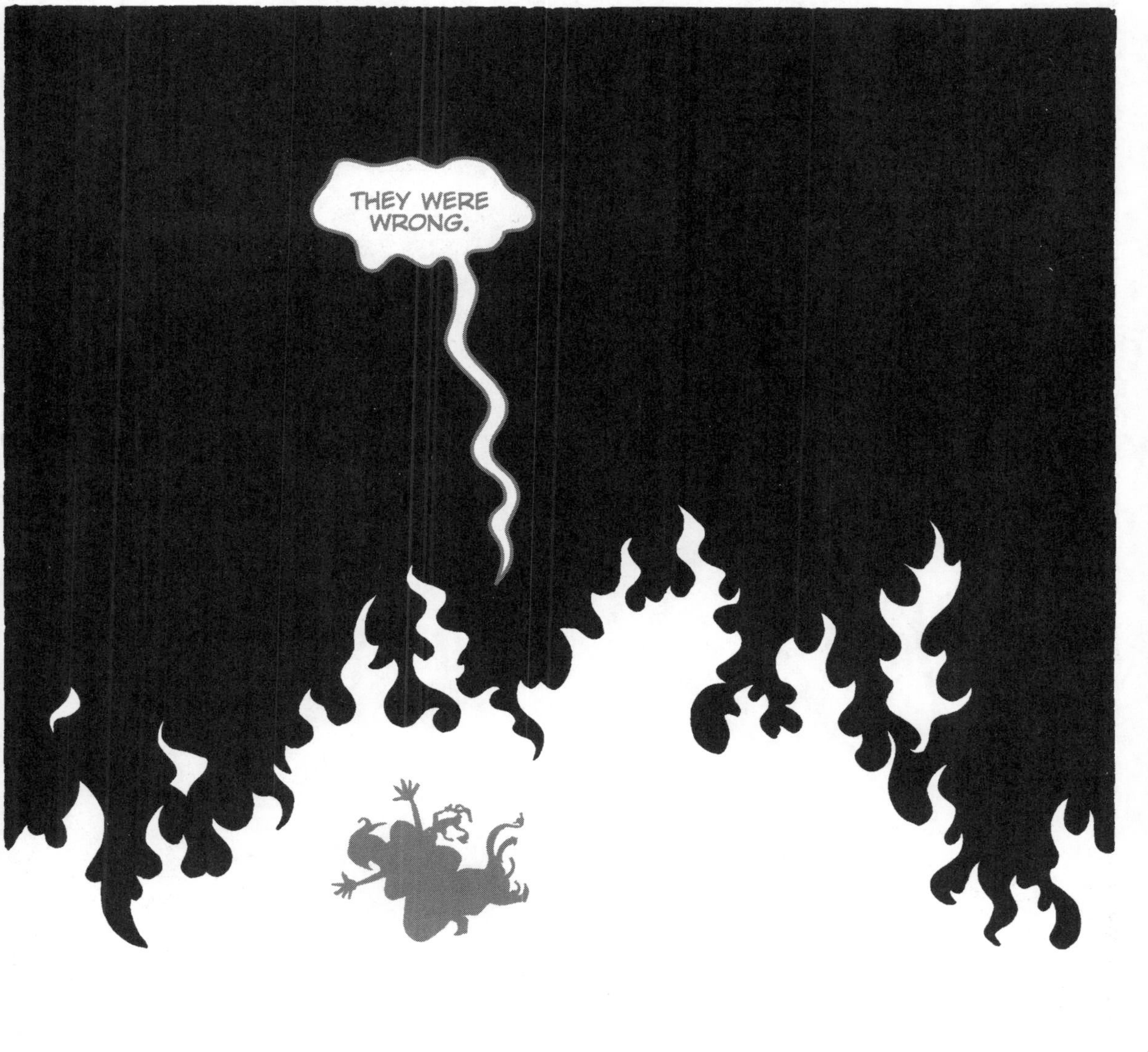
THEY WERE WRONG.

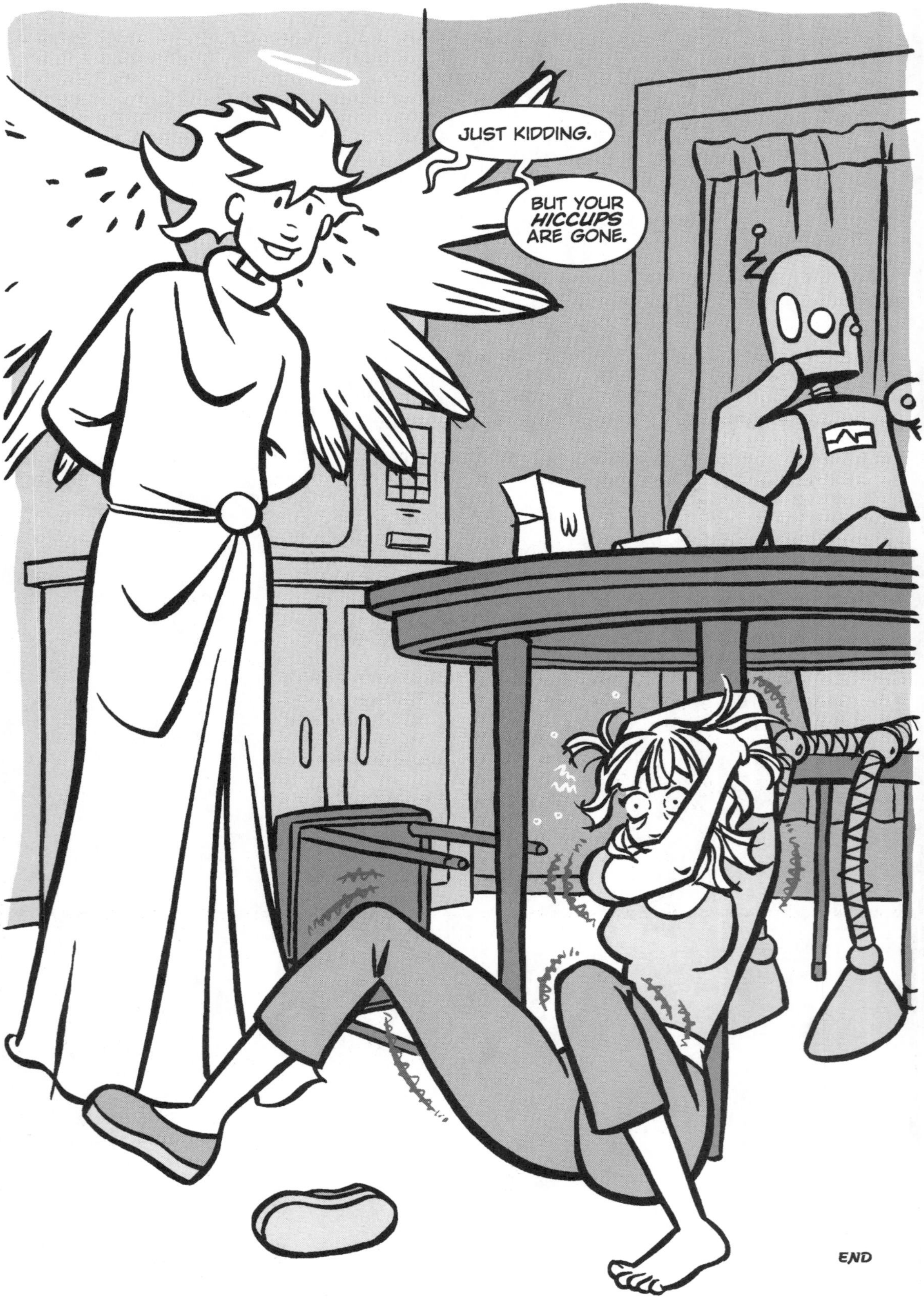
JUST KIDDING.
BUT YOUR *HICCUPS* ARE GONE.
END

HALO AND SPROCKET

"CLOUDY"

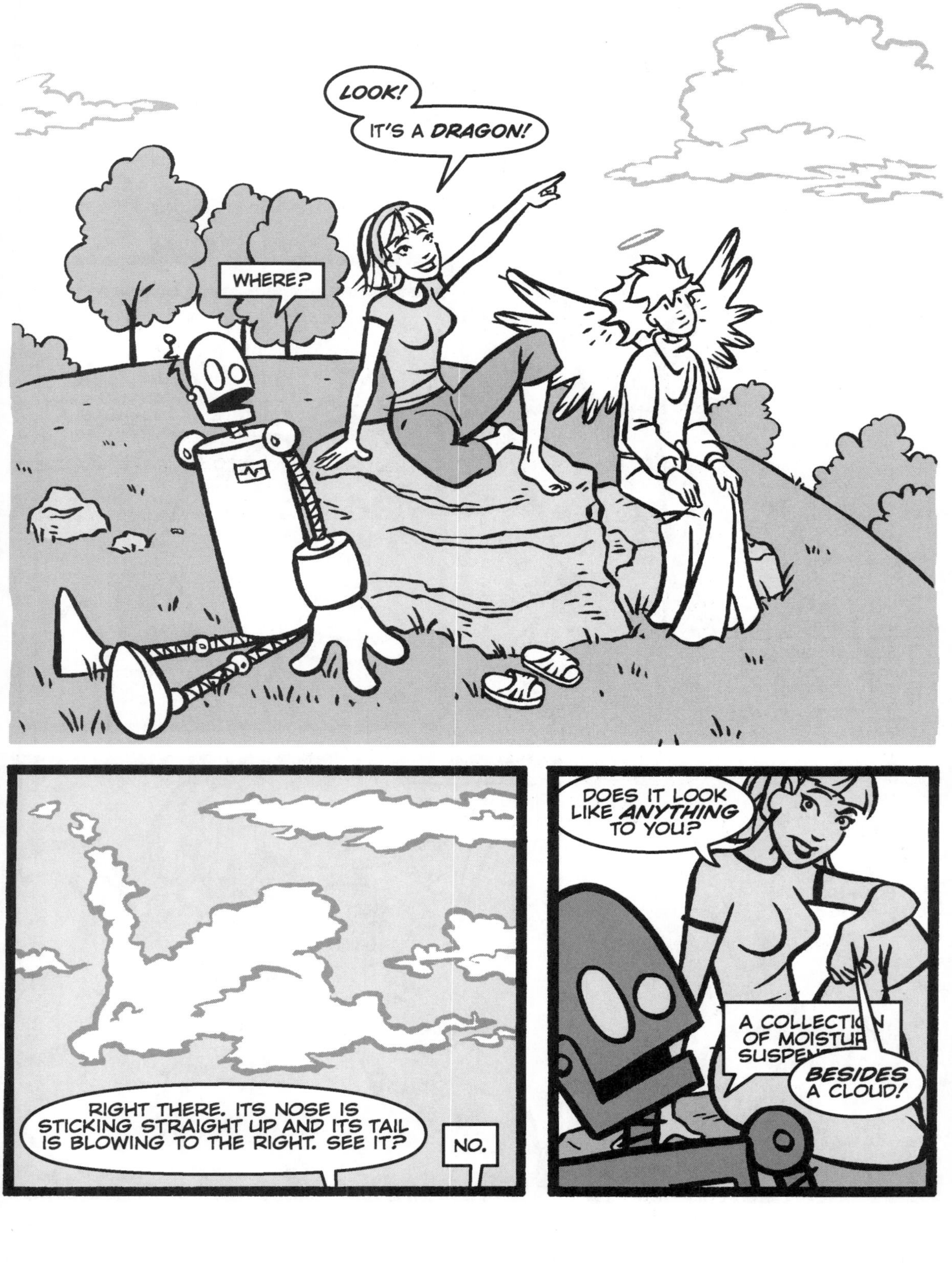

LOOK!
IT'S A DRAGON!
WHERE?
RIGHT THERE. ITS NOSE IS STICKING STRAIGHT UP AND ITS TAIL IS BLOWING TO THE RIGHT. SEE IT?
NO.
DOES IT LOOK LIKE ANYTHING TO YOU?
A COLLECTION OF MOISTUR SUSPEN
BESIDES A CLOUD!

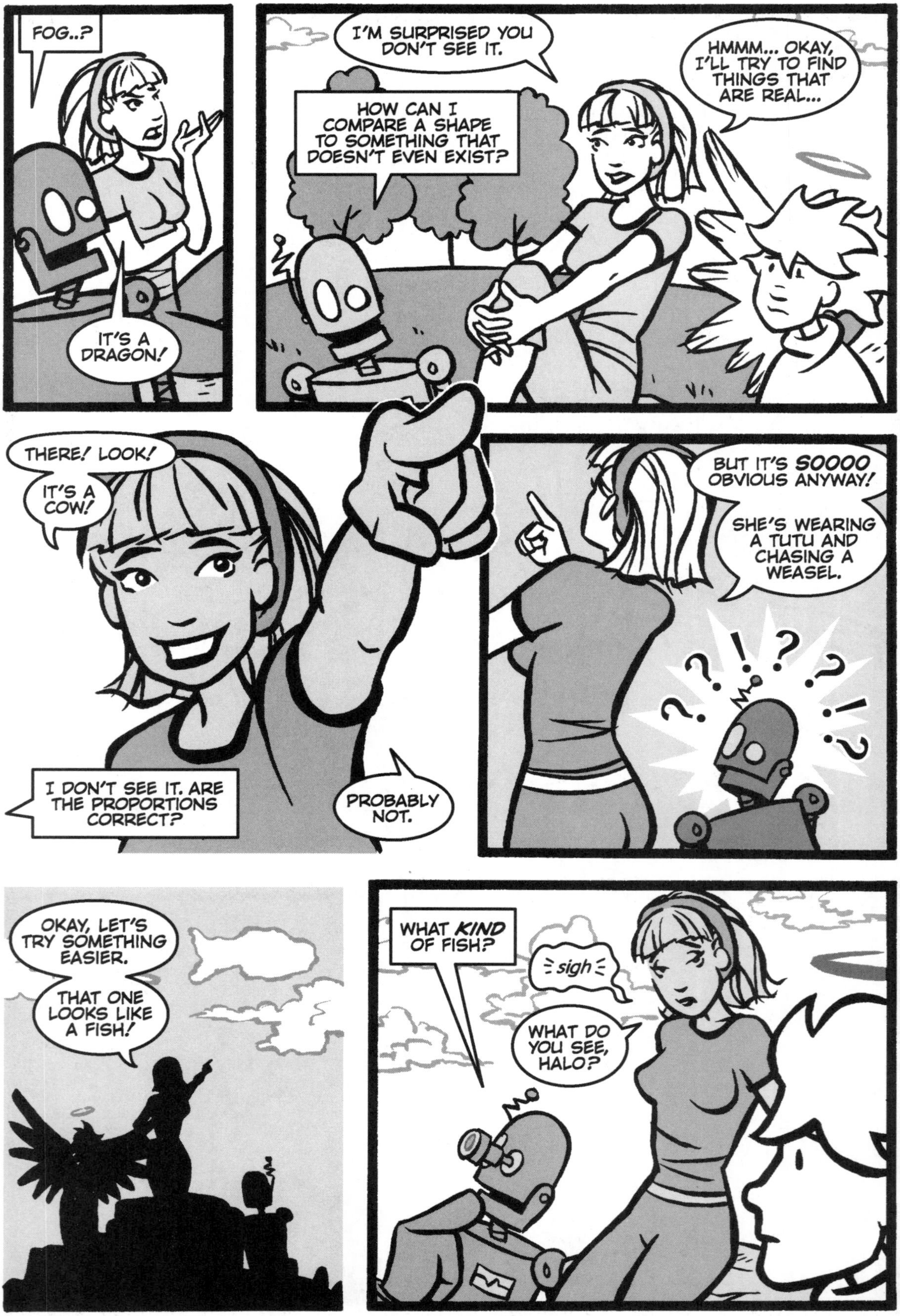
FOG..?
IT'S A DRAGON!
I'M SURPRISED YOU DON'T SEE IT.
HOW CAN I COMPARE A SHAPE TO SOMETHING THAT DOESN'T EVEN EXIST?
HMMM... OKAY, I'LL TRY TO FIND THINGS THAT ARE REAL...
THERE! LOOK!
IT'S A COW!
I DON'T SEE IT. ARE THE PROPORTIONS CORRECT?
PROBABLY NOT.
BUT IT'S SOOOO OBVIOUS ANYWAY!
SHE'S WEARING A TUTU AND CHASING A WEASEL.
?? !? ?! !?
OKAY, LET'S TRY SOMETHING EASIER.
THAT ONE LOOKS LIKE A FISH!
WHAT KIND OF FISH?
sigh
WHAT DO YOU SEE, HALO?

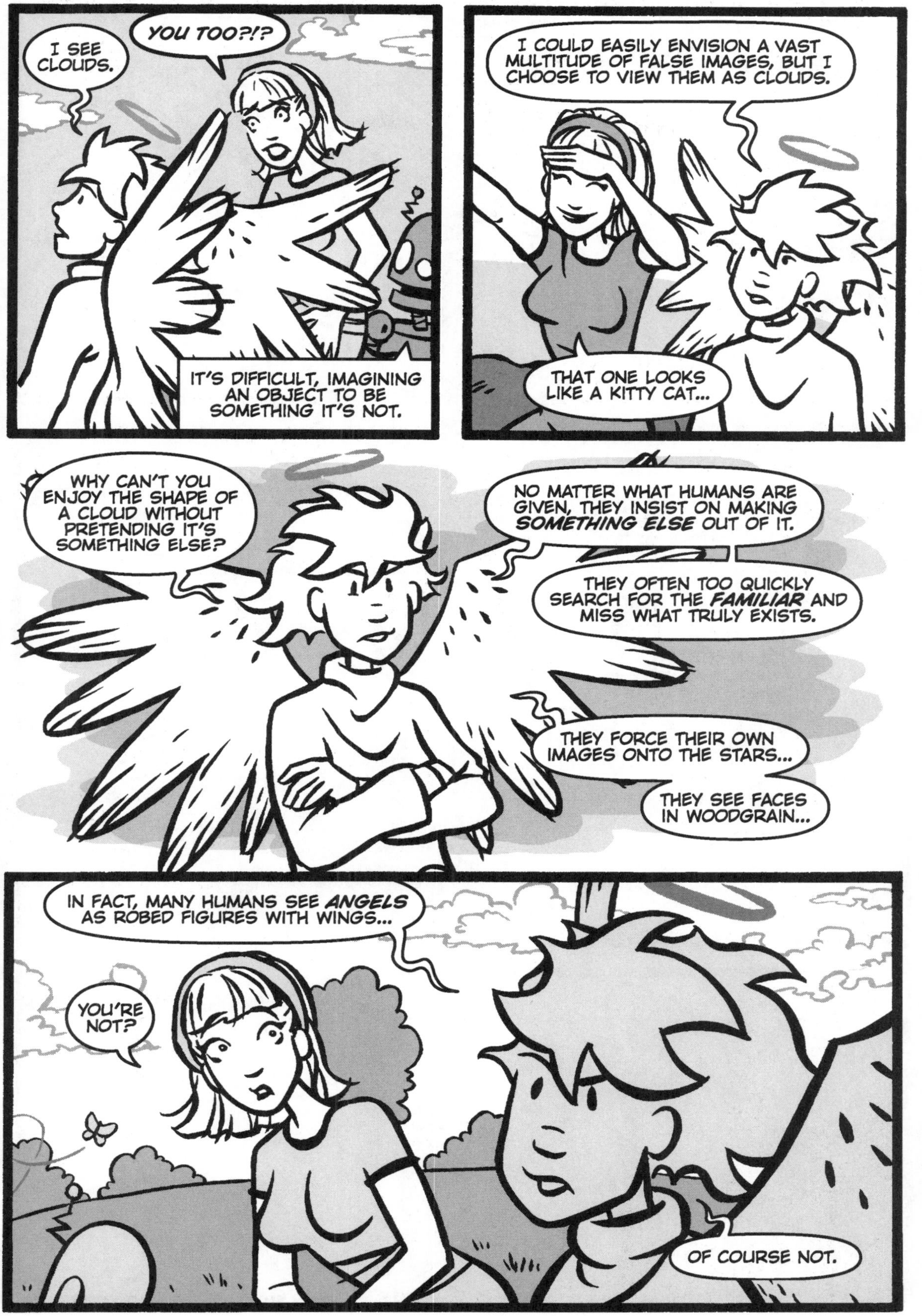
I SEE CLOUDS.
YOU TOO?!?
IT'S DIFFICULT, IMAGINING AN OBJECT TO BE SOMETHING IT'S NOT.
I COULD EASILY ENVISION A VAST MULTITUDE OF FALSE IMAGES, BUT I CHOOSE TO VIEW THEM AS CLOUDS.
THAT ONE LOOKS LIKE A KITTY CAT...
WHY CAN'T YOU ENJOY THE SHAPE OF A CLOUD WITHOUT PRETENDING IT'S SOMETHING ELSE?
NO MATTER WHAT HUMANS ARE GIVEN, THEY INSIST ON MAKING SOMETHING ELSE OUT OF IT.
THEY OFTEN TOO QUICKLY SEARCH FOR THE FAMILIAR AND MISS WHAT TRULY EXISTS.
THEY FORCE THEIR OWN IMAGES ONTO THE STARS...
THEY SEE FACES IN WOODGRAIN...
IN FACT, MANY HUMANS SEE ANGELS AS ROBED FIGURES WITH WINGS...
YOU'RE NOT?
OF COURSE NOT.

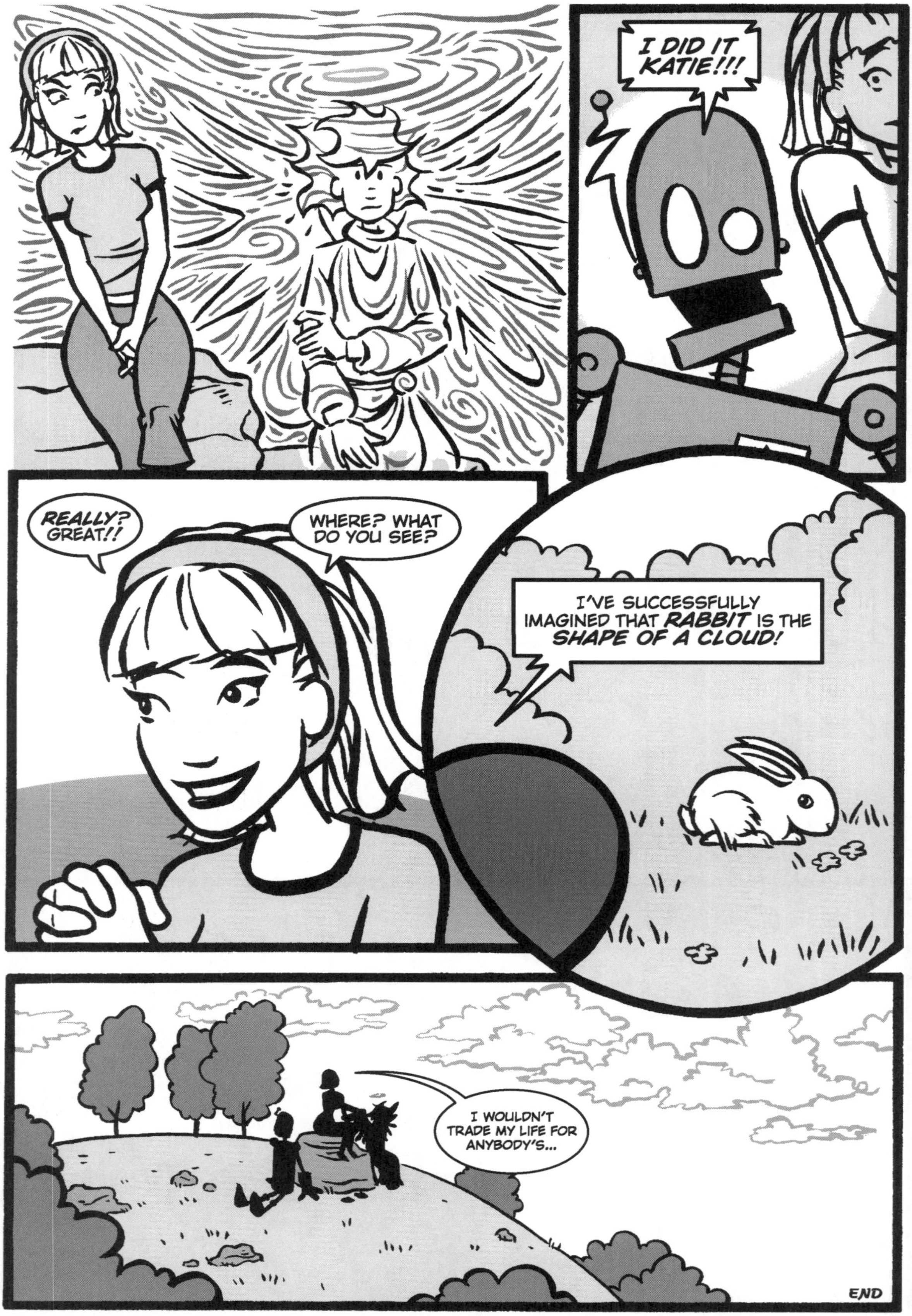
I DID IT KATIE!!!
REALLY? GREAT!!
WHERE? WHAT DO YOU SEE?
I'VE SUCCESSFULLY IMAGINED THAT RABBIT IS THE SHAPE OF A CLOUD!
I WOULDN'T TRADE MY LIFE FOR ANYBODY'S...
END

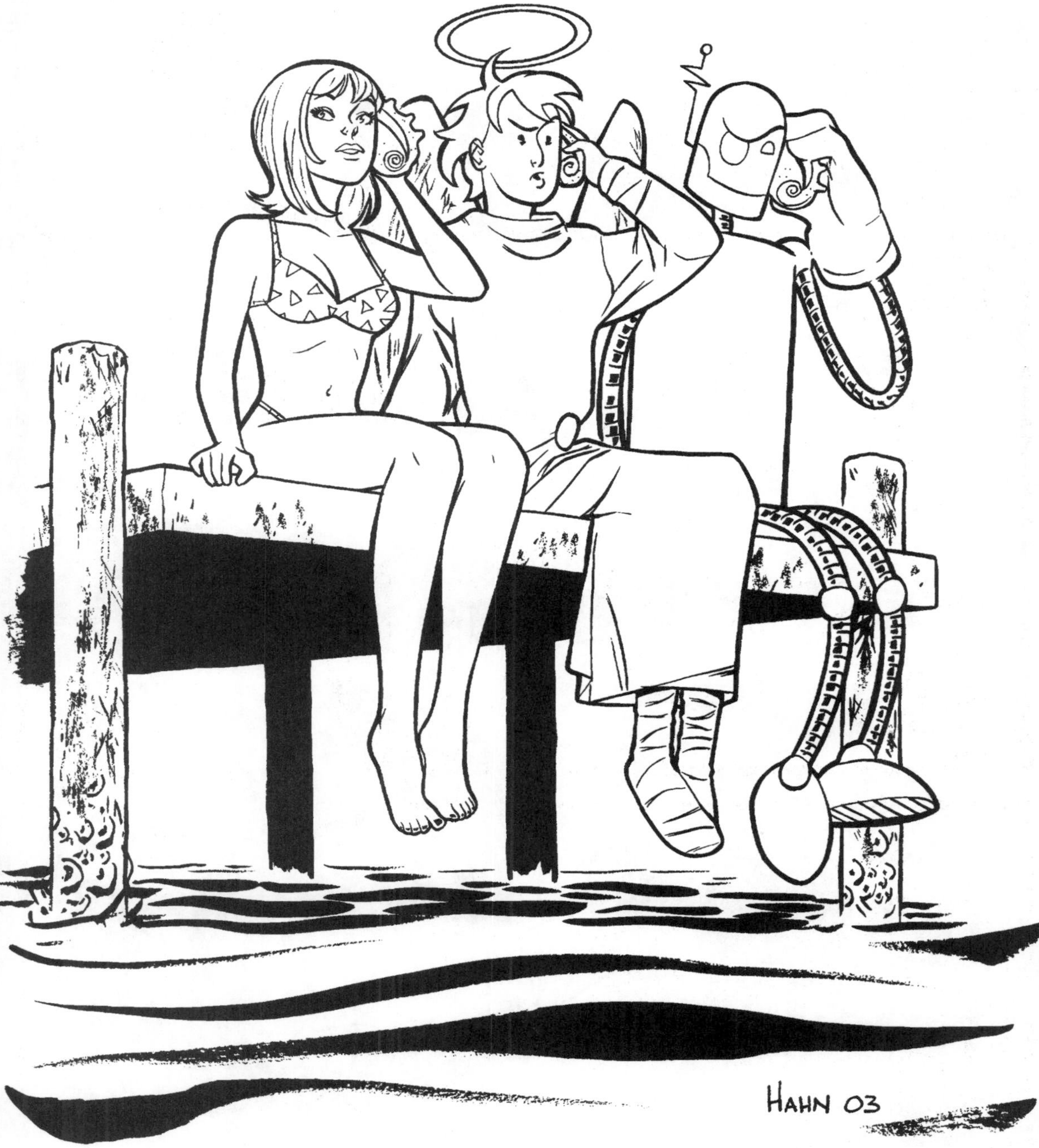
HAHN 03

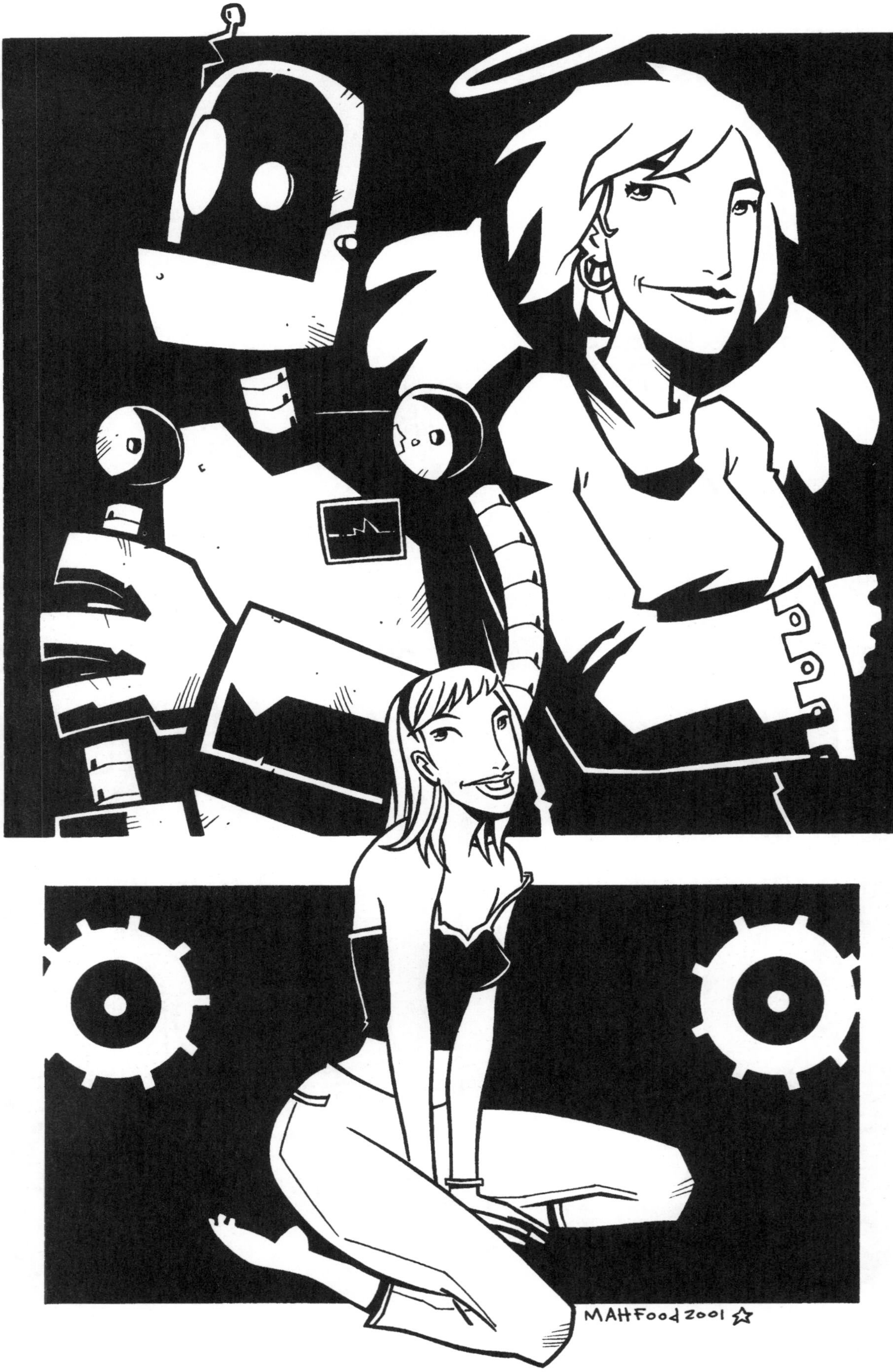
MAHFood 2001

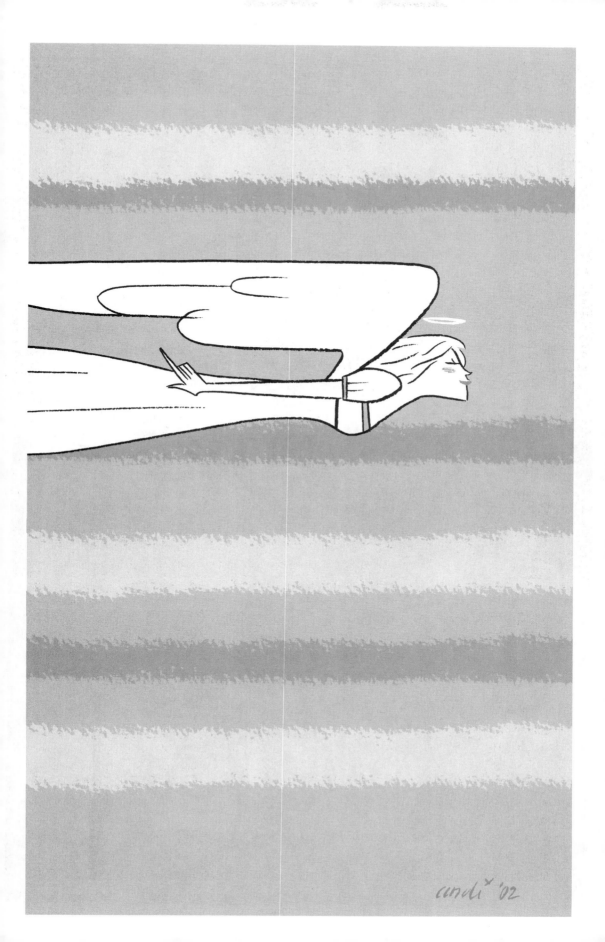

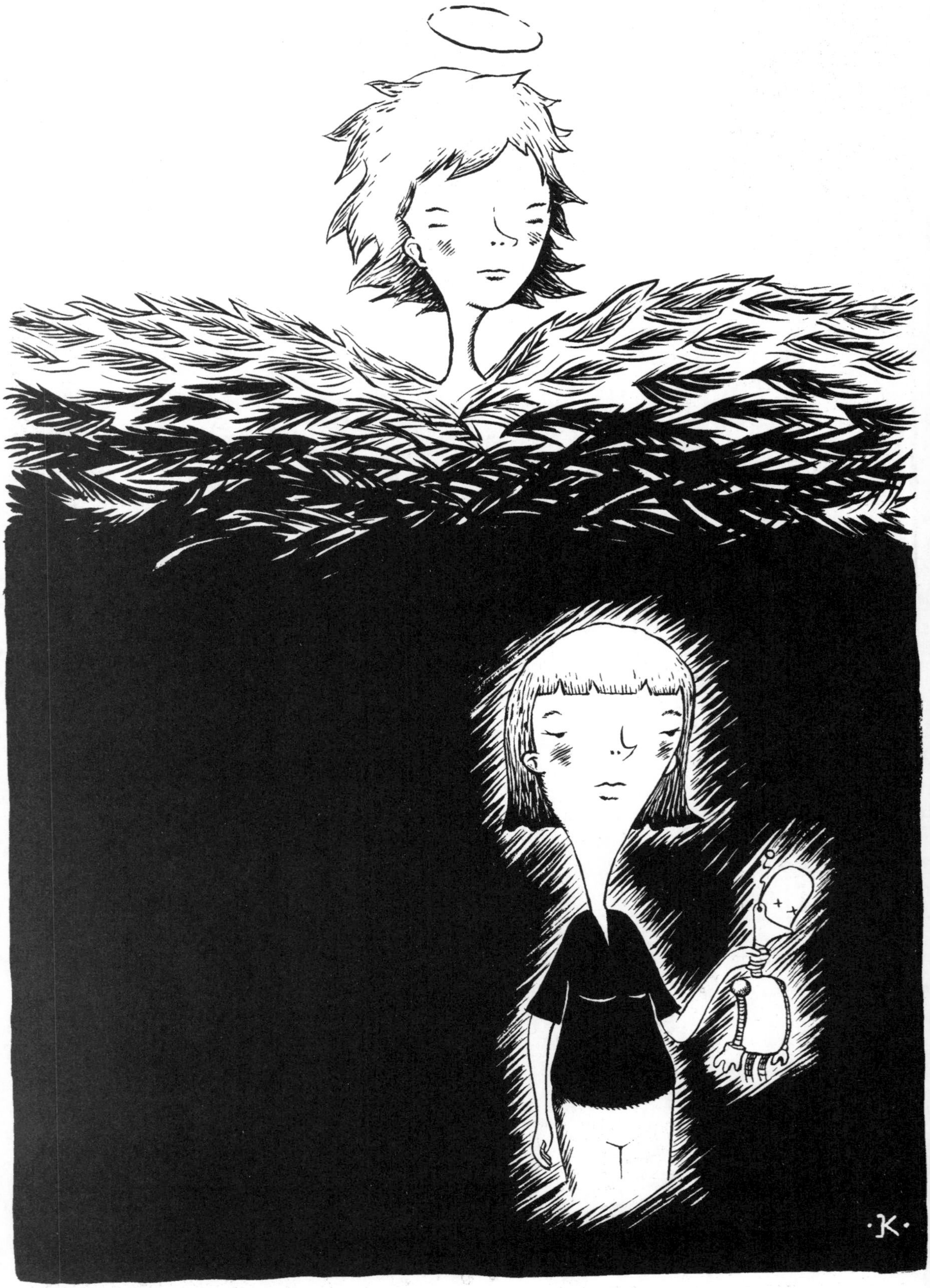
·K·

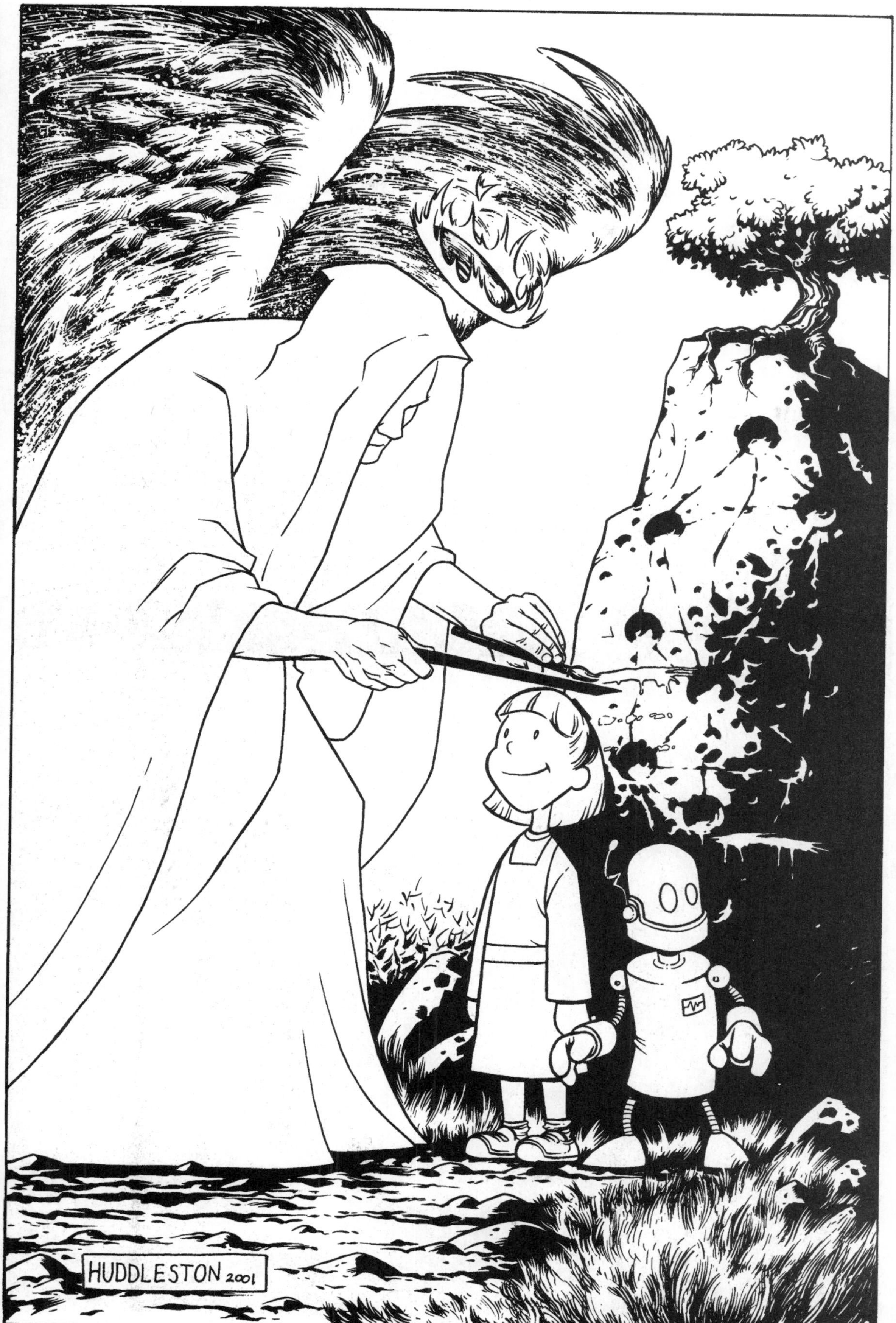
HUDDLESTON 2001

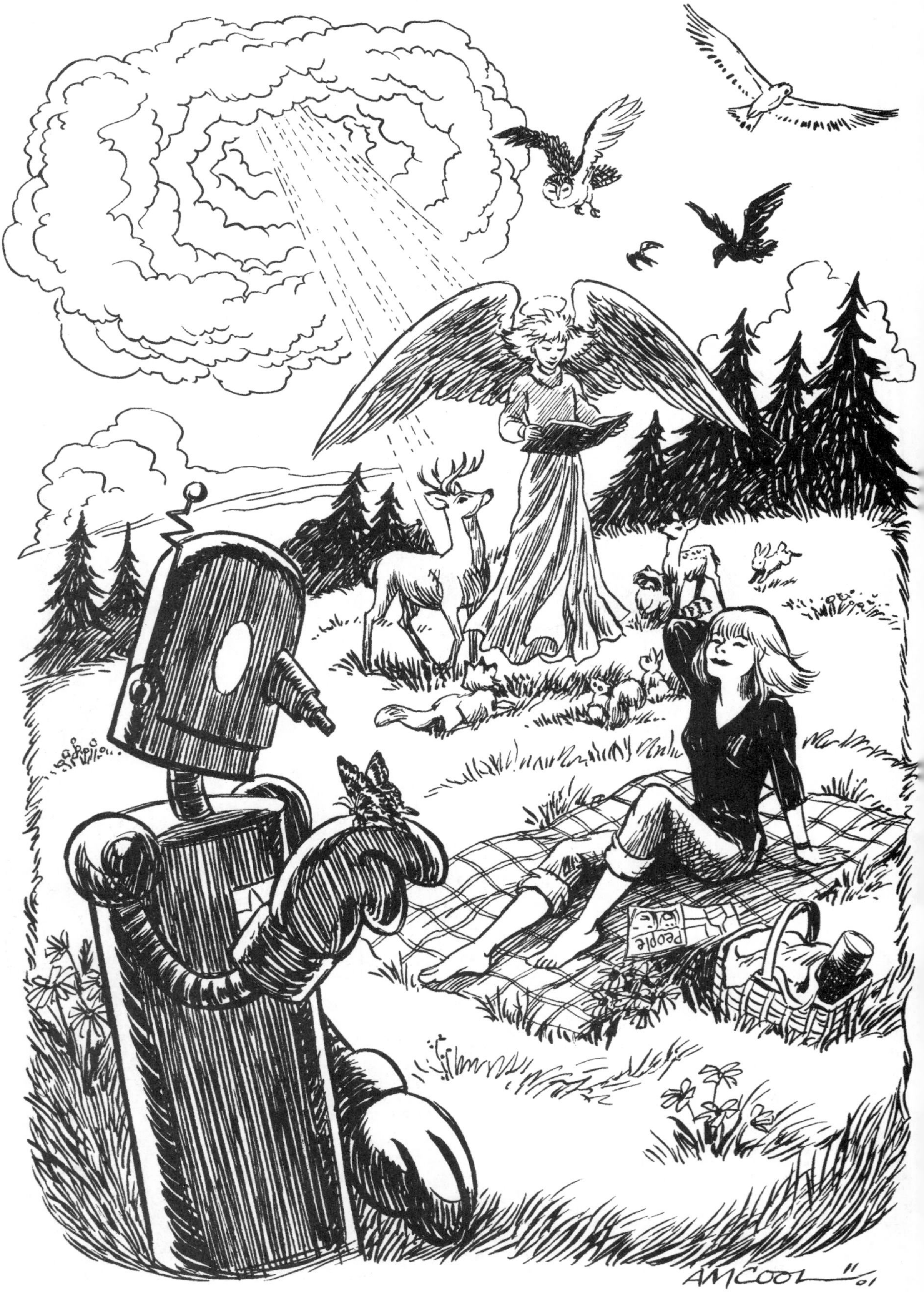
People
AMCOOL '01

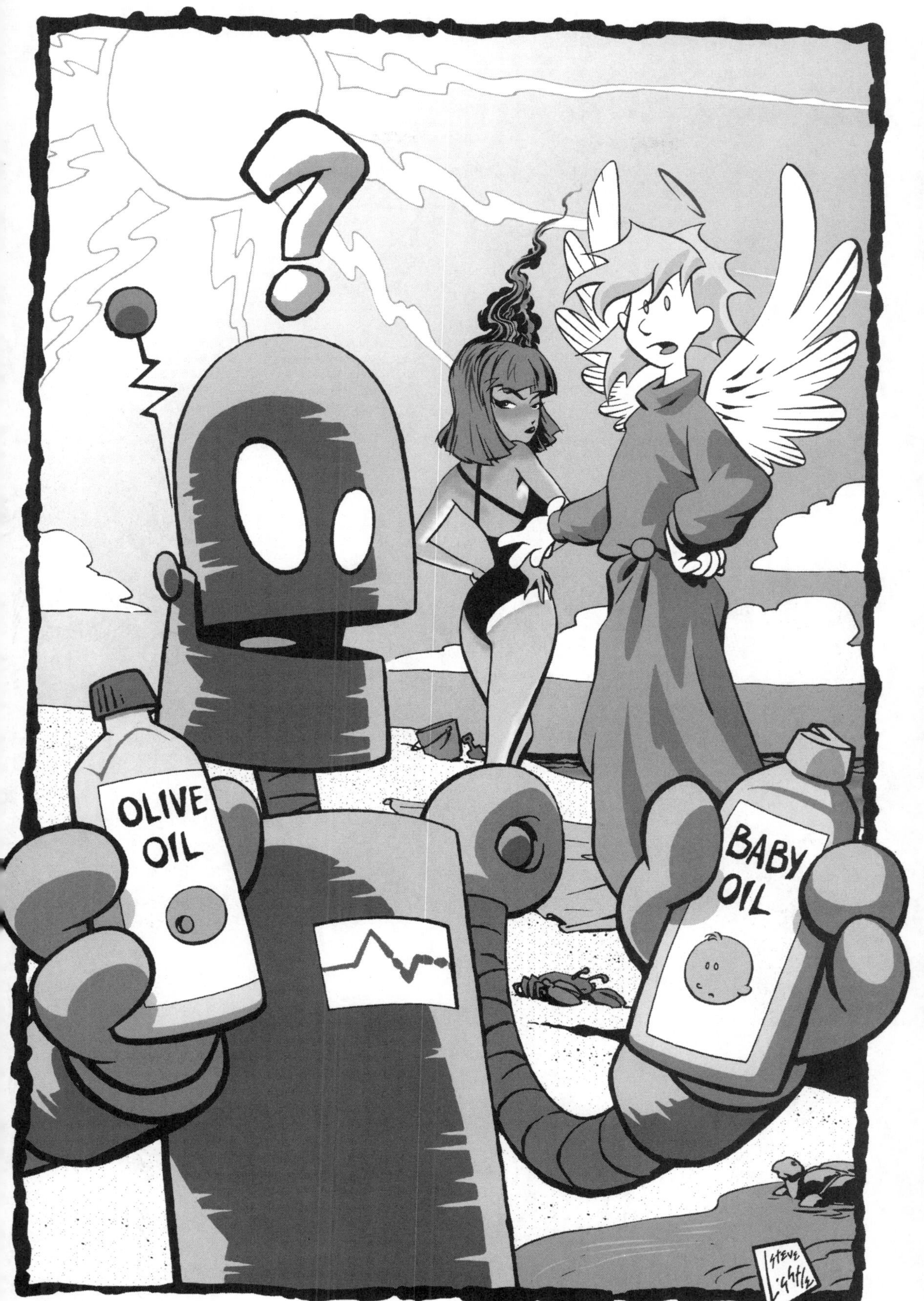
?
OLIVE
OIL
BABY
OIL
STEVE

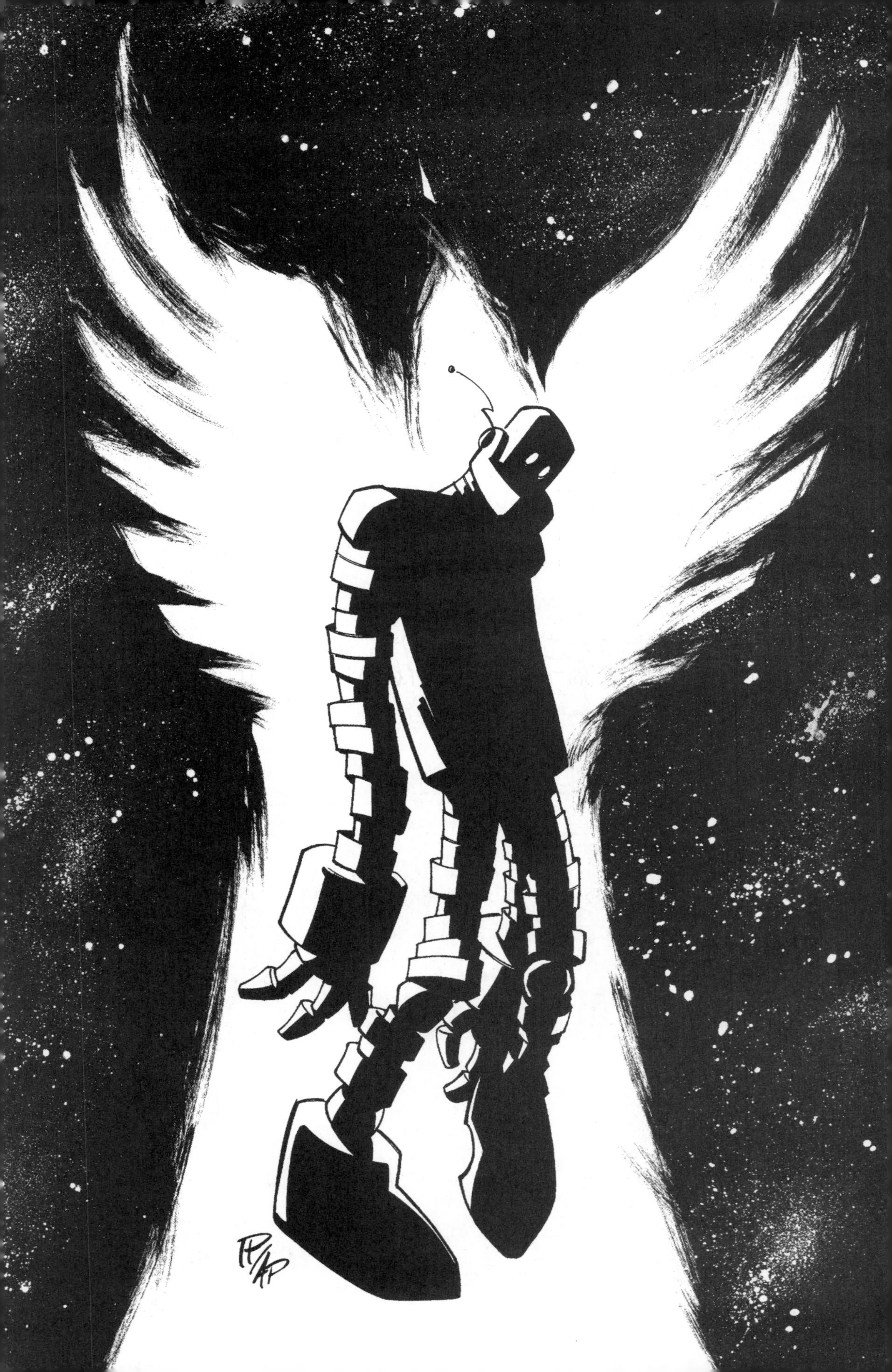

HOPE & GEARS

I thought it would be fun to share some of my work that lead up to the creation of **Halo and Sprocket**. I've called this section "Hope & Gears" because, at one point, that was what I had named my angel and robot characters.

The first time I drew an angel strip was in 1993 (shown below). It showcases my weird desire to have unknowable, worthless knowledge.

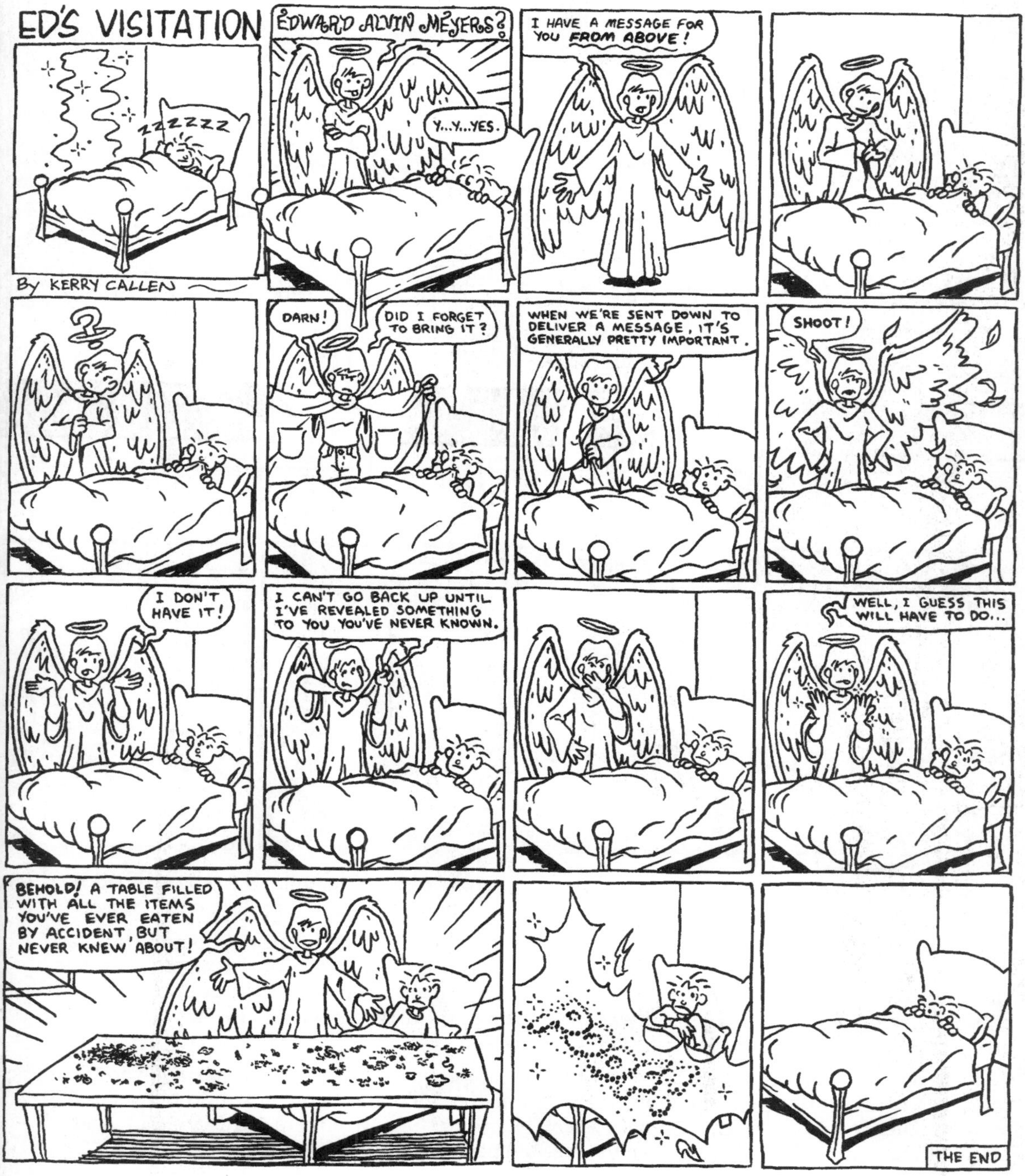
ED'S VISITATION
By KERRY CALLEN
ZZZZZZ
EDWARD ALVIN MEYERS?
Y...Y...YES.
I HAVE A MESSAGE FOR YOU FROM ABOVE!
?
DARN!
DID I FORGET TO BRING IT?
WHEN WE'RE SENT DOWN TO DELIVER A MESSAGE, IT'S GENERALLY PRETTY IMPORTANT.
SHOOT!
I DON'T HAVE IT!
I CAN'T GO BACK UP UNTIL I'VE REVEALED SOMETHING TO YOU YOU'VE NEVER KNOWN.
WELL, I GUESS THIS WILL HAVE TO DO...
BEHOLD! A TABLE FILLED WITH ALL THE ITEMS YOU'VE EVER EATEN BY ACCIDENT, BUT NEVER KNEW ABOUT!
THE END

In 1995, I blew out a knee during a game of volleyball and spent a couple of weeks recuperating from reconstructive surgery. To fill up the time, I decided to try my hand at creating a newspaper strip. I wanted it to be about an outsider to our society, but I didn't want to fall back on the obvious alien or robot. I decided to do a version of "Ed's Visitation" where the angel was stuck on Earth until it remembered its message. I wrote and eventually penciled 4 weeks worth of strips. I've taken the liberty of inking the following three...

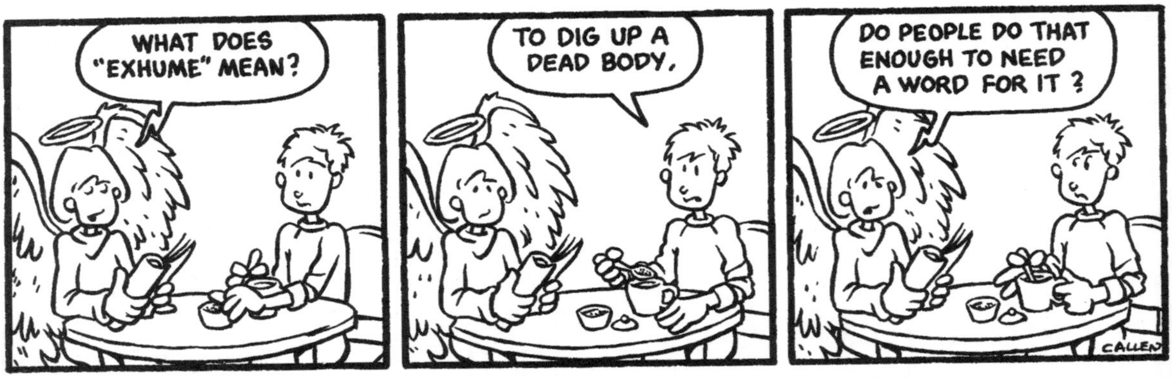
WHAT DOES "EXHUME" MEAN?
TO DIG UP A DEAD BODY.
DO PEOPLE DO THAT ENOUGH TO NEED A WORD FOR IT?
CALLEN

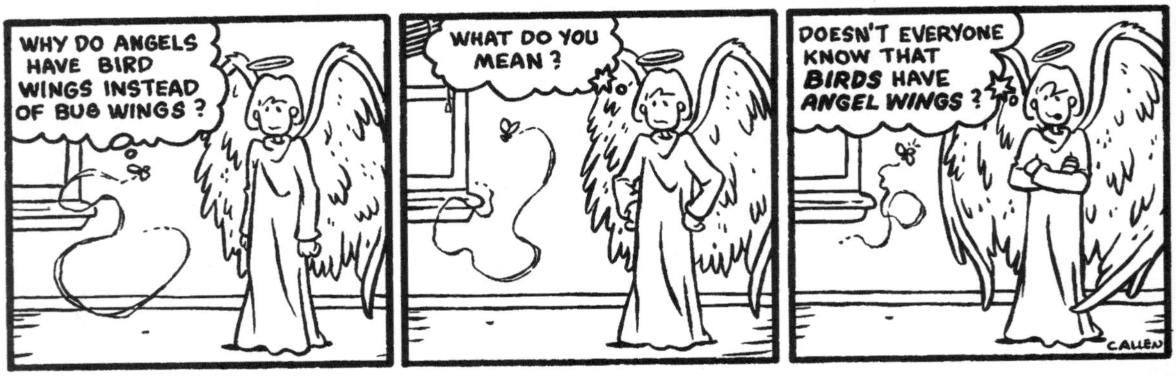
WHY DO ANGELS HAVE BIRD WINGS INSTEAD OF BUG WINGS?
WHAT DO YOU MEAN?
DOESN'T EVERYONE KNOW THAT BIRDS HAVE ANGEL WINGS?
CALLEN

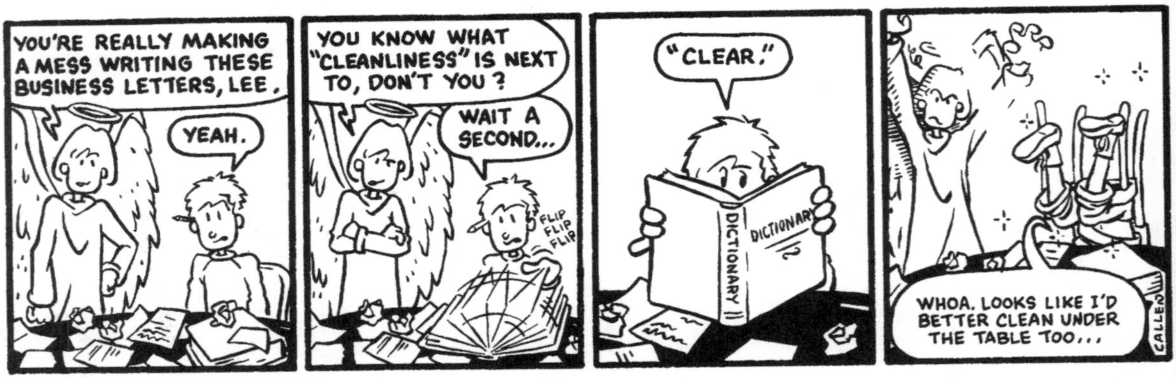
YOU'RE REALLY MAKING A MESS WRITING THESE BUSINESS LETTERS, LEE.
YEAH.
YOU KNOW WHAT "CLEANLINESS" IS NEXT TO, DON'T YOU?
WAIT A SECOND...
FLIP FLIP FLIP
"CLEAR."
DICTIONARY
DICTIONARY
WHOA. LOOKS LIKE I'D BETTER CLEAN UNDER THE TABLE TOO...
CALLEN

I liked some of the themes I hit upon, but newspaper strips are so limited in space, I had no room to truly explore an idea. After submitting the strip to a few syndicates, I scrapped the concept.

A few years later, I got the itch to do a comic book. I had dabbled in the field before, but had never attempted a series. Again, I wanted to create a character who was an outsider. (That doesn't say anything about *me*, does it?) Again, I didn't want to use any cliches. I had discovered that life viewed through the eyes of an angel was too limiting for the type of stories I wanted to tell. The creation of the proper character stumped me for over a year...

I was about to cave in to the cliche and do a series about a robot when, mysteriously in the night, it came to me. I could do a book about an angel **and** a robot! One character would represent logic, and the other would represent "things unseen." Perfect! The only obvious addition they needed was a human companion to introduce the real-life perspective...

I liked the visual juxtaposition of a robot and angel together, so I couldn't get too outlandish with their designs. If I did, they would look merely like two aliens hanging out together.

I did a few robot sketches...

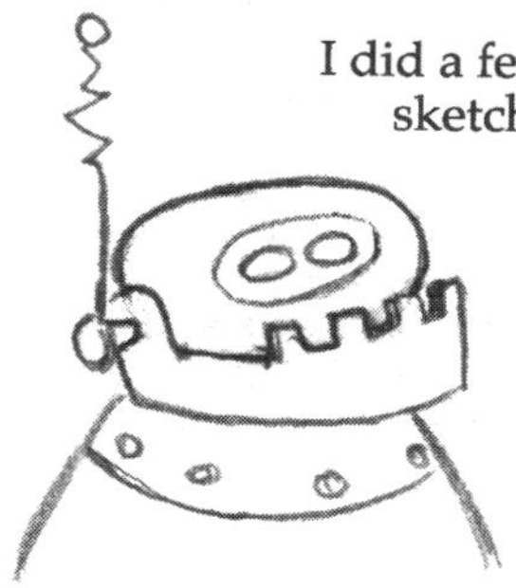

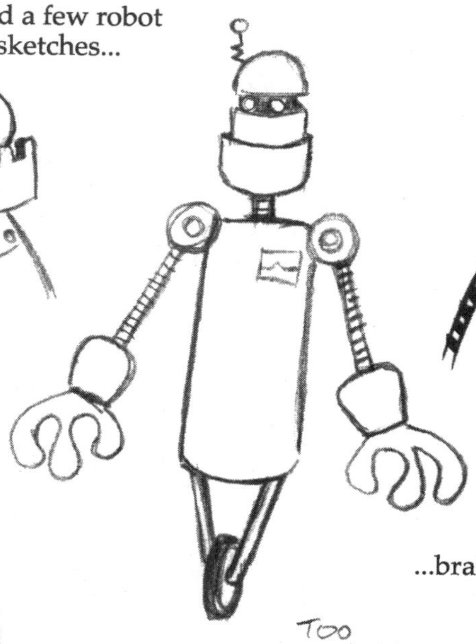

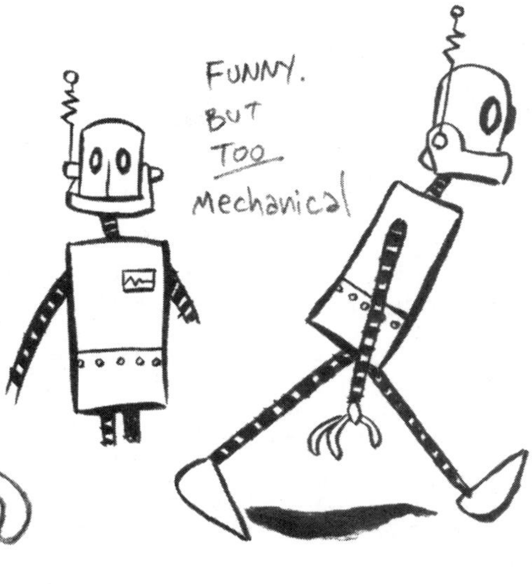
FUNNY.
BUT
TOO
Mechanical

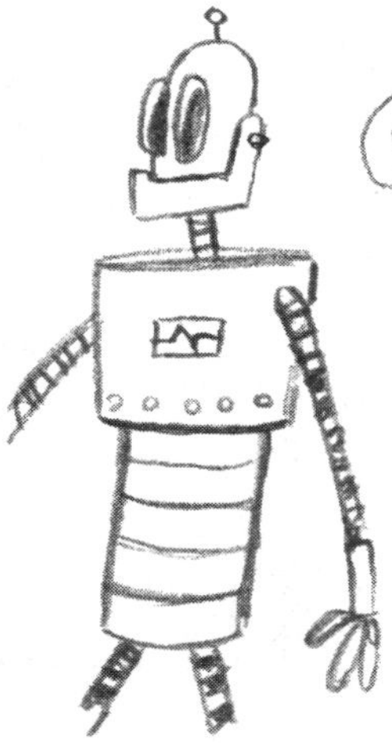

...brain-stormed a few names...

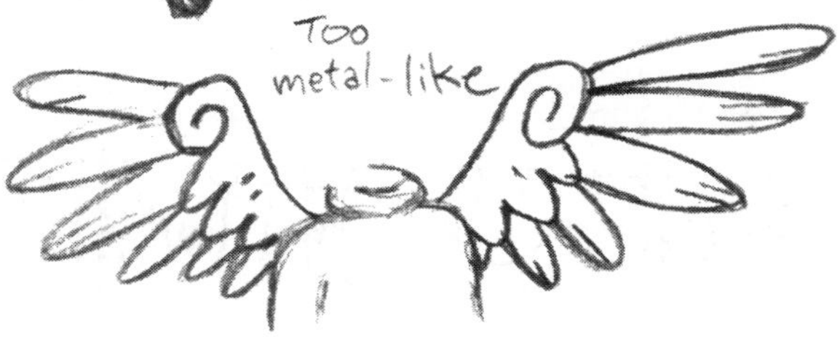
Too
metal-like

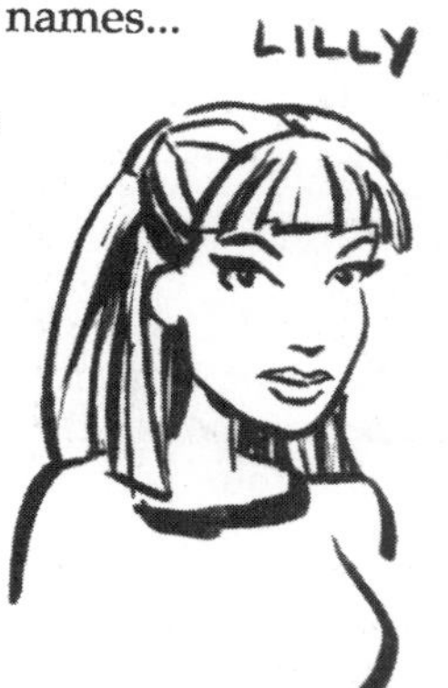
LILLY

...and ended up with the character sketches shown left and right.

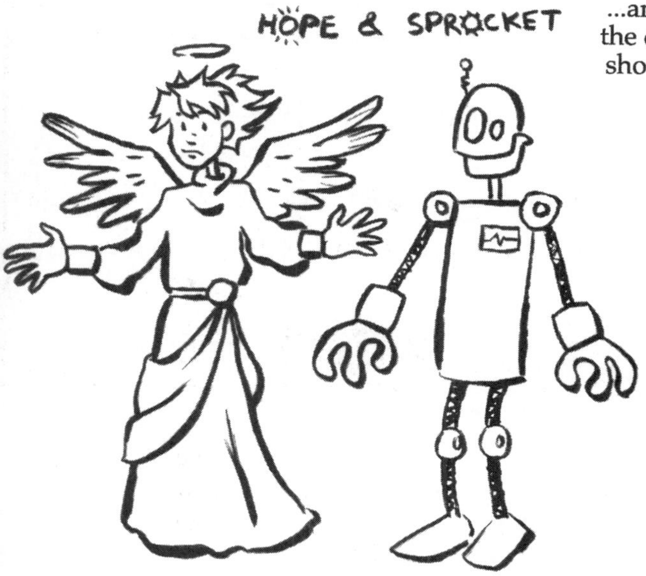
HOPE & SPROCKET

Then I jumped in and created the stories "Half Wits" and "Names." After a visit to my local copy center, I had *Halo and Sprocket* Mini-Comics! (Shown at right. Wow, that cover is boring.) Soon afterwards, SLG Publishing picked it up as the series you're now reading...!

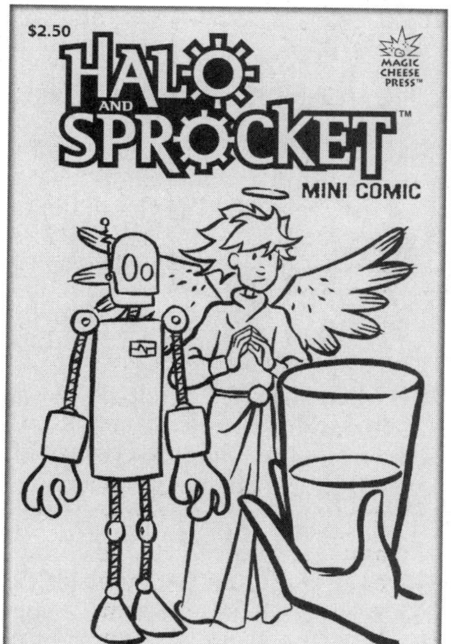
$2.50
MAGIC CHEESE PRESS™
HALO AND SPROCKET™
MINI COMIC

Story Notes

"HALF WITS" - This is the first story I drew. It's obvious to me that I hadn't quite yet figured out the look of the characters.

"NAMES" - I'm sometimes asked if the "Butter Crackers" box is based on a real-life incident. It's actually just something that occurred to me one day.

"EXHIBITIONS" - It was on the first page of this story that I decided that Halo doesn't cast a shadow.

NEW! **":)"** - This is the first of three "one pagers" I created to avoid having blank pages on the reverse side of the reprinted covers.

"BEING FRANK" - After writing the stories in issue #1 and "Suckers," I wanted to show that it can actually be a *good thing* to live with an angel and a robot.

"SUCKERS" - This possibly contains the quintessential Halo & Sprocket dialogue. (I'd love to redraw some of the art, however...)

"A DRIVING DILEMMA" - Why is it when someone inconveniences us, we assume it's on purpose...?

NEW! **"LOOK AT ME!"** - This is more about Halo perceiving time differently than we do, than it is about the consciousness of plants.

"ABOUT FACE" - I almost subtitled this book *"May I Borrow Your Flaming Sword of Vengeance?"*. Ultimately, I felt it was too long and changed it to *"Welcome to Humanity"*.

"THE LITTLE THINGS" - I gave Sam the hiccups in this story solely because I originally had "Aw Heck" planned as the last story in the same issue. "Aw Heck" started with Katie eating a spoonful of sugar as a way of avoiding blatantly showing she had the hiccups. I ended up using "The Telemarketer" instead of "Aw Heck" in the issue. When I later used "Heck," I had to rewrite the beginning. (I actually like the rewrite better!)

"THE TELEMARKETER" - I was interrupted by a telemarketer one night while drawing. After I hung up, this story wrote itself.

NEW! **"ALL'S WELL"** - I think all time travel stories where something "never happens" should be one page.

"ONE TO NOTHING" - A friend told me about "Xeno's paradox" after I had written this story.

"BUT IS IT ART..?" - In my mind, people in H&S comics don't make a big deal out of seeing an angel and a robot because Halo prevents it by slightly clouding their minds. As in all the stories, when Halo's eyes go hollow, something's going on...

"...CATS..." - I also have a dog strip I want to do someday.

"AW HECK" - This one was fun. I need to do more other-worldly stuff. I also like the vagueness of exactly what Halo was "kidding" about...

NEW! **"CLOUDY"** - I initially wrote this to appear in SLG's Free Comic Book Day comic (2003). I then decided to go with something that had more immediate impact and submitted "Aw Heck." I had "Cloudy" roughed out, so I finished it for this edition.

A BIG THANKS TO THE GALLERY ARTISTS! - David Hahn, Jim Mahfood, Andi Watson, Kelley Seda, Mike Huddleston, Anna-Maria Cool, Steve Lightle, and Phil Hester / Ande Parks.

"SPONTANEOUS HUMAN COMBUSTION EXPLAINED" - This was a doodle in my sketchbook that I redrew for an anthology released by a group of local cartoonists.

– Kerry Callen, October 2003